A DESTROYER SAILOR'S WAR

The True Story of a Destroyer Sailor's Life at Sea during World War II

With best wishes to Harry

Jerome S. Welna

Jerome S. Welna

HERITAGE BOOKS
2009

HERITAGE BOOKS

AN IMPRINT OF HERITAGE BOOKS, INC.

Books, CDs, and more—Worldwide

For our listing of thousands of titles see our website at
www.HeritageBooks.com

Published 2009 by
HERITAGE BOOKS, INC.
Publishing Division
100 Railroad Ave. #104
Westminster, Maryland 21157

International Standard Book Numbers
Paperbound: 978-0-7884-4928-4
Clothbound: 978-0-7884-8167-3

This book is dedicated to the thousands
of brave destroyer sailors who gave their lives
in defense of freedom during World War II,
December 7, 1941, to September 2, 1945.

CONTENTS

LIST OF MAPS, ILLUSTRATIONS AND PHOTOGRAPHS

Maps and Illustrations

Photographs

FOREWORD

In his introduction, Jerome Welna argues that the Navy's destroyers, especially regarding their heroic action at Normandy, did not get their fair shake for credit due in their role during World War II. To that I would have to agree. Certainly the narrative of the Navy's efforts, especially in the Pacific, has been well documented. Samuel Elliot Morison's fourteen volume *History of U.S. Naval Operations during World War II* followed by the *Victory at Sea* television series gave Americans an appreciation of the challenges the Navy faced during World War II. With the revelation of the role of the code breakers, more recent narratives, such as *Combined Fleet Decoded, the Secret History of American Intelligence and the Japanese Navy during World War II* by John Prados, provide a greater understanding of the factors that influenced the admirals to act as they did.

Perhaps because it was not a fleet-on-fleet engagement, historians have overlooked the naval component of Normandy. Navy demolition experts helped to clear the beaches of obstacles and without the close-in gunfire provided by our destroyers at Omaha Beach, our troops would have remained pinned on the beach. Yet there is no memorial at Normandy commemorating the Navy's role on "the longest day." In addition, most World War II narratives look at the war from the khaki perspective. For example, Evan Thomas's recent *Sea of Thunder: Four Commanders and the Last Great Naval Campaign, 1941-1945* looks at the battle of Leyte Gulf from the perspective of two Japanese and two American naval officers.

Only in recent years have the stories of enlisted sailors, who are the navy's lifeblood, begun to be told. Dr. Jack Haberstroh began collecting oral histories of sailors and published *Swabby I* and *Swabby II*—both volumes having the subtitle of "World War II Sailors Tell It Like It Was!" Sadly Dr. Haberstroh passed away before *Swabby III* could make it to press. Then there is Andrew Carroll who began collecting letters from sailors and soldiers and has published a series of books on the topic beginning with *War Letters*. Finally, there is the Library of Congress Veterans History Program that has captured the stories of thousands of World War II sailors in their growing collection—including two video interviews with Welna!

While the above provide much material for those interested in how it was to serve aboard a World War II combatant, few give as comprehensive beginning to end overview as Welna. As a sailor who served in destroyers, he was part of a unique breed as illustrated in Raymond Calhoun's *Tin Can Sailor*. Welna's memory, backed with research, offers a well crafted narrative, written in the voice of a sailor who served during his time when calling a woman a dame or a broad was part of the vernacular. Few have captured the experiences of going through boot camp at the Great Lakes Naval Training Center and the subsequent torpedo and San Diego advanced torpedo schools as well as he, and then went on to serve in the second USS *Barton* (the first having been sunk at Guadalcanal) which participated in the invasion of France and the subsequent operation to liberate Cherbourg. He then transferred to the USS *Sterett*, a destroyer that survived Guadalcanal, to see some of the war's most ferocious action as the Japanese launched kamikaze suicide plane attacks against the advancing American fleet as a desperate measure to defend their homeland. For its action, *Sterett* would earn a well deserved Presidential Unit Citation from both the Philippine and U.S. governments.

In 2004, the nation dedicated a World War II Memorial in Washington, D.C. After reading Welna's narrative, it will be quite apparent that this memorial dedicated to the service and sacrifice of those who served the nation during that conflict, was long overdue.

David F. Winkler, Ph.D.
Naval Historic Foundation
Washington, D.C.
November 2007

PREFACE

Much has been written about the great land and sea battles of World War II. Morison, in particular, chronicled the entire two-ocean naval war in fourteen volumes, while Ambrose, Costello, and other authors also contributed a great deal of information to the navy's role in fighting World War II. Most authors derived their information of naval battles from high ranking naval officers, and action reports that did not describe a picture of what the war was like for destroyer crews who spent months at sea engaged in multiple operations scattered over the great oceans of the world. One exception would be Calhoun's personal account of the sea battles of Guadalcanal (Third Savo) and Vela Gulf, on the same destroyer I served aboard later on in the war in the Pacific.

The newscasters and the press of the period did not report much detail of what was actually happening during the big naval operations in both theatres because of censorship. The army had the *Stars and Stripes* publication and the navy had the *Our Navy* publication. Reporters from the *Stars and Stripes* were allowed to travel with the army as they fought their war. Men from the *Our Navy* were not allowed aboard warships, especially destroyers. The navy was very secretive about its ships, where they were, and what they were doing.

To this day many people have no idea what the navy did in World War II despite what has since been published. The most frequent question asked of me is, "What did the navy do in World War II?" They are usually referring to the Normandy landings. More people are aware of the French invasion than the Pacific war. This is probably due to the fact that Hollywood has made several movies concerning the Normandy invasion, but has rarely mentioned much about the navy's role in that operation. Movie producers have made no attempt to create an accurate documentary of the navy at Normandy; however, when considering the complexity of the Normandy operation, I really don't know if it is possible to film it and do the story justice.

My first realization of this fact came to light during the celebrations June 6, 1994, of the fiftieth anniversary of the landings on June 6, 1944, at Normandy, France. In observing the television and printed news media coverage I noted that there was practically no mention of U.S. naval personnel that were involved in the landings that day. Even in the recent documentary, *The War,* there was hardly a mention of the navy's contribution to the success of Operation Overlord. There was no mention of the SFCP (Shore Fire Control Parties) that went ashore with the army assault troops to brave German fire and direct fire from navy ships. Was that because many of them were killed or lost their radios in the surf? There was no mention of navy beach masters who functioned as policemen during a hail of German fire in order to direct placement of the huge amount of equipment landed starting at the height of the battle and during the several days of the landings—everything from bulldozers to ammunition. There was little, if any, mention of the heroism of navy coxswains who transported troops in landing craft through mined beach obstacles and artillery fire to their beach destinations—many of them never survived. When it seemed that the Omaha landings were destined to fail, navy destroyers were finally called in and ordered to give the troops ashore the fire support they needed. Navy destroyer captains risked their ships and the lives of their crews to provide the only artillery support the army had at Omaha Beach. The navy destroyers saved the day by taking out German gun emplacements and reducing German firepower so that the troops could advance to the high ground and accomplish their objective for the first day.

There has never been a mention by the media of the four U.S. destroyers and one Norwegian destroyer lost during the first three days of the landings. The media has never mentioned the Cherbourg bombardment by the navy, and the ships hit and casualties suffered in that operation of 6-24-44, to aid the U.S. Army VII Corps in capturing the all important port of Cherbourg.

To be fair about the lack of information available at Omaha Beach on that fateful day of 6 June 1944, it is important to add that correspondents were prevented from going ashore with the assault troops; however, there was one correspondent who did manage to talk his way aboard a landing craft. He wanted to provide a first hand documentation of what the initial attack on the German defenses was like. When he finally arrived near the beach and saw landing craft and their soldiers being blown out of the water, he immediately jumped into the water, was picked up by a surviving landing craft, and returned to the safety of one of the ships anchored eleven miles from shore. The other correspondents were wiser and stayed put where they were safe. The high command did not provide them with any information concerning the progress of the operation.

To this day there is not one monument or historical marker at Omaha Beach, Utah Beach, or to the west at Cherbourg, to commemorate the navy personnel that fought and died there. The lack of publicity for the navy was probably due to the fact that the navy never had much of a vehicle (other than the *Our Navy* magazine) to publicize the navy's accomplishments. The attitude that prevailed in the navy from the admirals down to the lowest seaman was that we had a job to do, we did it, and that was that. For these reasons, and because I was a destroyer sailor whose battle station was on the bridge in both theatres of war (where I was privy to the entire action and communications), I decided to write this book based on my personal experiences and observations.

In war, the strength of the offensive is commensurate with the strength of the line of communications—the ability of supply.

Without the navy to solve the logistical supply problems that made possible the delivery of the tremendous quantity of materials produced by America's industry it would not have been possible to conduct the many amphibious operations, the continuous supply of troops fighting on land, and the resupply of task forces operating at sea for months at a time while seldom seeing a port of call. In addition to fighting enemy warships, aircraft, and conducting shore bombardments, the destroyers played a vital part in the protection of supply ships transporting cargo from the United States to the battle zones. Thousands of soldiers and marines were safely transported to their destinations over thousands of miles of ocean, while being protected from enemy submarines and surface ships by navy destroyers.

The modern destroyer of World War II had evolved over the years from the square-rigged frigates of Lord Nelson's day, and the torpedo boats of previous wars. They were small vessels averaging 350 feet in length with an average thirty-five-foot beam and a crew of 290 to 350 men, depending on the class of ship. These ships were commonly called "tin cans" because of their thin three-quarter-inch hulls—they were also known to navy sailors as the "tin can navy." With propulsion machinery capable of generating 40,000 to 60,000 horsepower, destroyers (DDs) were fast, highly maneuverable, and tough beyond expectations. They were able to absorb terrific punishment in battle—a tribute to the naval architects who designed them. More than one destroyer made it back from both war zones of the Atlantic and Pacific under its own power missing its bow, stern, or with a third of its guns and superstructure blown off due to enemy action. This is also a tribute to the superb training and performance of their crews. Destroyers were known as lethal attack vessels. The destroyers of World War II had the greatest concentration of firepower ever seen in a small ship. They were the most versatile of all fighting ships and mounted weapons for every type of offense—with their torpedoes they were able to attack battleships and cruisers to either sink them or damage them enough to put them out of action. With their 5-inch main batteries they were used to attack surface ships, shore installations, and provide artillery support for amphibious operations including fire support for troops operating ashore within their gun range. Their radar controlled guns provided the capability of downing enemy aircraft, and their ASW equipment allowed them to locate enemy submarines and sink them with depth charges.

There were more destroyers in commission than any other kind of combatant ship, and no other warship equaled the destroyer in the number of combat jobs these fighting ships did— this is why they were known as the workhorses of the navy. They were the eyes and ears of the fleet and considered indispensable in every operation— no task commander ever had enough of them.

In the early days of the war when most of our battleships lay in the mud off Ford Island at Pearl Harbor, it was the destroyers and cruisers of the United States Navy that provided most of the artillery support for the invasions of North Africa, Sicily, and Italy. In these operations the main burden supporting the infantry divisions in the initial assaults, and stopping counter attacks by German tank columns, fell to the navy.

During the Sicily operation General Eisenhower witnessed the power of the navy in supporting invasion forces establishing beachheads. Over a period of ten hours, two cruisers and eight destroyers fired on enemy tanks destroying most of them in range while completely demoralizing the German defenders, and making it impossible for them to stop our invading troops. The next day our cruisers and destroyers delivered naval gunfire support for our own advancing troops up to eight miles inland. The intensity, accuracy, and effectiveness of the navy firepower convinced Eisenhower and his officers that not only were navy guns suitable for shore bombardment, but they were indispensable to the success of amphibious operations. The lessons learned were employed in

Operation Overlord, the invasion of Normandy—the errors were not repeated.

During the Philippine Campaign, the Japanese Navy was restricted as a viable attack force due to lack of fuel oil and sufficiently trained carrier pilots. In an attempt to destroy our landing operations and prevent the resupply of our newly established beachheads, the Japanese introduced the Kamikaze Corps in the Sulu Sea just prior to October of 1944. Thousands of young men volunteered to sacrifice their lives to crash their planes into our ships with the hope of disrupting our supply lines and therefore thwarting further advancement of our forces. The kamikaze suddenly became a very formidable weapon, with supply ships and destroyer losses suddenly increasing at an alarming rate.

Prior to the battle of Okinawa, Rear Admiral Turner realized the need for destroyers to function as radar picket ships with the responsibility of protecting the supply vessels from kamikaze attack. To get to the supply vessels the kamikazes first had to penetrate the CAP, (Combat Air Patrol) destroyer picket screen, and put the destroyers out of action. These tactics resulted in the most difficult and costly naval battle of the war. When attacking in large numbers 100% of all kamikazes had to be shot down. If one penetrated the screen, a destroyer or transport vessel was almost certain to be hit. From admiral to seamen, men manned their battle stations until the kamikazes were either shot down, the ship was hit, or they were cut down. The action went on day after day, week after week, taking a heavy toll of ships and personnel. Crews manned their battle stations courageously pouring fire into oncoming kamikazes even when it was obvious that the suicider, dead at the controls, would hit his target. After six grueling weeks of constant battle with the CAP and destroyers shooting kamikazes out of the sky, the radar picket ships crews reveled in victory—but at what cost? By the time it was all over and victory was won, the loss in ships was greater than the total number of United States destroyers in commission at the beginning of the war. Our total naval casualties in killed and missing were greater than the combined marine and army forces fighting on land. The picket line had held and the destroyer forces had proven once again their spirit of "CAN DO"—no job being too big to handle. The destroyer sailors of World War II are justified in being proud of their battle record and contribution to victory. It is with great pride that I write this story which is as much their story as mine.

ACKNOWLEDGEMENTS

First and foremost I wish to acknowledge the patience of my wife Jeannette who put up with me for the five years I spent writing this book. During that long period of my life I was deeply engrossed in retrieving old memories of happenings that had at one time been put back into the deep recesses of my brain. I would often bore her with navy jargon that must have been a foreign language to her, and yet she never complained. On the contrary, she would now and then question me as to how my work was progressing—and then encourage me to keep on writing.

I also wish to acknowledge the great amount of help I received from Diane and Charles Kucera. Diane patiently read and edited every bit of my manuscript and made countless suggestions for improving its readability. She made many suggestions for improving readers' interest, while locating and correcting my typos and misspelled words.

Charles also read every word of the manuscript and was very helpful in assuring me that dates and historical information were accurate. Charles also aided me greatly in drawing my attention to navy terms or jargon that would creep into the manuscript from time to time and possibly confound or confuse the reader. He was extremely helpful in aiding me to adequately and clearly describe technical terms so that the layperson would understand and derive the true meaning. The help I received from both Diane and Charles is invaluable and will ensure that the lay reader will be able to understand and draw a verbal picture of events as they happened. To Diane and Chuck I will always be eternally grateful.

I wish to acknowledge Captain E. Raymond Calhoun, Retired, for his encouragement and consultation that stimulated me to write the book in the first place. I also wish to recognize the late Mr. Stephen Ambrose, Director of the Eisenhower University of New Orleans, Louisiana, who, when looking for stories from veterans of the Pacific war, encouraged me to write my own book of my wartime experiences. I wish to thank my daughter Jeannette Marie Welna for her unceasing interest and encouragement in helping me to complete my project. I wish to acknowledge the extensive help of David F. Winkler, Director of the Naval Historical Foundation, for his many fine suggestions and final editing of the manuscript for historical accuracy. I wish to thank Ed Fisher, my computer technician, who made it possible for me to create the manuscript while learning to use the computer. And last but not least, I wish to thank Kathleen Merriam for her edit and final review of the manuscript.

NAVAL TERMS AND ABREVIATIONS

Used in this text

ALNAV: Transmissions to All Navy Personnel

ASDIC: An ASW device for locating submerged submarines by using sound waves

A/S: Antisubmarine gear

ASW: Antisubmarine warfare

Baka: see Oka

Bangalore torpedo: Explosive charge for blowing barbed wire and other obstacles

BEF: British Expeditionary Force

Belay: an order to cancel an order; to stop

Blitzkrieg: Lightning war

Bofors 40: Antiaircraft-40mm guns

Bogie: Unidentified or enemy aircraft

Brow: Large gangplank leading from the ship to a pier, wharf, or raft and usually equipped with rollers on the bottom and hand rails on the sides

CAP: Combat Air Patrol

Capital ships: Largest warships such as battleships, cruisers, and carriers

CIC: Combat Information Center

CINPAC: Commander in Chief, Pacific Fleet (Admiral Nimitz)

CO: Commanding Officer

COMINCH: Commander in Chief, United States Fleet (Admiral King)

COMDESDIV 60: Commander Destroyer Division 60, etc.

CTF: Commander Task Force; **CTG:** Commander Task Group

CV: Aircraft Carrier; **CVE:** Escort Carrier; **CVL:** Light Cruiser

D--Date of the operation to commence

DD: Designates Destroyer; **DE:** designates Destroyer Escort

DF: Direction Finder

Depth charge racks: Located on the fantail to roll depth charges off during ASW attack

Dog: Small bent metal fittings used to secure watertight doors, hatches, etc.

ENIGMA: German designed code machine

German 88: Dual Purpose 88mm artillery piece

Gooseberry: Artificial harbor created for Operation Neptune

GQ: General quarters, battle stations all hands

Gun boss: Gunnery Officer

H: Time of day of the operation to commence

Hedgehogs: ASW device for hurling explosive charges forward of the attacking vessel to kill enemy submerged submarines

Higgins Boat: Landing craft

hm: Nautical mile equal to 6076.115 ft.

HMAS: His (or Her) Majesty's Australian Ship

HMS: His (or Her) Majesty's Ship, British Royal Navy

HQ: Headquarters Command

K-Guns: Guns that propel depth charges away from the ship

Kriegsmarine: The German Navy

Landing Craft: [(A) (G) (L) (M) (R) after LC indicates armor, gunboat, larger, mortar, rockets]

Lay-to: To hold a ship stationary in open sea

LCI: Landing Craft Infantry

LCP: Landing Craft Personnel

LCT: Landing Craft Tank; **LCTR:** LCT fitted with rocket launchers

LCVP: Landing Craft Vehicles and Personnel

LST: Landing Ship Tank

Luftwaffe: German Air Force

Magic: Code name for U.S. Naval Intelligence

Mark-9 Depth Charges: Standard navy explosives for killing submerged submarines

Milch Cows: German Oiler vessels stationed in the Atlantic to refuel their submarines

Mulberry: Artificial harbor created for Omaha Beach

NOB: Naval Operating Base

Oka (Baka): Japanese flying kamikaze bomb (meaning "stupid")

OOD: Officer of the deck

Ping Jockey: Soundman using A/S gear for submarine detection

Plank owner: Original crewmember at commissioning of a new ship

Port: Left side of ship looking forward

Potato masher: German grenade

Quarterdeck: That part of the main deck reserved for ceremonies and the station of the OOD in Port

RAF: Royal Air Force (British)

RN: Royal Navy (British)

RPS: Radar Picket Ship: A ship stationed away from the main force using radar to detect an enemy

SC Radar: Radar for locating and tracking aircraft

Schnellboots: German torpedo boats (called E-boats by our navy)

Scuttlebutt: Drinking fountain; also, unfounded rumor of questionable importance

Secondary Con: Duplicate emergency location amidships for conning the ship during bridge failure

SFCP: Shore Fire Control Party (for directing fire of bombarding ships from shore)

SG Radar: Radar for locating and tracking surface ships

SHAEF: Supreme Headquarters American Expeditionary Force

Single up: to reduce the number of mooring lines out to a pier preparatory to sailing; and, to leave only one mooring line in each place for easy cast off where previously there were two doubled up lines for greater security

Sound Stack: Part of A/S sound gear located on the keel about 1/3 back from the bow

SP: Shore Patrol

Splice the Main Brace: Having several tall libations ashore on liberty

SQUID: ASW device for hurling explosives forward from the attacking vessel to kill submerged submarines

Starboard: Right side of a ship looking forward

Stores: Food and other essential supplies

TBS Radio: Radio for talking between ships

TF: Task Force # 60 etc,

TG: Task Group # 57.5 etc.

Thermite Grenade: Grenade designed to melt steel

UDTS: Under Water Demolition Teams

USO: United Servicemen's Organization

USS: United States Ship

USS *ANCHON*: Command and Communication ship

USS *YOSEMITE*: Command and Communication ship

V-2 Rockets: German self propelled flying bombs

U.S. Navy Aircraft
Numbers in parentheses indicate number of engines

F4F – Wildcat, **F6F** – Hellcat; **F4U** – Corsair, Navy and Marine fighters (1)

OS2U – Kingfisher, scout observation float plane (1)

PBJ – Mitchell medium bomber (2)

PBM–3 – Mariner flying boat patrol bomber (2)

PBY – Catalina patrol bomber; **PBY-5A** amphibian Catalina (2)

SB2C, SBW – Helldivers; **SBD** – Dauntless dive-bombers (1)

TBF, TBM – Avenger torpedo-bombers (1)

Japanese Aircraft

Betty – Mitsubishi Zero-1, Navy high level or torpedo bomber (2)

Fran – Nakajima, Navy all purpose bomber (2)

Frances – Nakajima, Navy bomber (2)

Frank – Nakajima, Army fighter (1)

Jake-Aichi/Watanabe, Navy reconnaissance bomber (1)

Jill – Nakajima, Navy torpedo bomber (1)

Judy – Aichi, Navy dive bomber (1)

Kate – Nakajima, Navy torpedo bomber (1)

Oscar – Nakajima Army fighter (1)

Nick – Kawasaki Zero-2, Army fighter (1)

Sally – Mitsubishi, Army medium bomber (2)

Tojo – Nakajima Zero-2, Army fighter (1)

Tony – Zero-3, Army & Navy fighter (1)

Val – Aichi 99, Navy dive bomber (1)

Zeke – Mitsubishi Zero-3 Navy fighter (1)

To not know history is to remain a child.

Cicero 65BC

Chapter 1

PRELUDE TO WORLD WAR II

1938

I was born in September of 1923 in the little town of Lynch, Nebraska, about thirty-six miles west of the confluence of the Missouri and Niobrara Rivers. My mother had come to Lynch from International Falls, Minnesota, to be with the Welna family for the occasion of my entry into the world, even though her family lived on a farm near Niobrara. At Lynch there was some semblance of a hospital and a traveling visiting doctor. My father worked as a locomotive engineer on the railroad that operated from International Falls, Minnesota, north into the lumber camps of Canada which is why Mother decided to have me in Nebraska. Before returning to International Falls Mother spent some time with her family on the farm and I was already several weeks old before Dad saw the results of his handwork.

My mother was the daughter of Marie and August Jeannoutot, and one of six siblings. Grandma Jeannoutot had been the personal chef of a wealthy French family. Grandpa Jeannoutot was the head gardener for the same family. They came to Nebraska in the late 1800's with gold, bought a farm, and became successful farmers. Grandpa Jeannoutot was very knowledgeable in world history and politics. My mother and the other siblings were all home schooled in world history, U.S. History, politics, and geography in

1

addition to their public schooling. All of the siblings were bilingual in French and English. Both my mother and father were very knowledgeable and worldly-wise with an indomitable spirit. Both of my parents guided me well in my formative years.

When I was only three years old we moved to Minneapolis where we lived until the crash of 1929. Dad had been working on the Rock Island Line out of Minneapolis when he suddenly found himself out of work. My grandfather Welna had suffered a stroke about that time and could no longer operate his flourmill at Niobrara. We moved to Niobrara and Dad joined his three brothers to operate the mill; however there just wasn't enough cash flow to support us and the entire family. In 1931 we moved to Chicago and moved in with my great-uncle Anton Welna.

We occupied one bedroom and I slept on our trunk. Mother and Dad had to pay room and board. (Uncle declared to everyone that for the first three days they were guests, after which they were boarders.) Uncle did the cooking and my great-aunt did the baking. Uncle was a professional chef who had at one time cooked for John D. Rockefeller, and in better times had owned a restaurant on the southwest corner of State Street and Madison Avenue in Chicago. He had come to Chicago around the turn of the century.

It was now the depth of the Great Depression and it took Dad six weeks to find a job. He became a porter at the north side store of Sears & Roebuck on Lawrence Avenue in Chicago where he picked up the trash, washed the windows, and finally worked his way into the electrical department where he attracted the attention of the Chief Engineer of all Sears & Roebuck stores. That spring I came down with scarlet fever and was admitted to the Cook County Contagious Hospital run by the county. I was put in a ward with eleven other men and boys and left there to die. The night I was supposed to die my parents were allowed to visit me for a short while. I remember waking up for a brief moment, seeing them covered with white hospital coats looking down at me, and then falling back to sleep. I spent two months in that horrible hospital before being allowed to rejoin my parents, except that my mother wasn't there—she had acquired scarlet fever and was confined in a different hospital on the south side of Chicago. During the time I was in the hospital I thought I was in prison. When finally released I had only been home for a few days when I landed back in the Cook County Hospital for a mastoid surgery. Again I almost died. Because of complications with the first surgery I had to have a second one on the same side of my head forward of my right ear. When I found myself on the operating table again, and they tried to give me the anesthetic (ether) again, I put up such a fight that I tore up the operating room. The nurses and doctor finally subdued me, performed the procedure, and were sporting bruises for several days after. Several weeks later I was well enough to attend school. In the meantime winter set in and I outgrew the trunk, and so it was arranged for me to sleep in a feather bed on the floor next to a coal burning pot-bellied stove. That was fine with me and I was happy— I was no longer in the hospital!

Mother was finally released from the hospital and I had to get acquainted with her all over again. For over six months my great-aunt had cared for me and I had adopted her as my mother. I shall always be grateful to her for the loving care she gave me in my mother's absence. We then moved to the north side of Chicago where Dad could be within walking distance of work, and I could go to a school close by. It was still the depths of the Depression and Dad continued to work in the electrical department, but he didn't earn much money. My uncle George (Dad's younger brother) moved in with us and that made it possible for my parents to survive financially. Mother and Dad slept in the bedroom and Uncle George and I shared the "Murphy Inadoor Bed." Dad also had two other brothers, Bill and Alvin, who lived on the south side of Chicago. I loved all of my uncles as much as my dad. They were all brilliant engineers and were never out of work. They all had multiple patents, as did my dad. When I had questions about flight (I was crazy about airplanes) they explained the physics of flight to me so that I could understand it. Uncle Alvin even taught me the molecular structure of matter. Atomic science was a fledging science in those days, but I was introduced to atomic structure at a very tender age of eleven years old. They never pushed me, they just answered my questions in a way I could understand.

It wasn't until 1933 that I completely recovered from my mastoid surgery. During that period I was warned not to play too strenuously because of my incision which was not completely healed. I obeyed precisely because I didn't want any more to do with hospitals; however, several of the kids took this as an indication that I was a weakling and started bullying me. I didn't consider myself to be big and strong or a good fighter, but I did learn something of the art of street fighting when we lived with my great uncle in his Sicilian neighborhood. When it was finally determined that I had recovered enough to defend myself my father gave me permission to react to the hostile bullies. Three big bully brothers lived next door to us and when the oldest and toughest took out after me I hit him so hard with a right hook that I fractured his jaw. His younger brother tried to even the score and I hit him hard enough to knock him down a flight of stairs. Weeks later when all three jumped me I chased them all into their kitchen into the arms of their mother. Needless to say, my poor mother had a few verbal fights of her own with mothers defending their bully brats.

By the time I entered high school I had a head of black wavy hair and a baby face that caused me to look ten years younger than I was. Because of my extensive reading of good literature my vocabulary improved beyond my age. All of this seemed to give the impression to the would-be toughs that I was a sissy pants. This caused many a fight which I never instigated, but which I victoriously ended. Rarely did I enjoy the privilege of a fight on a one to one basis. Most encounters were two or three against me. My father felt that some of the neighborhood kids were just plain jealous of me—at the time I didn't understand it. To this day I can't make people believe my true age.

By 1934 Dad was now the Chief Engineer of Sears & Roebuck's north side store. In 1937 he was hired by Mundelein College as their Chief Engineer where he became known as the leading Power Engineer in the City of Chicago. He also became president of the National Association of Power Engineers for the City of Chicago.

In 1936 Germany invaded the demilitarized zone (Rhineland) between Germany and France—a military act that violated the Treaty of Versailles. Hitler, Chancellor of Germany, bluffed the French because the German army didn't have the strength to maintain the occupation should the French enforce the Versailles Treaty with a threat of military confrontation. Hitler's bluff worked because the French never challenged him! This set a precedent of appeasement for future German expansion plans and negotiations with France and Great Britain. That same year civil war broke out in Spain.

At the beginning of 1938 I was fourteen years old, an only child, and living in Chicago, Illinois with my parents. (I would not turn fifteen until September.) I was a freshman at Amundsen High School in Chicago, and while I was aware of what was happening in the world, suffice it to say that I did not realize the true significance of it all. I had some awareness of the ancillary ramifications of the civil war in Spain because I was studying the concert guitar, and suddenly most of my music, which came from Spain, was no longer available because of the war. However, the subject was discussed routinely at the dinner table. Other than that, my interests revolved around baseball, swimming, bicycle riding, ice-skating in the winter, and the Boy Scouts.

During my fist two years of high school Dad took Mother and I on two separate auto trips through eastern Canada and from New

England all the way south to Virginia, and to all of the famous historical sites including the Capitol in Washington D.C. During my third and fourth years Dad took us to all of the western states, many of the national parks, and Baja Mexico. Since we had already been in most of the Midwest states I had now seen three-fourths of the continental United States. These were trips that most people never thought of taking in those days, and our friends were astounded that we were so adventurous. During this time my knowledge of U.S. history and geography had considerably broadened.

My mother was first generation French descent, and my father was first generation Czech descent. Both sides of the family had strong interests in European history and current affairs, and the subjects we very much discussed in depth with my parents each evening. In addition, I was reading everything about the subjects that I could get my hands on. I didn't realize it at the time, but my knowledge and understanding of world politics was increasing day by day and I could hold my own in a discussion of world affairs with most adults.

In 1938 Hitler had declared an *Anschluss* (union of Austria and Germany). Hitler used the pretext of Germans living in Austria, who supposedly wanted to unite the two countries, to invade and occupy Austria. Hitler accomplished his objective in that year. In 1938, twenty-three percent of the population of Czechoslovakia was German, and they were located mostly in the Sudetenland. The Sudetenland Germans agitated against the Czech Republic for German rule after much prompting by Hitler. Germany then made demands for autonomy in the Sudetenland causing a crisis in Czechoslovakia, and Hitler mobilized his army threatening war if his demands were not met. At a meeting in Munich, Germany, Britain, France, and Italy all agreed to yield to Hitler's threats (despite their previous guarantee of Czechoslovak Republic sovereignty), and allowed Germany to occupy the Sudetenland without ever consulting the Czechs. Prime Minister Chamberlain lowered himself by going to Munich, Germany to beg Hitler not to attack Czechoslovakia. The little man with the funny mustache was amazed that the so-called powerful Englishman would come to him, instead of demanding that Hitler go to Chamberlain. Hitler immediately recognized Chamberlain as weak and used it to his advantage in the negotiations that followed. I still remember Prime Minister Chamberlain of Great Britain when he appeared at the door of his airplane upon arriving in London, following his trip to Munich to see Hitler proclaiming, "Peace in our time" and waving a white paper. He seemed thrilled at his accomplishment, when all he had actually done was set the stage for World War II. This underhanded, knife-stabbing cowardly appeasement (known as the Munich Pact) eliminated all Czechoslovak military defense fortifications leaving Czechoslovakia completely defenseless. This is precisely what Hitler wanted for his obvious plans of expansion. With the stroke of the pen Hitler set the stage for the acquisition of one of the largest munitions manufacturing plants in Europe and the expansion of his military machine. We now know that Hitler was bluffing—he didn't have the military strength at that time to wage war against the Czechs who had defiantly mobilized their army and only needed the French, British, or both to back them up. The German generals had orders to withdraw should the French or British challenge them. (More about that later.)

Day by day I became more and more infatuated with world politics, the history and cause of World War I, the tragic Versailles Treaty of 1919, and what I believed to be the root cause of a coming world war. I spent my study periods in the school library reading until I had a good grasp of the subjects including the then current state of European affairs of the time.

As time progressed Hitler was clamping down on the freedom of the German citizens. Even though it was peacetime, elimination of free speech, food rationing, and intense wartime military preparations were progressing at top speed in Germany. The

German Bund (a pro-Nazi German-American front organization for spies and propaganda) was well established and operating widely in the United States. Germany was already expanding their influence in South America, especially Argentina. Many German-American nationalized citizens were openly advocating German rule of the United States! Concurrently, the appeasers and isolationists were undaunted in their beliefs that we had two oceans to protect us, and therefore had nothing to fear from Germany, and should not become involved in the affairs of Europe. This almost fifteen-year-old kid thought otherwise! In the fall of 1939 I joined the R.O.T.C. at Amundsen High School—I had just turned fifteen years old.

Indeed, by the winter of 1939 Germany was a military power to be reckoned with. Germany had a large well trained, and led, modern army and advanced air force, and the nucleus of a small but modern impressive navy. President Roosevelt commissioned Charles Lindbergh to visit Germany and evaluate the German air force. Lindbergh was favorably impressed and declared the German air force to be the most advanced in Europe in both equipment and tactics, which earned him severe chastisement here in the United States; unfortunately, he turned out to be correct.

The British were not prepared for war in 1939. Their army was thinly spread over the world and they had not updated their equipment. Their air force, as their army, had been neglected and was poorly equipped with mostly outdated airplanes. The British Royal Navy, supposedly the largest navy in the world, had very well trained sailors, but was composed of many outmoded ships left over from World War I, never modernized, and too few destroyers and escort vessels. Their ships were pitifully lacking in antiaircraft defenses. Their ancient, slow, bi-wing carrier airplanes were still in use well into World War II. They were about to pay dearly for the neglect of their armed forces.

France had a very large army that outnumbered the Germans by almost two to one, and was superior in numbers of tanks and artillery short and long range. The French air force was, however, seriously outmoded. Their navy was much larger than the German navy but not completely modern. They were lacking in carriers and naval aircraft. The French were a "paper tiger" sorely lacking in leadership and low in morale—a fact that would contribute to their early defeat in World War II.

The United States Army was in worse shape in comparison to Britain, France, and Germany. The army was miniscule numbering less than 130,000 ground, air, and services. There was not one infantry division of full combat strength, and not one organized armored division; there were two horse cavalry divisions at less than half strength. The Army Air Force was small with well-trained pilots but outdated equipment.

The navy was in no better shape. Following World War I, the United States almost totally disarmed for all intents and purposes. Most of our battleships were of World War I vintage.

Of the period from 1920 to 1933, except for cruisers, no destroyers were added to our own fleet, hardly any combatant ships (no battleships during that period) and few were under construction. Moreover, advances in the science of naval construction were hampered by the lack of opportunity to prove new design. In addition, practically no auxiliary vessels had been built. I remember that in 1940 we were so short of auxiliary ships that only one oiler and one transport vessel were assigned to the entire Pacific Fleet.

This dismal situation of the American, British, and French navies had its origin in the infamous disarmament treaties of February 1922. This series of treaties, which also included Italy and Japan, served to lull both the American Congress and Britain and France—with their policy of pacifism—into a feeling of complacency. Japan renounced the naval limitation treaty in 1936. Yet, both Britain and the United States still considered themselves bound by the treaties; however, the United States Navy had been allowed to deteriorate to the point where it would take as much as ten years to even rebuild it to treaty limitations.

Franklin Roosevelt had been Assistant Secretary of the Navy early in his political career. As President, Roosevelt realized the deplorable state of the navy in 1933 when he first assumed office. Roosevelt, along with Carl Vinson (Chairman of the Naval Affairs Committee) and senior admirals immediately began pressuring Congress for money to initiate the rebuilding of the navy. The first new construction of modern warships in years was for *Brooklyn* class light cruisers, *Gridley* class destroyers, carriers *Enterprise, Yorktown* and *Ranger*, and four submarines. The purpose of this change in attitude concerning naval armament was supposedly to provide much needed employment and was somehow tied to the National Industrial Recovery Act of June 1933. I think the real reason was because Roosevelt was immediately branded as a "war monger" by the pacifists and isolationists of the time—it was the only way he could get Congress to authorize it.

The first five treaty "10,000 ton" heavy cruisers of the *New Orleans* class went into commission in 1934. Congress in their infinite wisdom refused to authorize an increase in navy personnel which forced the navy to operate their ships with 80% of their required crew complement—this in spite of the fact that there was still high national unemployment. By 1939 the first of the *Atlanta* class antiaircraft cruisers, several types of auxiliary ships, including minesweepers, were appearing in the fleet. It was about this time that the battleships *North Carolina* and *Washington* (known as the fast battleships) appeared in the fleet—the first modern battleships in eighteen years.

The Spanish Civil War ended in 1939 and I once again was able to buy a limited amount of music. Hitler broke his agreement made at Munich the previous year—surprise, surprise—and seized Bohemia and Moravia, completing his occupation of Czech lands and creating a separate pro-Nazi puppet republic out of Slovakia.

Italian troops invaded and conquered Albania. Hitler annexed Memel (Klaipeda) from Lithuania, which had been taken from Germany as one of the many surrender terms imposed on Germany by the Versailles Treaty.

One of the most obnoxious provisions of the Treaty of Versailles was the separation of Prussia from Germany. What came to be known as the province of East Prussia was separated from Germany proper by a Polish neck of land known as the "corridor to the sea." In an effort to nullify this, the most unpopular provisions of the Treaty of Versailles by negotiation and consent, Hitler proposed free access through Poland by building a railroad and major highway to the free city of Danzig in East Prussia, and the return of Danzig to German control. The Poles refused to negotiate and Hitler turned to Prime Minister Chamberlain of Great Britain— the former initiator of appeasement—to help in solving the problem. Chamberlain announced his unqualified support of Poland, and Daladier, Premier of France, agreed. Hitler then turned to Stalin and in April a Nazi-Soviet agreement was reached, followed by a final secret Nazi-Soviet Pact in August.

The Nazi-Soviet Pact provided for the German occupation of west Poland with the east half to be occupied by the Soviets, plus the Soviet annexation of Latvia, Estonia, and Finland; however, in 1939 the propaganda release to the world was that the Nazi-Soviet agreement was simply a non-aggression pact. This pact made war inevitable.

September 1, 1939, my parents and I were on vacation at the home of my mother's aunt Helen at Mount Vale, New Jersey. Mother and Dad were relaxing and I was reading because I couldn't con anyone into playing another set of tennis with me. Suddenly the radio program was interrupted by a special newscast announcing the invasion of Poland by the German Army. My mother looked at Dad and said "the war has started." This wasn't as big a surprise to us as it might have been had we not known of the Nazi-Soviet Pact which had been announced before we left on vacation. At the time we thought it was a big joke having Hitler and Stalin buddying up to each other, and we wondered which one of these cutthroats would get the knife in the back.

During the next three days we listened to news reports of the progress of the German invasion and the reports from Great Britain and France. September 3, 1939, I celebrated my sixteenth birthday. Aunt Helen baked me a cake and Dad took a moving picture of me holding the cake with sixteen lit candles on it. Again a special news broadcast announced that both Britain and France had declared war on Germany. World War II had begun! While it was somber news to all of us at my birthday party, it was not a surprise. The return of German territories surrendered by Germany to other nations as dictated by the Versailles Treaty, and the expansionist ambitions of Hitler since he came to power in 1937, had made war inevitable. He was pursuing his long-range plans as mentioned in his book *Mein Kampf (My Struggle)*.

German forces were not only superior in numbers to the Polish army, but superior in armor, mechanized and motorized divisions, and air force. They had gone through extensive training for a mechanized war—new tactics previously developed by the British but untried in modern warfare. The German ground forces were formed around infantry divisions of about 12,000 officers and men; Panzer Grenadier divisions of motorized infantry and artillery, comprising 14,000 officers and men; and Panzer divisions consisting of two Panzer Grenadier regiments, a tank regiment, a Panzer artillery regiment, infantry, and service troops. Their air force was integrated to provide needed support to ground forces on demand.

The Polish army, while adequate in numbers, was inadequately organized and equipped for modern warfare. The Poles ignored the lessons of World War I and had practically no tanks, motorized transport, no antitank artillery, and no antiaircraft guns. They had practically no air force. They very foolishly developed their defense strategy around twelve brigades of horse cavalry with which they planned to combat German mechanized units. The results were predictable!

In anticipation of a German attack, Polish forces were deployed along the entire 3,500 miles of the German Czechoslovakia border and corridor. A small number of reserves were located in the Lodz–Warsaw area. Polish Generals had also ignored the writings of Frederick the Great who wrote that *he who defends everything defends nothing.* The Polish government depended on help from Britain and France to come to its aid. Under the circumstances neither country could act quickly enough and was probably not strong enough.

The Polish High Command was so antiquated in the formation of the Polish army and its military strategy, that it had no hope of stopping the German onslaught. In addition, the topography of the Polish territory where the German forces made their assault was particularly well suited for their blitzkrieg. The open flat plains of the Polish countryside allowed the mobile German army to quickly cut through and behind the Polish defense positions, encircle large portions of the Polish army, and cut their communications and railway lines with their air force. The horse cavalry of which the Polish army was so proud was absolutely ineffective in delaying the advance of German armor. They heroically charged German tanks, but to no avail. One does not stop a German tank with a lance or sword. German forces had advanced over 140 miles during the first week to the outskirts of Warsaw.

By 17 September most of the Polish forces had either been captured or wasted in battle, but Warsaw defenders were still holding out against the German attackers when the Soviets struck across their eastern border. This backstabbing attack provided the *coup de grace* to the Polish army. Warsaw fell on 28 September and all organized resistance ended on 5 October. The Soviets now controlled eastern Poland and the Germans the western half. The British and French had been powerless to fulfill their empty promise to come to the aid of Poland. The Soviets next annexed Latvia and Estonia, and attempted to annex Finland. Russia went to war with Finland in November and the world now became aware of the true reason for the Nazi-Soviet Pact. Germany and the Soviet Union were able to carve up Europe and grab territory as they saw fit.

The Finns put up a real fight, which turned out to be a severe embarrassment to the Soviets. Stalin had previously purged (murdered) his best generals because he feared they might overthrow him because of the seventeen million people he had murdered in the Ukraine. His commissars were running the show in what came to be known as the Russo-Finnish war. The purpose of the commissars was to keep the army from revolting against Stalin. The small Finnish army stopped the Russians cold and was able to keep the Soviet hordes from advancing into Finland through the Mannheim defense line. Finally, in 1940, after inflicting severe punishment to Stalin's army, the brave Finns were forced to capitulate and cede part of their territory to Russia.

Chapter 2

THE BATTLE OF THE ATLANTIC, PART I

1939

We arrived home in Chicago around the tenth of September to learn that on 3 September the German submarine *U-30* commanded by Captain Fritz Julius Lemp, had torpedoed the British ship *Athenia* killing 118 passengers, twenty-two of which were Americans—there were 1,300 survivors. Captain Lemp then ordered two shots from his deck gun to be fired into the sinking ship, killing many women and children. He then totally ignored international law, submarine protocol, and his operating instructions by submerging, leaving the scene, and not offering assistance to survivors in lifeboats. This incident marked the beginning of the "Battle of the Atlantic" which was destined to become the longest battle of World War II, and one of the most important—lasting until Germany surrendered six years later.[1] Fearing the spread of hostilities close to our shores, and because of the growing German influence in South America,

---

[1] For additional statistics on ship losses please refer to Hughes and Costello, *The Battle of the Atlantic*, p. 304. "During the month of September 1939, German U-boats sank 105 merchant ships of over 16,000 tons bound for Britain. By 31 December the losses came to 810 ships sunk for the four month period. With accelerated losses for that same period, and ever increasing U-boat activity in the North Atlantic, it had already become clear that Britain had a real supply problem looming for the future."

President Roosevelt took immediate action to get around his isolationist Congress by invoking the Monroe Doctrine, (a policy of continued attitude of independence of the Western Hemisphere from European influence).

I had started my junior year in high school and was beginning to form my plans for post graduation. It had suddenly become apparent to me that my dreams of one day becoming a successful concert musician would not materialize because sooner or later we would be drawn into the war, and I would have to plan for military service. With Hitler's rhetoric and actions, and the unprepared condition of Britain and France, it seemed to me that the only way that these two nations could survive was by the aid of the United States. It also seemed to me that the preservation of Britain and France was essential to our safety if we were to survive Hitler's policy of divide and conquer. I therefore threw myself further into the studies of mathematics, military science and tactics, international politics, and history in preparation for a career in the military. I also qualified for and was accepted for the rifle team.

On 2 October 1939, President Roosevelt, in an attempt to keep the country out of war, and maintain neutrality on the seas, declared a neutrality zone which became known as the "Pan American Neutrality Zone," stretching one thousand miles from Greenland to the tip of South America. No belligerents were allowed in this area, and the U.S. Navy received responsibility for enforcing the declaration.

President Roosevelt's action was probably initiated by the fact that two German pocket battleships, the *Graf Spee* and the *Deutschland* were loose in the South Atlantic sinking merchantmen bound for Britain. They had left port 27 September for the South Atlantic. The *Deutschland* headed for the shipping lanes near Bermuda while the *Graf Spee* headed for the shipping lanes off the Brazilian coast. These actions were all taken in defiance of Roosevelt's Neutrality Zone and on 30 September Captain Langsdorff of the *Graf Spee* intercepted the British cargo ship

SS *Clement* and sank her. The *Clement's* warning signal was the first indication to the British Admiralty that a pocket battleship was loose in the South Atlantic. The British Admiralty immediately organized eight hunter squadrons to search the entire Atlantic from Greenland to the Falkland Islands, and Churchill (then First Lord of the Admiralty) cabled Roosevelt to inform him of the news and invite him to have the U.S. Navy take part in the hunt. It was alarming news to the British Admiralty to later learn that there were actually two pocket battleships loose in the Atlantic raiding the shipping lanes. The *Deutschland* had sunk the British freighter SS *Stonegate* near Bermuda about 6 October, but the Admiralty was unaware of this until the USS *City of Flint* arrived in Norway, 14 October 1939, having been forced to sail there at gun point after capture by the *Deutschland*. She had a cargo of tractors, fruit and grain bound for Britain, which the Germans claimed to be contraband. This incident did nothing to improve relations between Washington and Berlin. After sinking three ships Hitler ordered the *Deutschland* home.

By mid December the German surface raiders and U-boats had driven the British closer to starvation than they realized with continually increasing British sinkings. The German strategy of operating surface raiders in various areas of the Atlantic and Indian Ocean, was causing the British to disperse their fleet, making it difficult to locate the raiders.[2] HMS *Ajax* spotted the *Graf Spee* off of the Brazilian coast at 0614, 13 December. *Ajax* was a 6-inch cruiser in the company of HMS *Exeter,* an 8-inch cruiser, and *Achilles*, a 6-inch cruiser, all designated Group G commanded by Commodore William Harwood. At 0618 *Graf Spee* opened fire on *Exeter* with her six 11-inch guns. Two minutes later *Exeter* opened fire on *Graf Spee*, followed by *Ajax* and *Achilles*.

---

[2] For further details of the battleship raiders refer to Hughes and Costello, *The Battle of the Atlantic*, p.56.

Shortly after the opening salvos *Exeter's* B turret was put out of action from an 11-inch shell and the bridge destroyed. The captain survived and took command from the secondary con amidships. Other hits knocked the remaining two turrets out of action and the ship was on fire, so the captain ordered two torpedoes to be fired as the *Exeter* retired from the action and headed for the Falkland Islands for much needed repairs.

Ajax and *Achilles* continued firing while in hot pursuit of *Graf Spee* with *Ajax* suffering hits on two of her turrets. These two light cruisers were no match for the *Graf Spee*, and so Commodore Harwood ordered them to fire torpedoes and retire under smoke. *Graf Spee* turned away to avoid their torpedoes and headed for Montevideo to patch up a hole at her water line and make repairs to her superstructure. The battle lasted ninety minutes and the *Graf Spee* reached Montevideo that evening—she was now trapped.

The British Admiralty made a false news release stating that the carrier *Ark Royal* and battle cruiser *Renown* had joined Group G to block possible escape of the *Graf Spee*; actually they were about four days away. Having received orders from Berlin the *Graf Spee* was scuttled on 17 December—Captain Langsdorff committed suicide two days later rather than face internment. And so ended the career of the ship that had sunk thirteen merchantmen during a three-month cruise in the South Atlantic. Captain Langsdorff was not a Nazi.

As we entered 1940 I was devoting myself to intense practice each afternoon on the rifle range, and was rapidly becoming a marksman of significance. I was advancing in rank in the R.O.T.C. and was now a top sergeant. I was ushering at the Chicago Theatre in the evenings and dating the girls on weekends and having a great time in spite of my concerns about the war in Europe.[3]

---

[3] Information starting on this page and including all remaining pages of this chapter came from my intense study and note taking during my elective high school history classes in 1940-41.

The first three months of 1940 saw an ever increasing loss of British merchant vessels due to increased activity of German submarines. The situation was becoming worse with each passing month. Hitler was determined to protect Germany's supply of iron ore which came down from Norway through the North Sea, (an area called the "covered way") and was vulnerable to actions of the British Navy. Both Britain and Germany recognized the strategic location of Norway, and on 9 April, Germany invaded Norway, Denmark, and the lowlands. Germany was successful in easily executing a coup because the Norwegian traitor Vidkund Qusling was the leader of the Nazi party in Norway, and he was responsible for delivering the country over to the Nazis. In addition to the political activity, several naval engagements occurred in what became known as the battle of the Skagerrak. The British Admiralty was taken completely by surprise with most of the fleet anchored at Scapa Flow. They did manage to maul the German fleet where they had suitable warships especially at Narvik where the HMS *Warspite* and some destroyers sank ten German destroyers. The Germans accomplished their objective by successfully invading Norway and establishing their army, navy, and air force. They were now strategically positioned to not only protect their own supply lanes but to harass the British supply routes.

Following the German invasion of Denmark, the British seized the Faroe Islands on 13 April (a strategic Danish possession). On 6 May the British landed 25,000 troops and seized Iceland (another Danish possession). The fiasco of the Norwegian operation demonstrated the incompetence of Prime Minister Chamberlain as a wartime leader and he was forced to resign 10 May to be replaced by Winston Churchill that same day.

Events moved fast in 1940, and on 10 May what had come to be known as the phony war (the war of inactivity) came alive when the German army invaded Holland, Belgium and France. The initial assault on Holland was accomplished with airborne troops and so surprised the Dutch, that the Germans were able to capture strategic bridges, airfields, and the major urban centers the very first day of operations. Their success was followed by the support troops and the Dutch were defeated by the second day. French forces under General Giraud finally arrived after the fact, and were much too late to alter the ultimate outcome. The Dutch had no choice but to surrender unconditionally.

The Germans wasted no time in solidifying their success in Holland. They immediately attacked Belgium 10 May. Again airborne troops were used to secure important bridges, so that German ground forces could advance southward. By the second day of the invasion, Belgium forces were in retreat and British and French forces were rushed to their rescue, but once again, they were too late.

The French had mistakenly determined that the forest of the Ardennes was a natural barrier, which needn't be heavily defended. By shifting their best troops to come to the aid of the Belgians, the Allies left the Ardennes sector at the end of the Maginot Line lightly defended. The German armored units of Army Group B were able to break through the Ardennes 14 May between the end of the Maginot Line and central Belgium while encountering little resistance, turn west and race to the sea. Once at the English Channel they turned north to seal off the important seaports from which a retreating army would have to escape. The situation for the Allies was perilous with only two choices: attack southward to link up with their southern units, or evacuate the continent by escaping across the channel. Allied forces were under the command of French General Gamelin who ordered a strike south on 19 May, the day before German forces reached the channel coast; however, Gamelin was relieved of command that same day and replaced by General Weygand who immediately countermanded the order pending further consideration. With no further direction from headquarters the

Allied armies were paralyzed and lost whatever chance there was to reverse the situation.

Luck was with the BEF (British Expeditionary Force) because the German main force of their Army Group B was halted by Hitler's command just ten miles from their location at Dunkirk, the only port from which the BEF could be evacuated. The opportunity to escape the trap they were in was not lost on the British commanders. While the Germans and the French were vacillating, British General Lord Gort, Commander-in-Chief, BEF analyzed the situation and on 25 May decided to evacuate his forces back to England. On that same day French General Weygand now called for a counter offensive in a rapidly deteriorating situation—his decision seemed to be based more upon saving face than sound logic. As usual with the French it was too little too late.

By now the British had had enough of the French and on 26 May the British War Cabinet cabled its approval of General Gort's plan to evacuate the BEF by sea. There was no time to lose because on that same day the Belgian Army collapsed and the government gave up. With Belgium defeated, German commanders now had additional troops to move on Dunkirk.

Having been conceived 20 May as a back-up plan for evacuating British troops in case of entrapment, the actual evacuation started on 25 May and rapidly gained momentum with each passing day until 29 May when the Germans finally attacked. While under constant attack the evacuation continued until 2 June when German air attacks became so frequent and effective that the operation had to be suspended. By that time however, with the help of the Royal Air Force, the Royal Navy, the poorly equipped naval task force, private boats, and just about anything with a motor that would float, 235,000 British and 95,000 French troops managed to escape to England having left all of their equipment behind. Of the thirty-nine British destroyers used in evacuating the troops, twenty-five had been sunk or damaged. This left the Western Atlantic with no antisubmarine escorts. Britain was now faced with a U-boat siege, attack from the air, and invasion. Churchill pleaded with Roosevelt for the loan of forty or fifty destroyers and airplanes.

William Bullitt, U.S. Ambassador to France warned President Roosevelt: "if Hitler should conquer France and England he would turn his attention at once to South America and eventually attempt to install a Nazi government in the United States." This would have been in keeping with Hitler's method of world conquest. Ambassador Bullitt was not the only diplomat who had arrived at this conclusion—many members of Congress had reached the same conclusion.

The French government fled Paris for Tours, France, on 9 June and Prime Minister Reynaud immediately appealed to Roosevelt for aid in battling the Germans. This was panic logic and wishful thinking on Reynaud's part. After all, considering our pitiful state of military readiness, where was aid to come from, and how could possible aid get there in time? In addition, Roosevelt's hands were tied. Paris fell on 14 June precipitating a Cabinet crisis which resulted in Reynaud's resignation and the naming of Marshal Petain (the hero of Verdun in World War I) on 16 June. Marshal Petain formed a new Cabinet and immediately requested an armistice and cease-fire from Hitler—his request was granted four days later. Italy had declared war on France 10 June and immediately invaded Southern France. For France, this was the beginning of the end.

The battle for France ended on 25 June 1940 with the signing of the armistice agreement between France, Germany, and Italy. It had taken only six weeks for Hitler's army to defeat what was once thought to be the finest army in Europe. It now remained for Hitler to arrange a compromise with the British, and failing that, bomb them into submission. Here in the United States most people were astounded at the apparent ease in which the German army defeated France, even though the Germans were greatly outnumbered by the French in both infantry and armored units. I followed the progress of the German offensive on the western front with great interest during that entire period which culminated in the French defeat. I was knowledgeable concerning the battles of World War I and I had expected the French to put up a real fight; however, as German Panzer Commander Hans von Luck who participated in the German break out under the command of General Rommel summed it up, the French were caught completely unawares by the rapid advance of the German Panzer forces—the French soldiers felt abandoned by their generals and retreated. Marshal Petain and General Weygand had obviously not paid attention to the German campaign in Poland.

The opinion of this armchair military strategist is that the French generals were trying to fight the war as they did the First World War where advances were measured in yards, and communications were not advanced to the year of 1940. They were comfortably quartered in chateaus well beyond the front lines with obsolete communications that deprived them of up-to-the-hour information of German maneuvers. They never went near the front lines where they could appraise the rapidly changing fluid situation of the mobility and advanced communications of the modern German army. French General Weygand was continually issuing orders days after the fact. He had no idea where the German breakthroughs and advances were taking place until it was too late to initiate proper action.

Secondly, they were the victims of the pacifists in their own government who couldn't deal with the reality of their times, namely the ambitions of Hitler for conquest. Most people in the United States were stunned at the speed of the German conquest and the lack of fight on the part of the French, and I'm certain that our government and military leaders were disgusted with the French and considered their performance disgraceful. In defense of the French army I should like to state that the morale of a fighting force reflects, to a large extent, the attitude of their government. After all, we had the same problem in our military because of the general attitude of a large segment of our Congress. As you shall see, the performance of the French in 1940 created distrust between them and their allies, Britain and the United States, and had a profound negative effect on relations during the coming years of the war. My mother was furious at the deceitful performance of the French government. After all, we had relatives in the French Air Force who perished in the fighting.

Great Britain was in dire need of emergency aid and Roosevelt's ability was limited in giving sufficient help. Some members of Congress wanted to retreat into a fortress America, while others realized that Great Britain had to be supported. Meanwhile, Nazi sympathizers in the U.S. were active in attempting to derail Roosevelt's attempts to aid the British, and the communists organized demonstrations on many of the college campuses. Many military men believed Britain could not survive much longer against the Nazi onslaught and to deplete our small military resources was futile. In June the British ship losses from submarine action increased to 585,496 tons from 288,461 tons in May. German U-boats and raiders had scored a 102% increase in just one month, and Britain's life line of shipping was severely threatened. She could not withstand many more months of such losses and she was about to go down in defeat due to the severance of her shipping lines. At this period in the war Britain was saved by the fact that German Admiral Karl Doenitz had less than forty operational U-boats, with only ten to fifteen being at sea, and of these only six could be on war patrol at any one time; however, Germany was about to step up her U-boat production and greatly expand her U-boat service.

Under the terms of the armistice France was divided into two zones: Occupied France in the north and Vichy France in the south under a regime headed by Marshal Petain in the south. The French of the southern zone became known as the Free French (which was a misnomer) and the southern government as the Vichy government. The northern zone included the entire Atlantic seacoast, but left the

Mediterranean coast to the Vichy zone. The French Navy was left with the Vichy government. At the time of the signing of the armistice the French fleet was mostly anchored in the Algerian port of Mers-el-Kebir in North Africa. There were a few other vessels anchored in British ports and others out at sea destined to enter British or U.S. ports.

With Italy now in the war on the side of Germany, and the uncertainty of whether the French fleet would fight alongside the British or the Germans, both the British and the United States had a big problem. U.S. Naval Intelligence estimated that the combination of the German, Italian, and French Fleets would collectively have one-third more power than the combined British and American forces in the Atlantic, even if the U.S. Pacific fleet were reassigned to the Atlantic.

Italian dictator Benito Mussolini, (Il Duce) could now carry out his boast of controlling the entire Mediterranean which he often referred to as his private sea. With his navy's six battleships, strong cruiser and destroyer forces, and the largest submarine fleet in the world, he had reason to be confident in the future. The only thing missing was the answer to the question of the French navy commanded by Admiral Darlan. Which side would French commanders choose to fight on? What would become of the three modern battleships, an aircraft carrier, two cruisers, two heavy destroyers and some submarines under various stages of construction?

The French navy had provided valuable assistance escorting Atlantic convoys as well as providing a strategic role in maintaining the balance of Mediterranean sea power for Britain. The collapse of France combined with the entry of Italy into the war on the side of Germany created a negative balance of sea power against both Britain and the United States, the results of which could be cataclysmic.

The British navy had German seaports blockaded and their raiders and submarines had to use caution and stealth to gain open water so as to be able to prey on British shipping. Both Churchill and Roosevelt suspected that the Germans planned to seize the French fleet when it suited them. To combat that possibility, Churchill offered an ultimatum to the French navy commanders which included the choice to fight alongside British ships, accept internment, or scuttle their ships. If none of these choices were acceptable, French admirals were informed that the British navy would use whatever force was necessary to prevent their ships from falling into German or Italian hands. French ships in British ports were either seized, or their commanders agreed to British terms.

In Alexandria, North Africa, French Admiral Godfroy agreed to British terms on 3 July 1940. In the French North African base of Mers-el-Kebir Admiral Gensoul who commanded the most powerful units of the French fleet refused the British terms. That same day British Admiral Somerville ordered his powerful battle force to open fire on the French warships in the harbor either sinking or disabling all except the battle cruiser *Strasbourg* which made a remarkable escape to Toulon with four French destroyers. Both Churchill and Roosevelt were immensely relieved—Churchill's decisive action won him approval in the United States. The French suffered heavy casualties plus the loss of ships, which became a point of contention that played a significant role in the coming battles of North Africa. When the new Vichy government complained to Roosevelt about the odious aggression of the British he reportedly replied: *I would not have had it otherwise. I am a realist.* Britain had just demonstrated that she would not relinquish her sea supremacy. (See Plate 1)

French Deputy Premier Pierre Laval, Jean Giraudoux, and other Fascist intellectuals were all Nazi collaborators who were partially responsible for the fall of France. Many of them became part of the French occupied government in Paris, and a few became

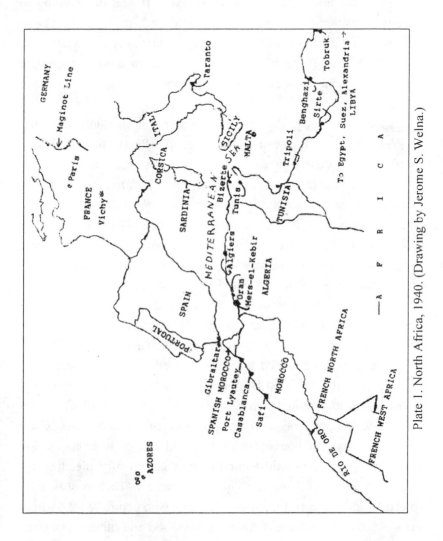

Plate 1. North Africa, 1940. (Drawing by Jerome S. Welna.)

part of the Vichy government. Their pre-war collaboration with the Germans continued throughout World War II and did nothing to improve relations between the British and the French. Their influence in the attitude of the French government is still apparent to this day. French General Charles De Gaulle refused to cooperate with the Germans and fled to England where he set up a Free French organization in exile.

Joseph Kennedy, Roosevelt's Ambassador in London, (father of President John F. Kennedy) advised the President that Britain should make an early peace with Germany. As early as September 1940 he reported to Roosevelt, *I have yet to talk to any military or naval expert of any nationality this week who think that England has a Chinaman's chance.* Joe Kennedy was either a sorry pessimist or a Nazi sympathizer. He was also on the wrong side of the great debate raging in the United States at the time—isolation or intervention. Roosevelt was definitely not an isolationist. Kennedy kept working against Roosevelt in belief that the British had no chance of wining the war, and that the U.S. would do well to forget about helping the British and side in with the Nazis.

Roosevelt became fed up with Kennedy's pessimistic reports and named Colonel "Wild Bill" Donovan as his personal emissary, who he sent to London with a team of high level staff officers to study and properly assess the situation of Britain's needs for survival. Losses of convoy ships from all causes were increasing with each passing month. Churchill was continually pleading for help from the U.S., especially escort vessels. Britain was now forced to defend herself from the Germans who controlled the whole French coastline and could challenge the food and other supplies of essentials by preying on British shipping with all types of surface craft, U-boats, and aircraft. In addition, Britain had to defend herself from the constant threat of a German invasion. The Committee to Defend America had placed ads in major newspapers such as *Between the U.S. and Hitler stands the British Fleet.*

Isolationist opposition was so strong that Roosevelt felt he couldn't release fifty over-age destroyers to Britain; however, a legal way was found to trade the destroyers for British bases in the Atlantic. It was a win-win situation for both countries. We needed the bases and the British needed the ships. In the deal we acquired the use of Newfoundland, Bermuda, the Bahamas, Jamaica, St. Lucia, Trinidad and British Guiana as naval and air bases. Some of these bases were leased and some were given to us. The *St. Louis Post Dispatch* declared, *Mr. Roosevelt today committed an act of war...Of all sucker real estate deals in history this is the worst and the President of the United States is the sucker.* So claimed the isolationists! When I heard this I thought of Randolph Hearst's father who purchased 1,600 square miles of land in the late 1800's in and around San Simeon, California, for a reported twenty-five cents an acre. He also was called a "sucker"!

The news of the deal was greeted in Britain, and with the majority of the population in the U.S., with enthusiasm. Many people in the U.S. were looking at the deal as strictly an economic benefit to the country, and not as a tactical defense matter. Even though I was now only seventeen years old, I considered it a great addition to our national defense. Later, as a seagoing sailor, my appraisal of the deal would prove correct. The first eight of the destroyers arrived in Halifax, Nova Scotia, 6 September to be taken over by the Royal Navy. These ships which were considered to be outdated were by no means outmoded for antisubmarine service. I had the pleasure of serving as a trainee aboard several of these ships during my training period and I can attest to the fact that they were fast, (they could make thirty-five knots) highly maneuverable, seaworthy, well engineered, and well armed for their intended use. They were equipped with torpedo tubes, depth charges, four 4-inch main battery guns, and several 20mm antiaircraft guns. Most destroyers of this age group were still in service in our navy when the Japanese hit Pearl Harbor 7 December 1941, and continued to see service in the South Pacific for the first two years of the war. Before being turned over to the British they were reconditioned, cleaned, and stocked with food and ammunition. I think the British sailors who took them over thought that they had died and gone to destroyer heaven.

The Germans and Italians were extremely angry over this deal. These fifty destroyers increased the destroyer strength of the Royal Navy to greater than it had been before Dunkirk. Also, the Germans knew all about these ships and their reputations as well engineered combat vessels. Germany would now have increased difficulty in maintaining their ability to strangle Britain's lifelines on the sea. In his rage Hitler ordered Doenitz to increase unrestricted warfare to the maximum. This meant that the German U-boats were to sink everything in sight with no warning.

As the American destroyers were absorbed into the Royal Navy they were given new names common to towns in both England and the United States. The USS *Aaron Ward* was renamed HMS *Castleton*, the USS *Phillip* became HMS *Lancaster*, and so on. These old greyhounds, as they were also known because of their gray paint, served the British navy well. There were seven of them lost in various engagements, but those same seven logged seven confirmed kills of German U-boats before the U.S. was even in the war.

On 5 November 1940, President Roosevelt was elected to an unprecedented third term. I remember the election well. The German Bund and the communists tried to sway the public with lies and misinformation but it didn't work. Churchill immediately cabled his congratulations to Roosevelt while at the same time informing him of the dire economic strait that Britain was in. Britain was close to bankruptcy, having exhausted most of its economic resources. Churchill pleaded for aid to hold off the Nazi hordes until the preparations of the United States were complete. In one of his famous radio fireside chats the President explained his new commitment to the nation:

If Britain should go down, all of us in all America would be living at the point of a gun, a gun loaded with explosive bullets, economic as well as military. We must produce arms and ships with every energy and resource we can command. We must be the great arsenal of democracy.

January of 1941 the Lend-Lease Bill was sent to Congress and became law 11 March 1941, after much heated resistance from the isolationists. As a result of this act American industry could now be mobilized for all-out production to aid the democracies and re-arm the United States.

Roosevelt's remarks of November 1940 were very poignant. After all, the Battle of Britain had started the preceding August with German Operation Sealion—the planned invasion of Britain. Hitler wanted Britain out of the war and was upset with Churchill because he couldn't bully him into a peace agreement. Germany was unprepared to cross the channel with an invasion army but Hitler wanted to do it regardless of the advice of his generals and admirals who knew that they were not ready for such an undertaking. Air Marshal Herman Goering felt that Britain could be forced to surrender by continuous air attack. It was finally decided to start the battle with attacks on British fighter bases and radar installations 13 August. Meanwhile landing craft, ships, barges and troops were being assembled for the actual invasion.

The German air force had been sporadically raiding Britain but this raid included 1,400 bombers and was the largest to date—it was to be the first in a series of raids designed to destroy the British air bases defending London. After crippling the Royal Air Force in these areas, Goering planned to shift bombing attacks to the seaports where he could destroy naval and merchant marine facilities. This would then pave the way for German airborne troops to be dropped, followed by the main army.

As Goering and Field Marshall Albert Kesselring soon found out, the British were not going to be an easy pushover as were the French and Poles. By this time the British had managed to build enough fighter aircraft and train enough pilots to equal the Germans in numbers and quality. The British Spitfire II and Hurricane fighters did not have as far to fly as the German M.E. 109s. The British had a well developed and effective radar warning system which allowed their fighters to scramble and lay in wait for their attackers who, with a low flying radius of 125 miles, now had a low fuel margin for combat. The British proved to have excellent fighter pilots—their problem at the beginning of the battle was that they didn't have enough of them. They were building fighter aircraft faster then they were training pilots. It was about this time that I started seeing British fighter pilot trainees in and near Chicago.

By 14 September Germany had assembled the necessary barges and other vessels for Operation Sealion; however, Goering was not making satisfactory progress in destroying British targets or breaking British morale. On 15 September, in a final effort to destroy London and crush British morale, Goering sent one thousand bombers over to London accompanied by five fighter planes for each bomber in a daylight raid. Because of their early warning system the British were waiting for them. The battle, which lasted most of the day, was a failure for the German Luftwaffe. In spite of their numerical superiority the Luftwaffe took a real beating. The British destroyed twenty-six German bombers while losing only twenty-six of their fighter aircraft, but best of all, they broke up the German formations so that the Luftwaffe never achieved their objectives, one of which was to neutralize the RAF. British bombers were now able to take the offensive and destroy the German assembly of invasion craft, thus destroying Hitler's dream of invading Britain.

Once again the Germans changed their tactics. Hitler was still bent on destroying British morale. The German air force now began using incendiary bombs, which proved to be more destructive than the conventional high explosive ones. They were dropped in night raids when it was more difficult for the RAF to get at the bombers before they were over London, or other principal cities. Incendiaries caused hot fires which were very difficult to extinguish, and which gutted whole blocks of buildings—many people were killed because they could not stay in their air raid shelters due to the intense heat.

Since Hitler couldn't break British civilian morale in and around London he ordered the Luftwaffe to attack smaller towns in the rural areas. Coventry, one of the first small towns to suffer the wrath of the Nazis, was located about ninety miles northwest of London and had absolutely no value to them as a military target. They knew there was no manufacturing or military base of any kind there. They knew the town, which was once the seat of Parliament during the fifteenth century, to be steeped in history dating back to 1043 when Lady Godiva took her famous ride naked through the streets to protest her husband's cruel tax. Coventry, the cathedral city, was rich in Shakespearean history and the legends of Henry VIII. Goering's objective was to destroy this beautiful historic town with its many historic buildings such as St. Michael's Cathedral which was totally demolished, and teach the British a lesson not to defy the great Nazis. They just about leveled the whole town in the attack, killing and wounding thousands of civilians and leaving most of the survivors homeless. They did the same to Birmingham, Bristol, and eight other towns of no military value before they returned to bombing London and the seaports. While their main objective was to bomb the English into submission, what they really accomplished was to bomb them into hatred. What the Germans did to Coventry on the night of 14-15 November 1940, was repaid to them with interest when the British and U.S. Air Force later bombed the German City of Dresden in retaliation for Coventry. The bombing with incendiary ordnance created such a tremendous firestorm that it completely reduced the entire city to rubble, while killing most of the population in the process. The British message to the Germans was, if you want to destroy our cities, we now have the bombers to do the same to you. This is what Hitler has brought you. Dresden was a communication center for the eastern front and therefore a military objective.

In the years that have passed since the termination of World War II, I have had the opportunity to work and talk with many Europeans. The British admire the Germans for their industrialist attitude in rebuilding their country following the war; however, they hate them for what the Luftwaffe did to Coventry and their wanton destruction of over thirty other cities. The Germans don't understand why the British leveled Dresden. On the contrary, they complain about the destruction of Dresden, but never make a mention about Coventry or any of the other cities the Luftwaffe destroyed, including London.

I can remember sitting in the movie theatres watching the newsreels of the German bombing blitz of Britain and thinking about those poor people having to live through that death and destruction day after day. I was also thinking about how lucky we were in the U.S. that we didn't have to go through that. Roosevelt was correct; Great Britain was all there was between the Nazis and the loss of our country, and we had better get busy and rebuild our military to protect us, as well as help the British as much as possible. We have to hand it to the English people. The blitz had already caused thousands of people to be killed, tens of thousands to be made homeless, commerce and industry to be completely disrupted, food and other essential shortages, and yet the people were more resolved than ever to fight and defeat Hitler and his fanatic Nazis for what he was having his military do to them. By this time the American people were recognizing the true dangers the Nazis presented to the world. Near the end of 1940 the mood in the

United States was definitely drifting away from isolation, although many members of Congress hadn't figured it out yet.

By January of 1941 it was apparent that the Luftwaffe had been unsuccessful in achieving its two main objectives, the destruction of the RAF and the breaking of English morale. Air raids would continue for months to come but it was quite evident that the days of the massive air raids were over. Hitler and Goering had shot their wad—they had lost hundreds of aircraft and trained crews with nothing to show for it but growing British strength.

While the air war over Britain was in progress, the sea war had escalated. German Grossadmiral Karl Donitz had developed a plan of submarine attack against convoys that would prove devastating to them. The Germans had broken the British Navy's code and were reading their mail in real time, thus HQ was able to direct their submarines to the convoys for attack. Previous to this time the submarine commanders were free to attack individually. With the new system they would surface attack as a group at night, break down the convoy's defense, scatter the ships, and pick them off. With their low surface profile and speed, and being so difficult to see at night, they could operate much like torpedo boats. The first submarine commander to sight the convoy would report the position to the others in the group, and after assembling they would infiltrate the convoy between ships and make their attack. Since they were on the surface, sound detection gear could not locate them. This system proved devastating to convoys—the British immediately termed them "wolf packs."

On or about 20 September a wolf pack of four German submarines attacked a fast moving convoy composed of forty-one merchant ships bound for Britain from the United States, escorted by four British corvettes and a sloop. The wolf pack attacked at night and sank eleven ships of much needed supplies.

Three days prior to this attack the passenger liner *City of Beneras* was sailing independently from Britain to North America with hundreds of children aboard being evacuated from the bombing of Britain. On 17 September, six hundred miles out, she was torpedoed at night by the German submarine U-48. Seventy-seven children perished! This incident was a perfect example of Hitler's unrestricted naval warfare.

On 27 September Germany, Italy, and Japan signed the "Tripartite Pact." This recognized the leadership of Germany and Italy in the establishment of a new order in Europe, in return for their accepting Japan's establishment of a new order in Greater Asia. The agreement's major objective was to ensure that the three nations would mutually co-operate in order to confine the United States to North America, thus blocking it from all other regions of the world. This agreement was tantamount to a declaration of war on the United States, which was not about to give up its economic influence in other parts of the world. More members of Congress (but not the entire Congress) were suddenly becoming more aware of the true aims of the Axis powers in establishing a New World order/control. I shuddered at the stupidity of the isolationists in the country. What would it take to wake them up?

The sea war continued to heat up in the remaining days of September and the entire month of October when in those two months the Germans sank more merchant tonnage than in any other two months of the war. This escalation of shipping losses rocked the British government, which could not withstand many more months of this kind of carnage. Plans to reorganize and reprioritize supplies for the Royal Navy were immediately initiated. There were two problems however; first, it would take at least six months to accomplish the necessary changes to combat the wolf packs, and secondly, Britain was running out of money. In August the Chancellor of the Exchequer had forecast that Britain would run out of gold by the end of the year. On 5 January 1941, the heavy cruiser USS *Louisville* arrived at Capetown, South Africa, to pick up 150 million dollars in gold bullion to be transferred to the United States for the purchase of much needed war materials. To add to the problem many defeatists in this country felt that the British couldn't survive another year, so why help them by extending credit? Many people in the country felt that if we were nice to the Germans they wouldn't bother us. That was immature logic for "we don't want our sons to go to war."

While fighting to keep the sea lanes open in the North Atlantic, the British were also justifiably concerned about the Italian Fleet cutting their life-line in the Mediterranean. On 11 November 1940, torpedo bombers operating from aircraft carriers attacked the Italian fleet that was at anchor in the shallow bay at Taranto, Italy. The Italian command evidently thought they were safe from attack because of the shallow water and difficulty of submarines and aircraft to launch a torpedo attack under such conditions. The British, however, had worked out a method for launching torpedoes from aircraft to run shallow. The results were devastating for the Italians. The British crippled the Italian fleet while only suffering the loss of two aircraft. This decisive battle was not lost on the Japanese who copied the technique and applied it to their attack on the U.S. fleet at Pearl Harbor 7 December 1941. With the Italian fleet disposed of, the British could now supply their 50,000 troops in Egypt (defending the Suez Cannel) through Gibraltar, rather then sending supply vessels the long tedious route around the Cape of Good Hope, and up through the Indian Ocean to Suez.

By the end of December 1940 the British, under the command of General Sir Archibald Wavell, had successfully defeated the Italian army in North Africa. During the period from mid September to year's end, Wavell received some reinforcements, including three armored regiments, which he used to successfully maul the Italian Army. In January 1941, while being outnumbered as much as three to one, he would almost totally destroy the Italian army and take 125,000 prisoners, while suffering few losses to his forces.

Christmas of 1940 was a bleak affair with the continuous sinking of all kinds of shipping by U-boats and raiders. The British were holding on by the skin of their teeth in hopes that Roosevelt would be able to get his Lend-Lease Bill #1776 passed in Congress so that he could help them by providing the necessary war materials they needed to combat the Nazi dictator. Roosevelt was also attempting to rebuild our navy so that we could defend our shores against possible attack from Hitler and Japan. With an isolationist pacifist Congress, and propaganda from the German (Nazi) Bund and the communists, both of whom were against helping the British, he was having his problems. With the Japanese threat and their expansion program in the Pacific, there was much talk of the need for a two-ocean navy.

January of 1941 found me a cadet officer in the R.O.T.C. and a member of the officers' club. There was much talk concerning the probability of all of us ending up in the military as a career. After all, the draft had been established by Congress earlier in 1940. The only question was, would I enter the army or the navy? At that point I was leaning toward the navy. To us, war seemed manifest. To some of our classmates we were excitable pessimistic kooks with great imaginations who lived in another world—others admired us for of our maturity and insight.

That same month, as a senior member of our rifle team, I competed in the Chicago Rifle Match. Each school's team consisted of thirteen riflemen, and each team competed against the entire teams of the city in this match. Our team placed third in the city—I placed second on our team with a score of 397 of a possible 400. My buddy, James Honan, placed first with a score of 398. We both were the best marksmen on the team, and on any given day one could beat the other, but never by more than one or two points. A few days later our team fired in the Sixth Corps Trophy Match. This event was a little tougher because there were only 200 possible points. I placed first and beat Honan this day by one point with a score of 199 out of a possible 200 points. Again our team placed third in the entire competition. Even though the team didn't place number one, we did some mighty fine shooting.

Chapter 3

THE BATTLE OF THE ATLANTIC, PART II

1941

In January of 1941 the United States was still unprepared for war, and it seemed questionable as to when our forces could be built up to a strength suitable for defending the country in the event of global war. This information was well known to the Axis powers, Germany, Italy, and Japan, and they were taking advantage of it. Germany hoped to defeat Britain within a very few months. Italy hoped to soon control North Africa and the Mediterranean countries. Japan was rapidly advancing in her objective of defeating China and was menacing all of Southeast Asia; furthermore, she was known to have one of the largest navies in the world, a fact that greatly disturbed Roosevelt and our admirals.

The situation concerning German aggressiveness in the Atlantic was growing more serious day by day. As a result, Roosevelt and Churchill decided that it would be prudent to have our naval representatives meet with those of the British in Washington to discuss strategy in the event of further expansion of the naval war. To appease Congress Roosevelt decided that the United States would assume the role of "belligerent neutrality." Hitler had declared a blockade around the British Islands and threatened to sink any neutral ship entering the area. His U-boats and surface raiders were also conducting an unannounced, unrestricted war throughout the entire Atlantic and the Indian Ocean.

On 15 March 1941 the *Scharnhorst* and *Gneisenau* sank fifteen freighters off the coast of Newfoundland and in American waters. In early March Hitler formally extended his war zone to Iceland and its surrounding waters, and in so doing stretched his war zone across the Denmark Strait to the three-mile limit of Greenland. As a result of this escalation of the sea war our navy transferred three battleships, an aircraft carrier, four light cruisers, and two destroyer squadrons, (eight and nine) from the Pacific to the Atlantic. On 9 April at the urgent request of Denmark's exiled government, the United States agreed to assume responsibility for the protection of Greenland until Denmark was free of the Nazi chains.

On 19 May the Egyptian steamer *Zamzam* with 150 American passengers aboard was shelled and sunk by a German surface raider in the South Atlantic. On 21 May the American freighter *Robin Moor* bound for South Africa with general cargo was torpedoed and sunk in the South Atlantic. On 24 May the British battle cruiser *Hood*, (the pride of the British navy) was sunk by the German battleship *Bismarck*, in waters between Iceland and Greenland in the North Atlantic. There were only three survivors of the crew of 1,419 officers and men. The next day Swordfish torpedo bombers from the British aircraft carrier *Victorious* located the *Bismarck* and torpedoed her but she was not seriously damaged and managed to slip away. The morning of 26 May a Catalina Flying Boat from British Coastal Command sighted the *Bismarck*. It turned out that Ensign Leonard Smith, USN was at the controls. The American officer was aboard as a "Special Observer" to help the British pilots become familiar with their new American aircraft. The *Bismarck's* location was immediately reported to Coastal Command and the main British fleet, which was looking for the *Bismarck*. Since the battleship was about 690 miles due west of Brest, France, it was possible for her to escape again, and gain the cover of the Luftwaffe, because the British main fleet was still 140 miles away and running low on fuel.

British Admiral Tovey ordered the carrier *Ark Royal* to launch Swordfish torpedo bombers for another attack. Fifteen bombers were launched and one torpedo struck her stern jamming her rudders and wrecking her steering gear. The *Bismarck* was in serious trouble and was no longer maneuverable. On the morning of 27 May Admiral Tovey arrived in the battleship *King George V* along with the battleship *Rodney*. The two battleships pounded the *Bismarck* into scrap iron and her guns went silent about 1015 when the cruiser *Dorsetshire* fired a torpedo into each side of the sinking hulk. *Bismarck* went to the bottom shortly after, taking a large part of her crew with her. The British picked up 110 survivors before they were forced to abandon the rescue because of reports of German U-boats entering the vicinity.

This battle jarred Washington, and the response was quick in coming. On 27 May Roosevelt declared an "Unlimited National Emergency.. That evening he warned in one of his famous "fireside chats":

> *The war is approaching the brink of the Western Hemisphere itself. It is coming very close to home.... It would be suicide to wait until they (the aggressors) are in our front yard.... We have accordingly, extended our patrol in North and South Atlantic waters.*

By 8 April Task Force 7.2 had been formed consisting of the carrier *Ranger*, heavy cruisers *Wichita* and *Tuscaloosa*, and destroyers *Kearny* and *Livermore*. This force, under the command of Rear Admiral A. B. Cook, was formed to operate out of Bermuda, one of the bases obtained from the British in the destroyer deal. It was soon expanded to also include the carriers *Wasp*, *Yorktown*, and *Long Island*, cruisers *Quincy* and *Vincennes*, and destroyer Division 11. It began patrolling the central Atlantic all the way east to longitude 30 west, almost to the Azores. The object of this force was to discourage Germany from attempting to seize the strategic Azores.

The U.S. Navy had already been operating out of San Juan, Puerto Rico, since 1940 with Destroyer Squadron 2 and twelve reconnaissance naval aircraft. In mid April this small force was enlarged to include two additional destroyers and twelve more Catalina flying boats. This small presence in the Caribbean was necessary because German U-boats had already surfaced to rake Dutch Curacao with shellfire and commit other atrocities. I have never learned what the motive was of the German high command for sending their submarines to shell these islands—other than their oil, the islands had no military value. Was the intent to draw destroyers away from the convoy routes of the North Atlantic? This may have been the best explanation.

An interesting development occurred in the French West Indies with the fall of France and the establishment of the French "Vichy" government. "Vichy" Admiral Georges Robert was left in control of Martinique and Guadeloupe, a small contingent of French ships including the aircraft carrier *Bearn*, a couple of cruisers, and some other warships. The question was, will he fight for Germany or Britain? Should he side with Germany that would be a threat to us. To combat this threat naval bases were established on the north coast of South America as the result of agreements with Britain.[1] They included Kingston, Jamaica; Port-of-Spain, Trinidad; Demerara and British Guiana. To augment these, others were established throughout the Caribbean.

As a result of Hitler's Icelandic war zone ultimatum Roosevelt directed Admiral Stark to reconnoiter the approaches to Iceland. Our high command recognized the strategic value of Iceland where

---

[1] I don't know if the French remained bottled up for the war or finally joined the allies.

British troops had been stationed since the spring of 1940, hopefully to prevent Germany from seizing it. Iceland was just 450 miles from the Scottish coast and only 530 miles from the coast of German occupied Norway. If Germany were to occupy Iceland they could all but shut down the northern trans-Atlantic convoy routes. Our leaders had no intention of allowing this to happen.

To expedite Roosevelt's directive the destroyer USS *Niblack* DD 424 was chosen for this delicate operation. Commissioned 1 August 1940, she was one of twelve of the new *Benson* class destroyers to join the fleet in that year. The *Niblack* was one of the first U.S. destroyers to be equipped with the new ASW sonar gear for locating submarines. In addition to Lieutenant Commander Durgin, captain of the ship, Commander D.L. Ryan, ComDesDiv 13 was aboard. The fact that Ryan was aboard is testimony to the sensitivity of the operation. Seldom, if ever, would there be a commodore commanding a division of one ship.

As the *Niblack* neared Iceland on 11 April 1941, three lifeboats were sighted—they turned out to be survivors of a torpedoed Dutch freighter. The *Niblack* had just completed the rescue of the survivors when her sonar gear detected the approach of a submarine. The crew immediately went to general quarters (battle stations). CIC (combat information center) determined that the range was closing indicating that the sub was positioning for an attack. Commodore Ryan ordered an attack on the submarine and depth charges were fired. This antisubmarine attack scared the submarine off. It is interesting that the fleet had specific orders not to fire on an Axis warship unless fired on first. For this to be allowed in this specific incident indicates the urgency of the situation. This incident is the first recorded incident of war concerning the United States Navy, even though we were not in an official state of war with Nazi Germany.

Niblack's mission combined with surveillance flights of navy planes prepared the way for U.S. forces to occupy Iceland, and on 15 June Admiral King named Iceland as an outpost of the Western

Hemisphere. Early in July U.S. Marines were landed at Reykjavik, Iceland, to reinforce the 25,000 British troops stationed there. U.S. Task Force 19, for the defense of the Icelandic area, consisting of two battleships, two cruisers, and nine destroyers was permanently stationed there in mid July 1941. Shortly after, the U.S. Army relieved both the marines and the British troops and construction crews arrived to commence building the necessary facilities for the new naval base. Late in 1940 the U.S. Navy had already selected the harbor of Argentia in newly acquired Newfoundland (from the British destroyer deal) as a naval base and naval air station. Construction units built the necessary facilities for base operations and on 15 July 1941, the United States Naval Operating Base and United States Naval Air Station were formally commissioned. Argentia became the command center for the destroyer forces and the forming area for convoys bound for Britain. (See Plate-2)

The beginning of May all British escort commanders were ordered to try to capture a German U-boat intact. What they were really after was the capture of the Naval Enigma code machine which would give their code breakers the information they needed to break the complicated codes used by the Kriegsmarine. This machine provided a highly sophisticated wireless secure system for transmitting unbreakable coded messages. Polish intelligence had done quite a bit of work on this machine prior to 1939, and had even built a similar machine which they used to try to crack the German codes. Before the fall of Poland in 1939 the British acquired the Polish machine, which even though rudimentary, helped their cryptographers warn the War Cabinet of the desperate situation in France. It was the key to planning the evacuation of Dunkirk.

The Enigma machines were electromechanical encoding devices, which resembled a typewriter. The secret of their operation was the constantly varying electrical path for the circuit completed when a letter to be coded was typed in on the keyboard. The signal passed back and forth through the internal wiring of rotors. A

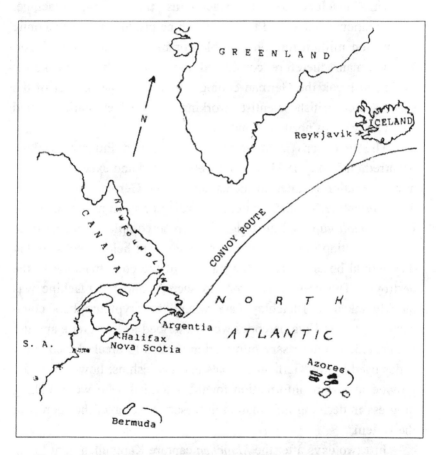

Plate 2: Convoy Route from Argentia, Newfoundland, to Reykjavik, Iceland, January 1941. (Drawing by Jerome S. Welna.)

plugboard was also included which together with the combinations and starting positions of the rotors determined the code. The meaningless jumble of letters in the coded message sent had to be sorted out by reversing the process through another Enigma receiving machine set up exactly as the sending machine. Mathematicians have said that the machine produced an astronomic six million million million possible combinations for every letter. The Germans therefore considered the code to be unbreakable. Trying to break the German coding system was the project of the super secret British scientists working at Bletchley Park, located about sixty miles north of London.

The first steps in attaining a sophisticated Enigma machine occurred on 7 May 1941, when a well planned and executed British naval operation resulted in the capture of the German weather ship *Munchen* in the North Atlantic. A boarding party from the destroyer HMS *Somali* captured an Enigma machine complete with its code book for setting the rotors. Prisoners were kept below decks so that they would be unaware of the transfer of the code machine to the destroyer. The crew was sworn to secrecy and the machine was quickly taken to Bletchley Park where the cryptographers could examine it. The Enigma codes were described as low grade and did not provide the necessary information needed to break the complex codes used by the German U-boats and battleships; however, it did provide important information for the scientists who were making progress in deriving information necessary to unravel the secrets of the system.

Just two days after the *Munchen* capture Kapitanleutnant Lemp in *U-110* (the man who sank the *Athenia)* attacked convoy OB 318 near the Hebrides. He was operating on the surface and had fired three torpedoes when the British corvette HMS *Aubretia* attacked him at flank speed with a medium pattern of depth charges. His boat suffered considerable damage from this first attack which was followed by two more successful depth charge attacks from HMS *Bulldog* and HMS *Broadway*.

The force of the depth charge explosions brought *U-110* to the surface. Faced with heavy shell fire from the corvettes, and fear of being rammed and sunk, the crew panicked and began abandoning ship. After the survivors had been picked up and ushered below decks so that they would be unaware of what was happening, a boarding party from HMS *Bulldog* went aboard the submarine and recovered its Enigma machine, code books, and other important logs, papers and manuals. The British also recovered spare rotor wheels, the current daily rotor settings, diary, and patrol signals. During the panic to be free of the submarine before it sank, Lemp was shot dead while trying to get back on board to scuttle his boat and destroy his Enigma machine. When notified of this success, the Admiralty notified the captain of *Bulldog* to maintain strict secrecy, make no mention of the operation, and to return to Scapa Flow at full speed.

The capture of this machine, complete with all documentation, proved to be the most important intelligence breakthrough of the entire war. The scientists working at Bletchley Park were now able to provide information so secret that it was given its own code name of "Ultra."

This breakthrough provided information that had a profound effect on the winning of the Battle of the Atlantic. Bletchley Park, later in the war, expanded their intelligence to read German signals in real time from no less than Hitler's command center. This breakthrough was so secret and important that the British didn't even tell, "those loose lipped Americans," as they stated it. I agree—it was a smart decision on their part.

The British Admiralty's Intelligence Center was linked to Bletchley Park by a private secret teleprinter line. The importance of this special intelligence at once became apparent when information on U-boat decoding signals concerning operational plans became available to the Admiralty. Vital information was also coming in concerning surface raiders such as the fast battleships *Scharnhorst, Gneisenau, Hipper,* and *Sheer* which were also responsible for sinking a large percentage of supply ships. Even though information being decoded was sometimes erratic, German success in sinking supply ships began to decline. Convoys were now being rerouted away from U-boat operation areas. What had been known to the Kriegsmarine as "the happy days," was temporarily declining; however, the battle was far from over and was destined to become more fierce for the next three years.

Hitler greatly underestimated the ability of American industry to develop and build modern equipment and ships for the army, navy, and supply of Britain, all at the same time. He must have been further surprised when Roosevelt agreed to furnish Russia with military supplies following the German invasion of Russia. Hitler also misinterpreted the mood of the majority of the American public. He was impressed by the isolationists in Congress (who were gradually losing credibility in the United States), a bad mistake made by many foreign leaders throughout our history. Americans were angered over the killing of American citizens as the result of Hitler's order to his commanders of U-boats and surface raiders to conduct unrestricted warfare in the Atlantic. The results of these atrocities caused Roosevelt to issue a declaration of "an unlimited emergency" on 27 May. With the approval of Congress he followed this on 14 June with an order which froze German and Italian assets in the United States—he also closed their consulates. The American public was mostly favorable to these actions. Roosevelt had the public backing, and therefore the congressional backing, if the Germans started a shooting war in the Atlantic. Hitler didn't attempt to retaliate because he didn't want to provoke a war with us on the eve of his planned invasion of Russia. The Japanese were rattling the saber and there was much talk of war in the Pacific against the Japs; however, Roosevelt didn't want to fight two simultaneous wars. He was quoted as saying, *It is terribly important for the control of the Atlantic to help* keep *the peace in the Pacific. I simply have not got enough navy to go around.* He was in constant touch with Tokyo, playing for time. The problem was, however, that the war clouds were gathering in both the Atlantic and Pacific, and those of the thinking public recognized it.

My parents and I recognized it, and such was the situation when I graduated from high school in June 1941.

My first job out of school was with the Jewel Food Co. I was hired as "Produce Manager" at fourteen dollars per week and reported for work in one of their grocery stores. It didn't take me long to figure out that this wasn't a get rich quick scheme. I had a title in lieu of money—this was my first lesson in economics. I hated the work and vowed to obtain an education so that I wouldn't have to work in what I considered to be undesirable jobs. I could see that industry was gearing up for war production and I wasn't prepared for any kind of factory work. In the fall I enrolled at Wright Junior College in Chicago for what I considered to be a waste of time. I was certain that war was inevitable and I just couldn't seem to concentrate. I was still entertaining thoughts of a career in the military, but I wasn't sure which branch to enter. I was following the international situation intensely, and I probably was getting ahead of my ability to use the acquired knowledge in some new vocation. Besides, I was only eighteen years old and who listens to an eighteen-year-old kid? My mother thought that I should prepare myself to be a history teacher. My father thought I would make a good engineer. Somehow, neither of these vocations appealed to me.

Hitler was so involved with preparations for his planned attack on Russia that he failed to recognize how rapidly the United States was rebuilding its military. He had dismissed as *"childish statements,"* intelligence reports that the United States was planning to produce 400 tanks a month and 18,000 aircraft by 1942. He also ignored his own intelligence information concerning the rapid build-up of the United States Navy. Here in the U.S. there was constant talk of a new "two ocean navy." All of this information was in our daily newspapers and radio news. For Hitler and his high command to ignore it all suggests extreme egotism.

At 0300, the morning of 22 June 1941, the German army invaded the Soviet Union with 120 divisions supported by massive armor, artillery, and 2,000 aircraft to begin Operation Barbarossa. While it did not catch Churchill or Roosevelt by surprise, it did astound most of the world including Stalin. We now know that the British had warned Stalin that the Germans were massing an invasion-size army on his borders. He was also warned by one of his envoys in Washington, and his spy in Japan—yet he chose to ignore the warnings.

Hitler had advised his generals that a blitzkrieg would result in the collapse of the Russian paper tiger as it did in World War I. The Fuhrer prophesized that Operation Barbarossa would destroy Communism once and for all. He also felt that a German victory in Russia would unnerve the United States enough to abandon Britain so that it would sue for peace. The German army immediately began driving deeply into Russia while military experts around the world predicted that Moscow would fall before Christmas.

On Saturday, 9 August 1941, President Roosevelt and Prime Minister Churchill met for their first historic meeting at Placentia Bay, Newfoundland. Roosevelt had escaped the press by going aboard the presidential yacht *Potomac* ostensibly for a vacation. Once at sea the *Potomac* headed for Martha's Vineyard where it rendezvoused with the heavy cruiser USS *Augusta* to which the President was transferred at sea. Both leaders had traveled in utmost secrecy with Roosevelt arriving first at Newfoundland aboard the heavy cruiser *Augusta*, escorted by the battleship USS *Arkansas* and the 17th Destroyer Division. Winston Churchill arrived next aboard HMS *Prince of Wales* together with his heavy escort of destroyers.

During this three-day meeting the United States agreed to provide escort protection for all convoys operating between Newfoundland and Iceland where they would be turned over to the Royal Navy. This agreement released over fifty British destroyers and corvettes for other operations. It was also agreed that some of the aid normally going to the British be diverted to the Russians. (See Plate 3.) While it wasn't publicized directly, the idea was to keep the Russians fighting the Germans as long as possible. This would prevent the Germans from invading Britain, and give both the United States and Britain more time to prepare for the Nazi menace. It was further agreed that the United States, under the "Lend-Lease Plan," would provide all of the aid possible short of war. If the British had any doubts about Roosevelt insisting that the United States would not commit to actual shooting unless attacked, they must have realized the true situation when the House of Representatives passed the very important bill to extend the selective army service by a majority of one vote! Notice of this vote was received at Placentia Bay during the meeting. It was also agreed that in the event the Germans invaded Spain, the U.S. would occupy the Azores. And finally there was a press release entitled "A Joint Declaration," which came to be known as the "Atlantic Charter." It was a declaration of Anglo-American war aims, which declared that the people of the world may live out their lives in freedom from fear and want.

When the news of the meeting was released to the world, the Nazi leaders had little to say—there was no effect on them. Hitler and his high command predicted that Moscow would fall before significant aid could be received. Hitler was right about insignificant aid before winter; but he was wrong about Russian resistance and he hadn't considered the Russian winter. He is supposed to have admired Napoleon, but he apparently hadn't read the history of Napoleon's defeat in Russia during the winter of 1812.

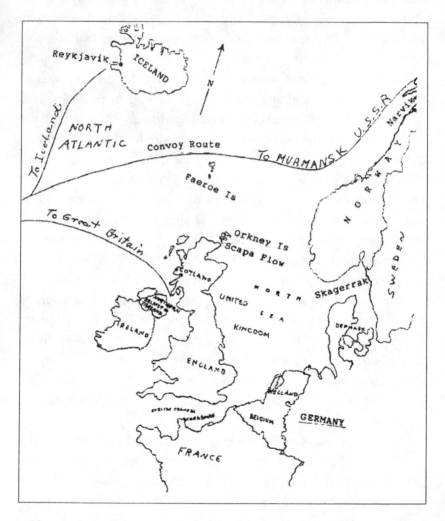

Plate 3: Convoy Routes from Newfoundland to Reykjavik, Iceland, and
beyond to the U.S.S.R. and United Kingdom, 1942.
(Drawing by Jerome S. Welna.)

We now know that the German admirals did not agree with the decision to invade Russia. Operation Barbarossa was requiring enormous amounts of resources which deprived the navy of materials needed to adequately carry on their operations against Britain's Atlantic life line. During the summer months of 1941 U-boat sinkings dropped by over seventy-five percent, due largely to Special Intelligence provided by the people at Bletchley Park. The Germans thought it was due to more escort vessels protecting the convoys. With more escort vessels and air patrol the convoys began to fight back. The end of June U-boats attacked a west-bound empty convoy, sank three empty tankers, and lost two U-boats for their trouble. Meanwhile, the British having received intelligence concerning the location of several German "milch cows" (surface tankers used to refuel U-boats) sank all of them operating in the mid-Atlantic. This forced the U-boats to return to port for lack of fuel.

About three weeks following the press announcement of the Roosevelt-Churchill conference, the USS *Greer* DD 145, was en route to Reykjavik, Iceland. *Greer* was an old four-piper, *Wicks* class destroyer, commissioned in 1919 and recommissioned for service in the North Atlantic in 1939. She was later refitted with antisubmarine sonar gear in 1941. While ships of her class were outdated in other armament, they were adequate for antisubmarine work, minesweeping, and other duties. Many of them served proudly all through World War II.

The morning of September 4, *Greer* was about 175 miles from Reykjavik when a British patrol bomber appeared and flashed a U-boat warning. The British bomber had spotted the U-boat about ten miles directly ahead of the destroyer. *Greer* acknowledged the warning, went to general quarters, (battle stations) increased speed to 20 knots, and initiated a zigzag course.

When she reached the submarine's approximate position, *Greer's* "ping jockey" (sonar technician) got a fix on the sub about 150 miles southwest of Reykjavik.

Greer's captain, L. H. Frost, was in a difficult position because the United States was not at war with Germany. We were at "belligerent neutrality" which was a somewhat ambiguous term; translation, our ships were not supposed to fire on a German vessel without express authority, or unless fired upon first. The skipper's dilemma was that he couldn't take aggressive action without express authority, and he couldn't ignore the submarine and hope he wouldn't take a torpedo. The only action he could take was to keep track of the submarine and notify all ships and aircraft within radio range of the sub's ever changing position. For over two hours he played cat and mouse with the submerged threat, always keeping his bow pointed at the submarine. At 1000 the British patrol plane inquired if the *Greer* was going to attack. The captain was compelled to answer in the negative. At 1032 the patrol plane attacked with four depth charges. The pilot then signaled that he was returning to base to refuel.

The tension among the entire crew must have been almost intolerable. Their air cover had disappeared and they had what was probably a very angry submarine commander to deal with. At the time it must have seemed axiomatic that the game they were playing would end in shooting. The only probable question was, who would score the hit? At 1240 the suspense was broken when the submarine turned and headed straight towards the *Greer*—at 1248 a lookout reported the wake of a torpedo off to starboard. The submarine had fired first!

The *Greer* immediately increased to flank speed and took evasive action to evade the torpedo which passed 100 yards astern. Exactly two minutes after the torpedo was sighted, *Greer* had authority to counterattack. At 1256 she fired a pattern of eight depth charges. At 1258 another torpedo was sighted coming straight for the ship. The destroyer did a hard left turn and the torpedo missed by 300 yards. Sonar contact was temporarily lost due to the noise of the exploding depth charges; however, the "ping jockeys" regained contact at 1312 and the search resumed. At 1315 another British plane appeared and dropped smoke pots on the spot where *Greer* had placed her depth charges. *Greer* continued the search until 1512 when she again made a submarine contact and dropped two more patterns of eleven depth charges. The sub evidently went deep and got away because there was no sign of an oil slick or debris, which would indicate a wounded submarine. She continued the search until 1840 when she received orders from Iceland to abandon the search and proceed to her destination.

Concerning the action of the *Greer*, Admiral King noted:

The action taken by the Greer *was correct in every particular in accordance with then existing orders.*[2]

In a memo to Admiral Stark, Chief of Naval Operations, President Roosevelt advised:

I think it is essential that two facts be made to stand out so clearly that they cannot be separated by any hostile press—first, that two hours elapsed between the bombing of the submarine by the British plane and the firing of the first torpedo by the submarine; and second, that no weapon was fired by the Greer *until after the torpedo attack began.*[3]

Three days after the *Greer* episode, the American merchantman *Steel Seafarer* was bombed and sunk in the Red Sea by German aircraft. On September 11, President Roosevelt made a historic radio address. Broadcasting to the world from the White House, he declared:

---

[2] Roscoe, *United States Destroyer Operations in World War II*, p. 33-34.
[3] Ibid.

*Upon our naval and air patrol-now operating in large
numbers over a vast expanse of the Atlantic Ocean-falls
the duty of maintaining the American policy of Freedom of
the Seas. That means...our Patrolling vessels and planes
will protect all merchant ships, not only American ships,
but ships of any flag, engaged in commerce in our defense
waters.*

*From now on, if German or Italian vessels enter the
waters, the protection of which is necessary for American
defense, they do so at their own peril.*

*The orders which I have given as Commander-in-Chief
of the United States Army and Navy are to carry out that
policy at once.*[4]

The above was Roosevelt's famous "shoot on sight" order.
From that hour on the United States was involved in a *de facto* naval
war with Nazi Germany.

Early in the morning of 16 October 1941, a distress call came
into Reykjavik, Iceland. A convoy of fifty merchantmen and their
escorts coming from Canada were attacked by a German wolf pack
about 400 miles south of Iceland and three ships had already been
sunk by the time the distress call was received in Reykjavik. Four
U.S. destroyers were immediately ordered to the battle scene to
offer additional screening protection to the convoy. The four
destroyers were *Plunkett* DD 431, *Livermore* DD 429, *Decatur*
DD 341, and *Kearny* DD 432. In addition, the British warship
Broadwater, the Free French corvette *Lobella*, and the *Greer* were
also ordered out from a separate location to join the battle. *Plunkett*,
Livermore, *Decatur*, and *Kearny* arrived on the scene about dusk on
the sixteenth to establish a screen 1,000 to 1,500 yards on the
starboard side of the convoy. The German submarines were waiting
for night to attack again.

---

[4] Roscoe, *United States Destroyer Operations in World War II*, p. 33-34.

The *Decatur* was an older ship refitted for North Atlantic A/S (anti-submarine) convoy duty. The other three U.S. destroyers were new *Benson* class ships of the latest design, armament, and fire control equipment including the most recent versions of radar and sonar gear. These were fast, highly maneuverable beautiful warships—a real advancement in ship design. The *Kearny* DD 432, had a well-trained crew and her captain, Lieutenant Commander A. L. Danis was well respected and competent; yet, a certain destiny will sometimes interpose when certain circumstances become evident during battle.

The wolf pack was still stalking the convoy, the *Kearny* was at her escort station in the screen, and the night was black with no moon or stars and little visibility. At about 1100 the wolf pack struck and one merchantman was torpedoed, lighting the seascape with flame and explosions. The escorts fired star shells, dropped ash cans, (depth charges) and broke up the attack. The Germans were not to be shaken off that easily and about 2315 the wolf pack struck again sinking two more merchantmen. At about 0200 the morning of the seventeenth the wolf pack attacked a third time firing a spread of torpedoes into the convoy hitting and sinking four more merchantmen.

Sinking exploding ships on fire created a fiery seascape that silhouetted escort vessels of the screen causing them to become perfect targets for submarine commanders. While operating outside the range of sonar gear, their close proximity to the merchantmen allowed the submarine commanders the advantage of a short torpedo range when firing torpedoes past screening escorts to hit merchantmen while disrupting the escort vessels' attacks all at the same time. It was during this foray that a torpedo struck the *Kearny* in a brief moment when she was vulnerable while silhouetted by a burning merchantman. The mistake of having escorts too near convoyed ships became apparent that night—navy commanders learned a costly lesson.

A torpedo hit on a destroyer is always severe, and *Kearny* was no exception. The explosion took out the forward fire room, ruptured the fire room cofferdam, severely damaged the bridge, ruptured the overhead deck, cocked the forward funnel, and damaged the deckhouse over the forward fire room. Four men were blown over the side from the force of the explosion. Seven men were scalded to death by live steam in the forward fire room. The ship was severely damaged with sea water pouring into the fire room through the huge hole below the water line on her starboard side; even so, she was able to regain power, maintain steerage, and retire to Iceland at 10 knots under her own power. This was all possible because of the design of the modern DD's with compartmentalization to seal off damaged areas of the ship, special structural reinforcement to absorb the shock of hits, and all kinds of back-up gear for maintaining power and communications in situations of emergency. Because of their design, and the extensive training of destroyer crews in damage control, it generally took more than one torpedo hit to sink a modern World War II destroyer. These ships, and the classes that followed, were a real tribute to the naval architects who designed them.

As a result of the torpedo hit *Kearny* lost eleven killed, and twenty-four wounded. The four men blown overboard were never recovered, even though the destroyer *Greer* searched for them at length. At Iceland *Kearny* was placed in charge of the USS *Vulcan*, a repair ship that took charge of repairs and had the ship back in service within a few months. The *de facto* naval war between the United States and Germany was now an absolute fact.

On 18 October 1941, the United States destroyer *Reuben James* DD 245, was part of an escort screen shepherding a convoy of forty-four ships to Iceland. She was an old World War I four piper destroyer of the *Clemson* class and was located about 3,000 yards from the convoy's port flank when, at about 0525, one of the escorts picked up a foreign radio transmission which appeared to be close to the convoy. The *Niblack* was positioned at the rear of the convoy formation and was the only escort vessel in the screen to be equipped with radar. *Reuben James* was just making a turn to investigate the DF (direction finder bearing) when she was struck by a torpedo at 0539. She was hit on her port side near the number one stack, probably near a magazine, because she immediately broke in two and sank. Only forty-five crewmembers of the entire compliment of 160 were recovered from the icy water. Some men in the water close to where the ship went down were killed in the water when pre-set depth charges exploded.

It has been suggested that the attacks on the *Greer* and *Kearny* might have been the work of Nazi fanatical sub commanders disobeying orders. But the attack on the *Reuben James* was considered to be deliberate. The Nazi Germans were obviously ready for an all-out war with the United States, and their U-boats were the conveyors of the challenge. If the Nazis were really looking for a fight on the high seas, they were about to get it.

On 1 November 1941, within thirty-six hours of the *Reuben James* sinking, President Roosevelt, with the authorization of Congress, transferred the Coast Guard to the Navy by executive order. The Coast Guard was now part of the Navy, and with the stroke of the pen Roosevelt had increased the navy's personnel, ships, and aircraft substantially.

Angered by the attacks on our ships on the high seas, Congress immediately amended the Neutrality Act. The first amendment declared that merchant ships could now be armed to protect themselves against attack. The second amendment did away with the restrictions, which denied American ships entry into European waters. Our navy could now convoy shipping into all ports of Great Britain. The unreasonable attitudes of "isolationism" and "belligerent neutrality" were coming to an end. American navy men had been fighting the Battle of the Atlantic for months, and those Americans who still believed that the United States was still at peace were refusing to acknowledge the facts and were about to be jarred into reality by both Japan and Germany.

Chapter 4

THE SEEDS OF WAR

W hile the Battle of the Atlantic was escalating, the United States, Great Britain, Free French, and the Dutch in the East Indies were all in conflict with Japan. The European war was considered by the Japanese as an opportunity to expand its policy of "New Order in Asia," which was in direct conflict with that of the United States Open Door Policy with China, established in 1899.

Japan's "New Order in Asia" was started in 1876 when, in quest for new markets, she sent warships to the independent kingdom of Korea to demand trade concessions. She used gunboat diplomacy in her search for markets and influence over Korea. The United States could do nothing about it because the navy, after the Civil War, had been neglected and allowed to deteriorate to the point of being incapable of challenging any modern navy including the Japanese fleet.

Captain Alfred T. Mahan had extensive experience in Asia with the U.S. Navy Pacific squadrons, and therefore had first hand knowledge of the deplorable state of disrepair of our outdated navy ships, plus the lack of service and coaling stations in the Asiatic Pacific area. By 1880 he was acutely aware that the United States had little leverage in competing with the European nations for markets in the Pacific. From history he had derived that sea power was a necessary component of national greatness, and he used Great Britain as the prime historical example of this philosophy. Mahan was appointed to the newly founded Naval War College in 1884 because of his extensive knowledge and intellectual abilities. He is famous for his lectures to young naval officers concerning the future of American sea power. Lecturing them on the lessons to be learned from Britain's successful use of maritime power and world trade to become the world's greatest empire of the time, he summed it up by stating that "War is not fighting but business, and a power not just military but economic." He constantly reminded the Congress that a strong navy was essential to commerce.

Mahan was influential in convincing then Assistant Secretary of the Navy Theodore Roosevelt of the wisdom of his theories concerning the navy and territorial expansion in the Pacific for the purpose of expanding commerce there. He had little trouble reinforcing his arguments when in 1890 Germany annexed the Bismarck, New Guinea, Mariana, Marshall, and Caroline Islands, all of which became part of the Hohenzollern Empire. In 1888 the United States and Germany almost engaged in a shoot-out over the strategic island of Samoa. The Germans were about to annex Samoa by force when a typhoon sank all but one of their warships, thus avoiding a military conflict.

Germany was maneuvering to grab Hawaii in 1894 when the islands became a republic. The United States declared that the island republic fell within the jurisdiction of the Monroe Doctrine and out-maneuvered the kaiser (Emperor William II of Germany) in his ambition to annex them. In 1898 they were formally declared a possession of the United States, and became a United States Territory in 1900. This was very important to the United States because it gave the navy a permanent base, which the admirals considered far enough away from Japan to thwart any attempt to ambush the American fleet. It was thought that the U.S. fleet could defend the Philippines from Hawaii in the event of a Japanese attack, and also the Panama Canal, which was then under construction.

In 1896 China had agreed to allow Russia to build the Chinese Eastern Railway across Manchuria to Vladivostok. In 1898 Russia leased land from China on the Liaodong Peninsula and built a naval base at Lushun (Port Arthur) and a port at Dalian. In 1899 the United States initiated the "Open Door Policy" with China, the purpose of which was to secure a fair share of trade for American businessmen. The United States hoped that it could win an agreement of the rival world powers to accept the principle of free trade and investment in China. In the spring of 1899 Washington contacted the world powers concerning the "Open Door Policy"— asking for recognition of the right to free commercial access to China. It was also hoped that Japan would be encouraged to refrain from more military intervention in China. The "Open Door Policy" was given a cold reception in Russia, because it was seen as part of an Anglo-American plot to thwart the Czar's plan to build the great Manchurian railway and establish control over the mineral-rich province of Manchuria.

Japan was working to establish her own sphere of influence on the Chinese mainland and when Russia constructed extension lines of the Trans-Siberian Railway through more of Manchuria, down the Liaodong Peninsula to Lushun (Port Arthur), she considered it a direct threat to Korea. Without warning the Japanese attacked the Russian fleet at anchor in the harbor at Port Arthur and sank it February 8, 1904. Japanese troops captured the port and advanced up the Darien Peninsula to defeat the Russian army. The following May the Russian Baltic fleet was transferred half-way around the world to even the score with the Japanese, but was defeated in the battle of Tsushima Strait.

As a result of Japanese successes in Korea and China, President Theodore Roosevelt petitioned Congress for funds to build twenty-eight battleships so that the U.S. Navy could have a two-to-one superiority in the Pacific. On December 16, 1907, Roosevelt reviewed sixteen battleships and their escorts at Hampton Roads,

Virginia, as they weighed anchor and departed down the James River for their trip around the world. Roosevelt wisely knew that for any nation to maintain industrial and military prestige in the world, an impressive show of sea power was absolutely necessary. The "Great White Fleet" was therefore the nucleus of his "speak softly and carry a big stick" policy. It did indeed put the world on notice that the United States was now a nation to be reckoned with. It also put Japan on notice that their expansion policies in Asia should not include the Philippines, which the United States had acquired after defeating Spain in the Spanish American War of 1898.

Roosevelt was aware of Japan's imperialistic attitude towards Asia in 1904 and he made no secret of the fact that the United States was not supportive of her aggressive policies. Japan had practically no natural resources such as minerals or oil, and had to purchase her needs from other nations. For the next thirty-seven years she would have to depend heavily upon the United States for raw materials required for her heavy industries, and since she was lacking in goods for export, she had a strapped economy. To gain more independence in the modern world she continued looking at China as an additional source of minerals, and the Dutch East Indies for oil. The only problem was that she didn't want to secure her needs through trade, but by the old feudal system of conquering her neighbors. Since this policy conflicted with the "Open Door Trade Policy" of the United States and China, Japan was now on a collision course with the United States. It was an imperialistic "New Order in Asia" policy that would eventually cause the Japanese government to commit national "hara-kiri."

When the fleet was welcomed home by Roosevelt he exclaimed, *never again will they laugh at Uncle Sam.* While the German kaiser expressed sour grapes regarding the world cruise, which had never been attempted before, and while Great Britain was miffed about Australia welcoming the U.S. Fleet over Great Britain as their protector, the display of power was not lost on the Japanese.

They never attempted to include the Philippines in their plans of Asiatic dominance until 1941.

From 1904 to the end of the twenties, the Japanese economy continued to improve. Trade with the United States kept increasing and the country was enjoying good times. The imperialists were unable to attain power in the government in such good economic times. In 1929 the American stock market crashed, along with the world economy. Many countries erected high protective tariffs which exacerbated the situation. As the U.S. economy deteriorated along with the world economy, Japan's trade with the U.S. collapsed. The value of the yen fell so far that it drove Japan off of the gold standard. Silk was the Japanese main export, and when the market for it collapsed, it bankrupted most small farmers who depended on the silk trade for their livelihood.

One effect of the great world depression on Japan was to create dissention between the democratic government, the industrialists, and the imperialists who controlled the army and navy. In China, General Chaing Kai-shek came to power and immediately went to work battling the local Chinese warlords to bring them into the national government. When in 1928 he marched north with his Kuomintang Army—reaching Peking the following year—he received the United States' recognition of the extent of the Republic's authority. He also received recognition from the Soviet Union. Washington's recognition of Chaing Kai-shek's "anti-imperialist crusade" infuriated the Japanese imperialists who saw the Kuomintang's march north as a threat to Japan's economic and industrial interests in Manchuria. Faced with the resistance of the military faction, the democratic faction of the Japanese government began to crumble—with the result that the military imperialists came into power. On September 18, 1931, the generals of the Japanese Kwantung Army defied the central government in Tokyo and invaded Manchuria. After a change in government by assignation and successive coups initiated by the warring factions against the Premier, imperialists managed their installment in the new cabinet—Japan was once again on the road to imperialistic expansion in Asia.

The German-trained Kwantung Army easily defeated the Chinese and conquered and annexed all of Manchuria and two other provinces. Japan created the state of Manchukuo out of three northern Chinese provinces. Manchukuo was not recognized by the United States and Secretary of State, Harry Stimson, wanted to retaliate by imposing sanctions—including oil embargoes—on Japan. Then President Herbert Hoover rejected the suggestion fearing that it would lead to war, for which the United States was totally unprepared. After more appeasement and bluffing the Japanese responded by sending their fleet to Shanghai. With the world depression worsening in both Britain and the U.S., military budgets were slashed to the bone, inspiring Hitler and Mussolini to embark on their policies of militaristic aggression. This exacerbated the ever-decreasing Anglo presence in the Far East, which gave the Japanese a green light to resume their "New Order in Asia" policy.

Franklin D. Roosevelt assumed office in January of 1933 and was faced with all of the old problems of his predecessor. Ambassador to Japan Joseph Grew warned that *the military and the public through military propaganda are prepared to fight rather than surrender to moral pressures from the West.* He warned that the non-recognition policy regarding Manchukuo would result in one side or the other having to eat crow. The Japanese were not about to give it up! Roosevelt was concerned about a century of commitment to the China trade, especially its impact on the weak U.S. economy; however, America's commitment was also a moral one. Rather than abandon the Chinese it was decided to step up technical and financial assistance to Chaing Kai-shek's government. The result was an ominous tough protest from the Japanese government. The Japanese considered the United States as another Western power attempting to exploit the resources of Asia.

As the rift between the two nations grew ever wider when Japan withdrew from the League of Nations and the Washington Naval Treaty system, she started a dramatic expansion of the Imperial Navy and air force. The Japanese had occupied Shanghai and Peking; and, Tokyo continued to insist that these aggressions were only incidents of little importance. By 1937 Ambassador Grew was warning Washington of the futility of issuing "moral warnings and threats" to check the aggression of a nation that could now be stopped only by a concentrated stand of the Western powers.

In 1937 a clash between Japanese and Chinese troops in Peking rapidly escalated into the Sino-Japanese War which was to continue until the Japanese surrendered in 1945. The Japanese continued their push into China. On 12 December 1937 a squadron of Japanese Navy bombers were hunting for Chinese river boats moving up the Yangtze River transporting Chinese soldiers retreating from besieged Nanking when they attacked the USS *Panay*. She was well marked as a United States Navy vessel and there was no difficulty in identifying her as such. American citizens were outraged over the sinking. The Japanese government remembering how the sinking of the USS *Maine* resulted in war with Spain, paid the United States Government compensation of $2,214,007.36. The incident was then forgotten except by the crew of the *Panay*.

Japan's military bureaucracy continued escalating the undeclared war against China and set up an Imperial General Headquarters to manage the China campaign. Even though Chaing Kai-shek's army was retreating up the Yangtze, he refused to yield to the Japanese and accept their demands of the "Imperial Way" as stated by Tokyo. In January of 1938 Japan sent another 100,000 men to the Chinese mainland to join the eight divisions already there fighting the officially described "incident."

The "incident" was in fact a full-scale war, and Japan became the first nation to mobilize. Controls were imposed on industry, food and gasoline was rationed, and the press was censored. The

Japanese military leaders were in power and had completed their stranglehold on the country by the end of 1938, had successfully killed democracy, and turned the country into a fascist state. They stated that conduct contrary to the interest of the nation must be eradicated. The nation was arming for a complete war of territorial expansion.

The army and navy agreed on territorial expansion but disagreed on which sections of Asia should be annexed first. The navy wanted to first take the rich British, French, and Dutch colonies in the Far East—they were especially after the Dutch oil. The army wanted to strike north against their old enemy Russia in Siberia, rather than continue the costly campaign to finish off China.

On 29 July 1939, the officers of Japan's Korean Army defied orders from Tokyo and attacked and overran Soviet frontier ports at Lake Kashan, where Siberia bordered Manchuria and Korea. The Russian port of Vladivostok, less than sixty miles east, was now vulnerable to Japanese attack. Fearing further aggression by the Japanese, the Red army hit back, and hit back hard with tanks and aircraft. Having no armor or aircraft the Japanese were forced to make a bloody retreat (more of a rout) back across the border while suffering very heavy casualties. On 11 September 1939 the Japanese were happy to agree to a border truce—they had suffered a solid humiliating defeat by the Red army.

That same year the Japanese seized the Hainan and Spratly Islands in the South China Sea. They were now in position to attack the Philippines, Hong Kong, and Indochina. By now they also controlled all of the major seaports along the China coast, and they were also well positioned to strike at Indonesia for the Dutch oil. It was imperative that they seize the Dutch oil if they were to go to war with the United States.

President Roosevelt was fuming at the audacity of the Japanese as they continued their policy of annexing more and more territory in Southeast Asia; however, there was little he could do about it because he still didn't have enough navy. In January of 1940 the Japanese-American Treaty of Commerce lapsed and was not renewed by the U.S. Roosevelt then prohibited, except under license, export of certain materials to Japan including steel, scrap metals and petroleum. The object was to force the Japanese to alter their policies of creating a new order in Asia.

The Japanese were taking every advantage of the European war, and were well aware of the preoccupation of Great Britain and the United States with Hitler. Roosevelt was playing for time until he could build a two-ocean navy suitable for meeting both the Nazi threat in the Atlantic, and the Japanese aggression in Asia. Meanwhile, the Japanese had occupied northern French Indochina, and were all set to occupy Burma, Thailand, Malaya, and Singapore.

Through most of 1940 Japan tried to use gunboat diplomacy to coerce the Dutch into selling them oil and high-octane aviation gasoline without restrictions. They also demanded the right to explore and develop additional untapped oil deposits. The Dutch refused and attempted to get assurances from both the British and U.S. to defend them in case of attack by the Japanese. This, of course, neither country was in a position to do. The Dutch finally agreed to sell the Japanese small quantities of petroleum products, but not aviation gasoline. The Japanese considered this unacceptable.

With the signing of the Tripartite Pact between Germany, Italy, and Japan, 27 September, 1940, the way was now cleared for the Japanese conquest of Southeast Asia. The only problem to be considered was what to do about the United States. The Japanese government finally decided to resort to diplomacy with the United States, rather than force, in attempting to gain control of the Dutch oil. When diplomacy failed as a result of the Japanese refusing to abandon their expansionist policies of conquering all of Southeast Asia, they began thinking seriously of using force to pursue their objectives. That meant going to war against the United States and Great Britain.

United States Navy code breakers had broken the Japanese diplomatic code and Roosevelt had a good idea of what the Japanese were up to. Our military commanders were planning for the inevitable war with Japan, but their plans anticipated the attack to come against the Philippines, and not Pearl Harbor. It was decided that the Philippines, Guam, and Midway couldn't be defended; therefore, the Atlantic theater was given priority over the Pacific, and Pearl Harbor was made the permanent home of the Pacific fleet. During this period new classes of ships were under construction for what would become the new two-ocean navy.

Early in 1940 stories began appearing in the press about the hostile Japanese. By 1941 the attitude of much of the public was not whether there would be war against Japan, but when.

Japanese-American relations had deteriorated to a new low by the summer of 1941 when the Japanese invaded and occupied the rest of French Indochina (now called Vietnam). Roosevelt's response was to issue an executive order freezing all Japanese assets in the United States, thus ending all trade between the two countries. President Roosevelt made a public statement to the effect that no more Japanese aggression would be tolerated. The Japanese were getting closer to the Dutch oil. Why was the Dutch oil so important to Japan? The answer was quite simple. The Japanese navy was now one of the largest in the world and it required huge quantities of oil for its necessary part in Japan's planned expansion and control of Southeast Asia.

In early August Premier Konoye Fuminaro requested a meeting with Roosevelt in a final attempt to avoid war. Roosevelt rejected this offer, informing the Japanese Ambassador to the United States that Japan would have to cease their aggression in Southeast Asia before any more discussions could take place. With this rejection, war between the two countries became inevitable. Both sides were playing for time, but for different reasons. Roosevelt wanted time to build up the armed forces, and Japan wanted time to get their forces into place for its strike on Pearl Harbor, and other targets in Southeast Asia.

Preparations for war in the United States began in earnest with the Conscription Act of 1940 implemented. Soldiers, sailors, and marines began appearing in the cities, and on the trains and buses in ever greater numbers. Factories were being retooled to manufacture all of the requirements necessary for rearming the nation for war. The feeling of war was in the air. In Japan a general mobilization was taking place and operational plans were being updated for an invasion of the Philippines, Malaya, and the Dutch East Indies. Simultaneously the Japanese navy began rehearsing their planned attack on Hawaii. Our navy code breakers were able to read enough Japanese ciphers to determine that there definitely would be an attack by the Japanese, but they couldn't acquire enough information to determine where or when.

Kurusu Saburo, a special Japanese envoy, and Admiral Kichisaburo Nomura were sent to Washington in mid November to attempt a last-ditch agreement with the United States. Neither envoy knew that their navy was on the high seas bound for the attack on Hawaii. Our naval intelligence noted that the Japanese navy suddenly changed all of their codes. This was interpreted to mean "almost imminent attack"—but when or where? Since the Japanese fleet was maintaining radio silence our intelligence people had no idea of its location.

The Japanese plan of attack was drawn up by Admiral Isoroku Yamamoto, and called for a four-pronged attack against the Western allies in Southeast Asia immediately following the discussions in Washington. The first and second stage of the offensive called for the invasion of Malaya, Siam (now called Thailand), and Burma. Simultaneously a second force would overrun Hong Kong and the Philippine Islands. Phase three would involve the seizure of

American bases in the Pacific. Phase four would complete the occupation of British Malaya and the Dutch East Indies.

The key to the success of this operation required the neutralization of the United States Navy before it could counter-attack Japanese forces, especially in the Philippines. The plan therefore called for a preemptive surprise attack on Pearl Harbor, the home of the American fleet.

The Japanese strike force was composed of four fleet carriers, two light carriers, two fast battleships, three cruisers, a flotilla of destroyers, eight tankers, and several submarines.

The strike force went undetected by sailing far enough north of normal shipping routs to avoid ships and land-based reconnaissance aircraft.

At 0637, 7 December 1941, the antisubmarine boom defense at the entrance of Pearl Harbor was opened to admit the entry of a U.S. navy target towing vessel. While the boom was open a small midget Japanese submarine slipped in. It was spotted by the guard destroyer USS *Ward* DD 139. Her captain immediately ordered a depth charge attack at full speed while sending a voice transmission over his TBS radio to Naval Control Center. He confirmed: WE HAVE ATTACKED FIRED UPON AND DROPPED DEPTH CHARGES UPON SUB OPERATING IN DEFENSIVE AREA. This then became the first shot fired by a ship of the United States Navy less than two hours prior to and against the Japanese attack on Pearl Harbor.

At 0600 on 7 December 1941, the Japanese fleet was in position 275 miles north of Pearl Harbor when it began launching attack aircraft. By 0750 the first wave of aircraft were over their targets and making their bombing runs. Japanese pilots knew exactly where to find their targets because their spies operating in Honolulu had transmitted the information to the fleet the night before, detailing all of the necessary information. Seven battleships were all lined up neatly in a row at Ford Island, and the aircraft were all crowded up on the airfields. It only took the Japanese a little over two hours to sink or damage the battleships of the American fleet, cripple the air force, and kill over two thousand military personnel. The results were catastrophic for the Pacific fleet which had lost much of its fighting ability, except for the aircraft carriers that were away from Pearl Harbor at the time conducting training exercises. Most of the army air force and navy aircraft on the ground were destroyed. It was all over by about 0930 Honolulu time.

It was almost 1500 Chicago time when it was announced on the radio that Pearl Harbor was under attack by aircraft of the Japanese Navy. I was sitting in the boiler room of Mundeline College on Chicago's north side reading a magazine when the news came over the radio. My father was showing two soldiers, my cousin's husband and friend, around the building and they were unaware of what was happening. I was stunned! I had expected war with the Japanese, but never dreamed that it would start as it did. We lived within ten minutes of the college and at home we all remained glued to the radio reports of the damage inflicted by the attack. I had a hard time believing the immensity of it all. How could this happen when everyone seemed to know that war was imminent?

The same day (it was 8 December in Manila, the Philippines) the Japanese attacked the Philippines with land, sea, and air forces. On 8 December Japanese forces invaded British Malaya. Within a very short time Japanese forces had conquered a significant part of Southeast Asia.

On 8 December the United States Congress, acting on a request from President Roosevelt, voted a declaration of war against Japan. There was only one pacifist, (in the House of Representatives) who voted against it. On 11 December Germany and Italy both declared war on the United States. On 12 December the United States declared war on Germany and Italy. Roosevelt now had a two-ocean war to deal with, a situation he was certain would eventually happen, but was trying to avoid until the nation could be suitably prepared—and unprepared we were!

Chapter 5

WORLD WAR II BEGINS

December 7, 1941

ith the start of officially declared war, the nation was
immediately put on a wartime footing. Shipyards and all
industry were immediately mobilized to produce all of
the required war materials. I felt like a fish out of water because I
wasn't prepared for any way of aiding in the war effort. As I
contemplated the shock to the nation, and the magnitude of it all, I
wondered if I should enlist in the military. I was advised to continue
my education until I was old enough for the draft—I entered Loyola
University to major in mathematics.

During the first four months, the war in the Atlantic and
European theaters had not been going well for the United States and
its allies. As the news came in over the radio, and the reports
appeared in the papers, it was one demoralizing shock after another.
The German army was rolling over Russia. The Russian army had
been defeated at Kharkov in the Ukraine and the Germans were
threatening the Crimea and Caucasus. Stalin was clamoring for a
second front to take the pressure off of the Russian Army.

German submarines operating off the East Coast were sinking
our oil transport vessels faster than they could be built. Because of
the shortage of navy destroyers and other classes of escort vessels,
the CAP (Civil Air Patrol) was formed to hunt and identify German

submarines from the air. Navy air could then follow up and attack them.

With the Japanese running unopposed and taking territory all over the South Pacific, morale was running low in the United States. Wake Island and Guam had been lost to the Japanese invasion forces the first week of December. Our forces in the Philippines were fighting magnificently; however, they were not receiving reinforcements and all of the supplies needed for an army to fight in the field because of the acute shortage of untrained men, merchant ships to deliver supplies, and warships with air cover to protect them. They had no air cover and no armor, yet they held on while inflicting heavy losses on the Japanese invaders. Our military was now paying the price for years of neglect, isolationism, and pacifism. General Wainwright on Corregidor in the Philippines was forced to surrender on 6 May 1942. His men were starving— dysentery, beriberi, and malaria were rampant among the troops. For many men it was a supreme effort to lift a rifle. His forces were about to be overrun by superior numbers of the Japanese army, and he had completely exhausted his food and medical supplies—further resistance would have resulted in the slaughter of thousands of good men. Even so, it finally ended with the agony of the sixty-five-mile Bataan death march that killed over 25,000 men as they were herded like cattle to Camp O'Donnell— another 22,000 died in the first two months at the camp. General MacArthur summed it up in a press conference, *no army has ever done so much with so little, and nothing became it more than its last hours of trial and agony. I shall return.*

In February of 1942 I attempted to enlist in the Army Air Corps. They turned me down because I failed the eye examination. I have worn glasses since I was five years old because of an eye problem inherited from my maternal grandmother. I thought I could pass the eye test because I had, and still have, 20/20 vision with corrective lenses. I thought goggles could be ground with corrective lenses, but the army said no! I then tried to enlist in the U.S. Army and failed the eye examination again. I tried the Merchant Marine, but they wouldn't take me because I was still too young and had no experience that they could use. I began to feel totally inadequate and I didn't want to be classified as 4-F. I realized that at the age of eighteen I wasn't quite physically or mentally mature for officers' training, even though I might have qualified for the Navy V-Officer Training Program in college—that is, if I could get by the eye exam. I was working in a grocery store part time, had saved my money, and I had enough to purchase a train ticket to Seattle, Washington, when I finally decided to leave school and home at the end of my first college year to strike out on my own for the first time in my life. Dad concurred completely with my decision, and so I boarded a train bound for the state of Washington and I was on my way to freedom and fortune.

In Seattle I discovered a state-run employment office where plenty of jobs were advertised. I signed up to pick apples at a ranch in Wenatchee, was placed on a bus with other fellows, and arrived at the ranch in time for a supper of pork chops, potatoes, vegetables, bread, butter, and coffee (all you could eat). I grabbed a bunk in the bunkhouse and began to get acquainted with the other fellows who made me feel right at home. The next morning we were all up before sunup for a breakfast of sausage, eggs, pancakes, fruit, and coffee. The excellent food was cooked by women who served us at a very long table. We could eat as much as we wanted—I always felt like they lost money on me because I had a voracious appetite.

I enjoyed picking apples—it was something I could do with my meager experience, and it didn't bother me to work on a tall ladder. The ranch was located in the scenic mountains, the air was clean and crisp, and the scenery beautiful. We were paid by the boxes of apples we picked and the pay was good. The ranch foreman was a pleasant fellow and I enjoyed working there.

After about six weeks the apples had all been harvested and so I was paid off. I then ventured back to Seattle where I went to work for the Great Northern Railroad and moved into the YMCA. I was determined to prepare myself to enter the military, and while living at the YMCA I took the opportunity to develop my own physical training program.

The YMCA was located about a mile or so up the hill from the Great Northern Railroad Station where I worked. I would get up at 5:00 every morning, get dressed, and then start for the baggage area of the station. I would run all of the way to the station, eat breakfast in the station restaurant, and report for work a little ahead of time. As the trains arrived we would enter the baggage cars and unload them of trunks, miscellaneous shipments, and mail. Every Thursday we would get a boxcar load of magazines packed in mailbags. These bags were very heavy and usually averaged about 85-95 pounds. It would take us about half a day to unload a full boxcar—meanwhile, we would be unloading additional baggage cars as other trains arrived.

I was supposed to work eight hours a day, but since they were short of help I frequently worked as much as twelve hours a day except on Saturday. That was date night. I would swim a mile two or three nights a week and take jujitsu lessons the other three nights. On Sunday I would play chess with whomever showed up from the chess club. Those guys were always good players and they always beat me; however, it did serve to sharpen my game by playing with better players.

At the Y I had to share a room with another man who was employed in a shipyard—I don't know what his job was. I seldom saw him because he worked nights while I worked days. I lived there for some time before I finally got to meet him. My roommate turned out to be a very nice guy about a year older than I was. The second time I met him he informed me that he was entering the army—I never saw him again. My next roommate was a member of naval intelligence and a graduate of the University of Oregon. He didn't hang around too long before he disappeared. In the short period while he was there we had some very interesting conversations. He diplomatically gave me some fatherly advice, and we discussed how I might pass the navy eye exam. He was responsible for my decision to attempt to enlist in the navy.

In November of 1942 I decided that is was time to try to enlist in the navy. I returned home to Chicago and spent some time getting caught up on the progress of the war. The more I learned the more determined I became to enlist in the navy. I was determined not to be classified 4-F! I had been discussing my intentions with my buddy Bob Benson and the two of us decided that we would try for enlistment one day in December. Early one morning we went downtown in Chicago to the navy recruiting station to start the process. After doing the necessary paperwork we started the physical examination—the first stop was the dentist. Bob never got further than the dentist—I went all the way to the eye exam with no problem. I read the eye chart without my glasses and by some miracle passed it; however, the corpsman advised me to drink carrot juice before reporting for duty at Great Lakes. He suspected that I had an eye problem.

I spent a real nice Christmas at home with family members and friends—a holiday I was not destined to enjoy again for the duration of the war. I was able to visit with a couple of my friends who were now in the army and my uncle, Al Welna, who had been in the navy for some time and was already a Chief Petty Officer. I was now feeling better knowing that I soon would be called for active duty.

While I was working in Washington, the navy was on the offensive in the Pacific with the news of a bombing attack on Japan. On 17 April a task force code-named Mike and consisting of the carrier USS *Hornet* with cruisers and destroyers was headed for Japan. The *Hornet's* deck was loaded with sixteen modified land based B-25 bombers. The Army Air Force's bomber group was headed by their crack pilot and air speed record holder, Lieutenant Colonel James Doolittle. As the task force approached within 700 miles west of Kyushu, Japan, their discovery by a Japanese fishing boat required the premature launching of the B-25's for their scheduled bombing run on Japan with Colonel Doolittle personally flying the lead airplane. The fishing boat was subsequently sunk by our escort cruisers. The group's individual targets were Tokyo, Nagoya, Osaka, and Kobe. After bombing targets in these cities, the pilots proceeded on to land in China, but unfortunately bad weather caused all of the bombers to crash in areas of Nationalist China rather than their designated airfields. All but eleven airmen avoided capture by the Japanese in China. Of the eleven, three died in crash landings, eight were captured by the Japanese, two pilots and a gunner were executed and only four survived prison.

The raid did very little damage to Japan other than leveling ninety buildings and killing fifty civilians; however, as predicted by Roosevelt, the raid was a great morale booster to the American population who had been hearing nothing but bad news since 7 December. When asked by our press where the airplanes came from, Roosevelt added a bit of mystery to the question by replying *Shangri-La*.

The Tokyo Raid had a far-reaching psychological impact on the Japanese General Staff. They had all suffered a tremendous loss of face and were overcome with a sense of shame. They had underestimated the will of the Americans. The idea that U.S. warplanes had the audacity to violate Japanese air space, and especially the space over the Imperial Palace, was unthinkable. Their angry over-reaction caused them to make a succession of blunders. Their first one was to transfer fighter groups from the Chinese mainland to the homeland to beef up their island defenses. The raid had also made them fearful of more raids on the home islands if they didn't capture the mid-Pacific islands. They therefore decided to commence with Yamamoto's plan to capture Midway while at the same time drawing out the American fleet and destroying it once and for all. They feared that if they didn't do it, the Japanese fleet would be continuously on patrol to defend the country from American carrier raids. The date for this operation was set for the first week of June, after their planned capture of Port Moresby in New Guinea, Tulagi in the Solomon Islands, and the establishment of an air base in the Solomons near Honiara on Guadalcanal. They were drunk with victory and were anxious to avenge Doolittle's raid. What they didn't know was that Commander Layton of Magic (code name for Naval Intelligence) had broken their code and was reading their mail, and that Admiral Nimitz, Commander and Chief of the Pacific Fleet, was planning a suitable response.

The first step in the Imperial Navy's plan was to simultaneously establish troops on Port Moresby and Tulagi. They had already occupied Florida Island in the Solomons, and Rabaul in New Guinea. Their time plan for the occupation of the Solomons to command the Coral Sea approach to Australia was an overly ambitious one. It required the establishment of a key air base for launching an advance south to Noumea, in New Caledonia, to threaten the sea route of the United States, and was time-wise so tight that it didn't allow for possible resistance and counter moves by the United States Navy. The Japanese were suffering from "victory syndrome" as a result of their super egos.

The first four-day engagement between Admiral Fletcher's carrier group and the Japanese attempt to land troops at Port Moresby and Tulagi, 4 May 1942, was the start of many battles that would occur for control of the Coral Sea and the Solomon Islands for the next six months. During this first engagement the Japanese were forced to abort their planned landings on Port Moresby and Tulagi because their main carrier cover could not reach Tulagi in time due to bad weather. More clashes occurred before the week ended. This engagement was the first ever fought by opposing aircraft where surface ships never saw each other. Official records indicate that the Japanese lost seventy-seven aircraft and 10,074 men, plus the 12,000-ton light carrier *Shoho* and the severely damaged carrier *Shokaku*. The U.S. Navy tallied its loss at sixty-six aircraft, 543 men killed, a tanker and a destroyer lost, in addition to the 42,000-ton fleet carrier *Lexington* sunk, and the damage suffered by the *Yorktown*. In terms of tonnage lost, the battle was a tactical success for the Imperial Navy. When the outcome is measured against the Japanese objective of the battle, there is no doubt that it was an important victory for the U.S. Navy, and was accomplished with insufficient numbers of inferior aircraft, and lack of pilot training in coordinated attacks. The Japanese were prevented from establishing control of the strategic Solomon Islands, a situation from which they were never able to recover. Without control of the Solomons, they could never hope to control the Coral Sea and the approaches to Australia. This engagement demonstrated that the Imperial Navy was not invincible, as claimed by some pundits back home.

The civilians of industry were doing a masterful job of developing, building, and introducing newly designed ships, airplanes, and radar necessary for making the U.S. Navy competitive with the Imperial Navy of Japan; however, there just wasn't time to update the Pacific carrier force of the navy in time for the upcoming battle of Midway. Admiral Nimitz had to depend upon his code breakers of "Magic," radar, and the skill and ingenuity of his admirals to overcome the Japanese advantage of better and more aircraft—he was outnumbered by ships of all classes.

On 1 June the entire Japanese fleet of 145 warships was at sea for the planned destruction of the U.S. Fleet. It consisted of four separate attack groups comprised of eight carriers, seven battleships, eighteen cruisers, three seaplane tenders, twenty-two destroyers, eight supply tankers, many submarines, auxiliary vessels and many transports loaded with invasion troops. To meet this huge fleet, Admiral Nimitz had a small force of three carriers, eight cruisers, fourteen destroyers, and several submarines. He did, however, beef up Midway with additional land-based fighters and bombers.

Japanese carrier aircraft attacked Midway Island 4 June 1942, and what became known as the battle of Midway started. By the evening of 4 June the Japanese task force was in retreat having lost three of their fast carriers, the *Akagi, Kaga, and Soryu*. Two days later the heavy cruiser *Mikuma* was sunk by U.S. Navy dive-bombers, and the cruiser *Mogami* was severely damaged.

The Battle of Midway was won by the heroism of carrier- and land-based pilots flying outmoded airplanes, superior naval intelligence, and very competent leadership by our admirals. In an official press release Admiral King said:

> *The battle of Midway was the first decisive defeat suffered by the Japanese Navy in 350 years. Furthermore it put an end to the long period of Japanese offensive action, and restored the balance of naval power in the Pacific.*[1]

Even though I was still a civilian when this battle occurred, I chose to mention it in this text because of its extreme importance in boosting the morale of the American public. This humiliating defeat of the Imperial Japanese Navy is considered by most naval historians to be a turning point in the war that the Japanese never recovered from. The Japanese were drunk with past victories and egoism and that may have had something to do with their defeat. The great Imperial Japanese Navy was again proven to be not invincible—the positive effect on public morale was incalculable.

The public euphoria over the defeat of the Japanese at Midway had hardly subsided when a heated debate between the U.S. Joint Chiefs of Staff erupted over what action to pursue for the immediate

---

[1] For a detailed account of the battle please refer to Hughes and Costello, *The Pacific War*, p. 271–309.

future. Admirals King and Nimitz recognized the strategic importance of the Solomon Islands and wanted to continue on the offensive to block Japanese advances in that area and preclude the possibility of an Australian invasion. To prevent a Japanese invasion the Australians wanted to invade Timor and reinforce a small contingent of their troops, who along with a contingent of Dutch soldiers were fighting a small Japanese invasion force. To preclude an Australian invasion MacArthur was for attacking Japanese held Rabaul with a large sea, land, and air force.

Both Roosevelt and Churchill feared that the Red army might be defeated and that the bulk of the available U.S. military buildup available be allotted to the Atlantic and North African theaters. Admiral King reminded Roosevelt and General Marshall that the Pacific theater was only receiving fifteen percent, and that the navy was fighting a formidable foe. Admiral King requested an additional fifteen percent to bring the total up to thirty percent. Admiral King prevailed in these arguments and on 7 August 1942, the U.S. 1st Marine Division, with the support of the U.S. Navy and a couple of cruisers from the Royal Navy Australia, invaded Guadalcanal in the Solomons. Marines were put ashore on Tulagi Island in the Florida Island group, and Guadalcanal near the nearly completed Japanese airstrip which they captured the next day.

This battle had the code name "Watchtower," but the marines renamed it "Operation Shoe String" because a series of events deprived them of much of their equipment and food. The first event to befall them was the evening of the second day, about 2330, 8-9 August when a powerful Japanese force of five heavy and two light cruisers attacked the U.S. cruisers and destroyers covering the 1st Marine Division landings. The result of the ensuing night battle was the worst defeat ever suffered by the United States Navy. That night the Japanese attack force sank the heavy cruisers *Chicago*, *Quincy*, *Vincennes*, the light cruiser *Astoria*, and the HMAS *Canberra*.

One reason for this disastrous defeat was that the Japanese had changed their battle codes, and intelligence at CINPAC hadn't had time to crack it. Also, none of our ships had radar, and none of the lookouts had sighted the Japanese reconnaissance floatplane that spotted and identified our ships in that black night. There was also the problem of training. At that point in the war our navy was inadequately trained for night actions, while the Japanese navy was well practiced in night fighting. This lesson was not lost on our admirals, and practice in night gunnery immediately became an essential part of total training.

The Marines were saved, but this engagement deprived them of their naval fire support from the lost cruisers. Admiral Fletcher had lost twenty percent of his fighter planes in air battles, and on 8 August he was forced to withdraw his carriers to save them. After his defeat the night before, Admiral Turner continued unloading the transports until noon in the face of heavy air attacks, when he was finally forced to withdraw his transports and remaining warships in order to save them from destruction. The Marines were left without their heavy artillery, bulldozers, (except for one) mines, most of their barbed wire, and half of their rations. On 15 August U.S. destroyers slipped in under cover of darkness to deliver more ammunition and aviation fuel. The Marines were in a tough spot but they still managed to complete the airstrip by 17 August to welcome in the first of navy Dauntless dive bombers—two days later fighter aircraft arrived from the new escort carrier *Long Island*. These new "baby flat tops" (as we called them), were used to ferry aircraft and provide CAP (Combat Air Patrol). By this time the Marines were living on captured Japanese rations. They used captured equipment for the completion of, and enlargement and repair of, the airstrip from damage caused by air attacks and constant rainsqualls.

The public was delighted with the reports of the invasion and the fact that our navy was finally on the offensive. What the official censored navy press releases didn't say was that we had lost four cruisers and over a thousand sailors in a half-hour battle. What was said was that one of our submarines had sunk a Japanese light cruiser off of New Ireland near Rabaul; and, that a Japanese cruiser was sunk (it was lightly damaged) at Savo Island midway between Florida Island and Guadalcanal in the New Georgia Sound. This battle became known as the "First Savo," (there were to be two more) and the New Georgia Sound was to become known as "Iron Bottom Sound," because so many ships of both navies were destined to meet their end there in subsequent battles.

At Guadalcanal the Marines upheld their reputation for being the best fighting men in the world. The Japanese recognized the strategic importance of the location but after many attempts to retake the island, admitted defeat and began their withdrawal for good on 14 January 1943. By 7 February, they were totally annihilated. The Marines had inflicted heavy losses on them, and they had experienced the fighting spirit of the United States Navy. There were to be many more battles in which a little valiant destroyer, the USS *Sterett* DD 407, played a major role including the night of 13 November 1942 at the battle of Guadalcanal, Third Savo, where she assisted in the sinking of a battleship and heavy cruiser—she also sank a destroyer unassisted. During this engagement she suffered eleven major projectile hits resulting in twenty-eight killed and fifteen wounded. The night of 6-7 August 1943 she sank a Japanese destroyer and assisted in sinking another one at Vela Gulf in the New Georgia Islands. This was the second destroyer I was destined to serve aboard during four major battles from 1 October 1944 to the war's end in the South Pacific theater.

I chose to discuss the Battle of Midway and the two battles in the Solomons because it demonstrates the faulty logic of those who thought that pacifism/isolationism was the best defense policy for the country, rather than spending money on the military. Our military did a magnificent job in those battles, and it was no secret that they did it at the cost of thousands of unnecessary casualties because of lack of up-to-date equipment, while being outnumbered and outgunned. It wasn't until 1943 that our armed forces began to get the modern equipment they needed to match the Japanese.

I reported for active duty at the navy recruiting station in downtown Chicago on 11 January 1943. There was a whole group of us sworn in that morning and transferred to the Great Lakes U.S. Naval Training Station that same day. It was a cold, cloudy, blustery day in Chicago and I was suitably dressed for the weather; however, when we arrived at the Great Lakes Naval Training Station it was much colder with a stiff east wind coming off Lake Michigan that seemed to cut right through me. My Chicago clothes were not adequate protection from Great Lakes weather and I hoped I wouldn't freeze solid before being issued proper navy clothing—I envied the navy personnel enjoying their warm clothing. After collecting our orders of enlistment, the first stop was the chow hall where we were fed lunch and got thawed out before going for our next complete physical examination. By the time we finished our physical exam (complete with a few questions from a psychiatrist), it was time for chow again. We were assigned to a temporary barracks where we spent the night. I didn't sleep too well that night because I wasn't used to being with other guys snoring. Also, there was a sailor who would appear now and then who I later discovered was on duty as a fire watch. It was all part of the navy's super organized routine.

At precisely 0600 a sailor came through and got everybody up and made certain that we were all ready to be herded over to the chow hall for breakfast. The weather was colder than the day before and I couldn't wait to get into warm navy clothes. After breakfast we were herded over to another building that was quite a distance from the barracks and chow hall where we were ushered into a huge room with stacks of clothing and many tables. A sailor grabbed me, measured me up, and told me to start taking my civilian clothes off. He handed me long underwear that was stenciled with my name and said "put it on." To my amazement it fit perfectly! We went through the same procedure with each article of clothing until I was completely dressed including a wool skullcap, gloves and shoes. My civilian clothes went into a special box with my home address on it, and it disappeared to arrive at home a few days later. Everything fit perfectly. I was given a sea bag with all of my uniforms, a ditty bag (for personal items such as shaving gear), a mattress and covers, two blankets, pillow and covers, and a hammock; another sailor then guided all of us to our barracks.

At our barracks we caught up with all of our gear and a chief petty officer who awaited us to assign us our bunks. Our Chief was a no-nonsense guy who had been an athletic coach at the University of California before entering the navy. He immediately started our indoctrination concerning the care of our clothes and bedding. Every piece of clothing, including towels, etc. had to be rolled properly and secured with clothes stops—(small sections of rope about eight inches long.) We laid out everything in front of us for inspection by the chief to prove that we were doing it correctly. We were also introduced to the watch list, watches and watch protocol, and some navy terminology. We had a brief introduction to some knots that were needed immediately. More knots were introduced as we proceeded through our training. Mattresses had to be rolled up on our bunks during the day and we couldn't occupy our bunks during the day. All of our gear had to be properly stowed in our sea bag and ditty bag and lashed to a horizontal rail during the day.

We were advised that the biggest complaint from the fleet was that personnel were not in good enough physical condition; therefore, the navy hired Gene Tunney, the world boxing champion, to design a physical training program for recruits. The program involved calisthenics in the gym every morning before breakfast, with lots of running, and some wrestling.

I had enlisted in the regular navy as an Apprentice Seaman, USN, for six years. One day an officer came in and called off some names and mine was one of them. He informed us that Congress had passed a law stating that there would be no more voluntary enlistments in the navy—only draftees, and that we had all enlisted on a day that wasn't covered by any law; therefore, we could be of any classification we wanted. We could choose between USN, USNR, or USN-I (Inductee). I asked for the quickest way out of the navy when the war ended. He said, "be an Inductee." I said, "I'm an Inductee."

Needless to say, I breezed through the physical fitness program of boot training hardly breathing hard. This drew the attention of a fellow from Indiana who couldn't figure out my physical ability and baby face. I seemed to be too young to be in the navy. Most people always judged me to be ten to fifteen years younger than I was. This attribute, which I acquired from the Welna side of the family, has followed me all of my life. In some cases it was positive, and in others it was negative. My father always suffered from the same problem. Since I can't remember the name of the man from Indiana, I will call him "Indy" for short.

"Indy" started bugging me from the start, and since I wouldn't pay attention to him, his attitude became more and more abusive. It finally became so bad that one evening in our free time, two of the fellows pushed me towards him and demanded that I fight him and settle things once and for all. "Indy" threw the first punch, which I avoided, and I went after him. I didn't dare use any of my jujitsu technique for fear of hurting him seriously. Had I thrown him he would have landed on the edge of the picnic table and we both would have been in deep trouble. I simply used a few old fashioned wrestling maneuvers and pinned him down on his back and kept him there until he admitted defeat. That took the starch out of him and increased the respect of the other guys for me.

One other troublemaker in the group was a guy from Boston named Sam. Sam was an Inductee in his early to mid thirties who believed he should run the whole company. I avoided him as much as possible and he didn't mess much with me, especially after I decked "Indy." One Sunday afternoon he organized a poker game and insisted I also play. I think he thought that I was just a young punk "pigeon." I didn't trust him, I didn't like him, and I wasn't anxious to play, but I finally relented and joined the group. We played five-card draw with nothing wild. I was doing fairly well and the other guys dropped out. Sam had the deal and I wound up with four queens, all natural. Sam had what he thought was a good hand and he tried to bluff me; however, I wouldn't be bluffed, and in an attempt to force me out he reached in his pocket and put an extra twenty-five dollars on the table. I raised him and he chickened out and called me. When I showed those four queens he turned white. I made a couple of month's pay on the hand and Sam never got over it. He really hated me after that. He cried about me taking all of his money! We both wound up in torpedo school and I'll explain more about that later.

We were not allowed liberty for the twelve weeks of boot camp, but we could receive visitors at the visitor center each Sunday afternoon. My parents and my girlfriend did visit me on those occasions. My parents were typically very supportive and interested in navy routine, and what I was doing and learning. My girlfriend was mostly "shook up" because the navy had cut off all of my wavy black hair to one-quarter inch. Upon graduation we all received a ten-day leave. I went back to Chicago to visit my parents, uncles, girlfriend, and my buddies who weren't yet in the service.

While in boot camp I passed an examination for service school and chose torpedoman because I had heard that they were an elite group on destroyers and submarines. After graduating from boot camp I was assigned to the torpedo school at Great Lakes for sixteen weeks. The course was intensive—we were not allowed to take any material out of the classroom or take notes because all information was considered top secret—everything had to be memorized. We were threatened with a court martial if we revealed any information concerning torpedoes to any one, including other sailors.

In torpedo school the physical training was superior to that of boot camp. Each afternoon we would run a mile to the assembly center, then a mile to the beach of Lake Michigan, where we would run through a quarter of a mile of loose sand, then run up a ladder to the top of a sixty-five-foot cliff where we would reassemble. We would then run back to the commando course and run through it—this was more my speed. We also had to demonstrate swimming and water survival ability. We had to swim 500 yards while dressed in our white uniforms, tread water for fifteen minutes, then remove our pants while in the water, tie each leg in a knot, and then blow air into the pants so that they could be used as a life preserver. We then had to float for a prescribed amount of time. Having grown up swimming in Lake Michigan during my summers in Chicago, I had no trouble qualifying for a life saving card to add to the one that I had previously received from the Chicago YMCA.

One day in class the instructor left the room for a few minutes. When he opened the door to re-enter the room Sam immediately directed a question at me as if to indicate that he was directing the class while the instructor was out of the room. (The question was meant to embarrass me.) I was infuriated and yelled that if he ever tried a dirty trick like that on me again I would beat the hell out of him! We had three marines in the class and they had been testing me to see what I was made of. That day they found out because I also laid into that idiot with a few choice adjectives. When the instructor told me to shut up I told him to shut that slime ball up! I think the instructor then realized that he had one nasty situation to deal with.

That afternoon, back in the barracks, Sam made an insulting remark to me—which I can't remember. I jumped up on one of the tables and called him every filthy name I could think of. I told him that he was yellow clean through, and that if he was half a man he would knock me off the table for all of the rotten names I called him.[2] He turned white and just looked at me.

---

[2] Sam was the most despicable man I have ever met, and most of what I said is unprintable.

Chapter 6

USS *Barton* DD 722

December 1943

Upon graduation, most of our class was transferred to the destroyer base in San Diego for advanced schooling. We packed our gear in seagoing fashion, threw it on a truck, got on a train and went to Chicago. We had a leader provided by the navy who led us to the elevated train once in Chicago. Normally this would be a public train, but this one was just for the navy personnel. It was summer and all of the train windows were open, and I heard a girl call my name while we were briefly stopped at a station. I looked out to see one of my steady girlfriends standing on the platform waving at me. We exchanged a few quick comments and as the train pulled away she ran after it for a short ways and yelled for me to write to her.

Mae was a dark-haired slender beauty of a girl that I had dated for a couple of years and taken to several formal dances before I entered the navy. While I was in boot camp she had stayed in my room with my folks a few times so that she could ride up to Great Lakes with them to visit me. (This isn't the one that complained about my navy haircut.) The guys were all shook up and started yelling and whistling—my reputation enjoyed considerable improvement that day.

Our next stop was the Illinois Central Station where we transferred to another train. We were put in a Pullman car and fed dinner in the diner. After dinner our berths were all made up for sleeping. We were traveling first class to California.

We woke up the next morning in St. Joe, Missouri—the train was stopped at a station across from a Fred Harvey's restaurant. We all descended on the restaurant for orange juice, eggs, sausage, toast and coffee. The breakfast was excellent, and the ladies that served us were very efficient and polite. (Motherly would be a better description.) After breakfast we stood on the station platform and watched the railroad personnel add several cars to the train. I remember listening to the hand and whistle signals of the railroad men as they changed cars around and formed the new train that would take us to San Diego.

It turned out that some of the cars that were added to the train were special cars. (Specially designed cars with bunks jammed in them, crosswise to the beam of the car, with the aisle on one side to accommodate soldiers.) The soldiers referred to them as "cattle" cars. By noon we were over 250 miles west of St. Joe, and our leader advised us to go forward to the diner for lunch. To do this we had to pass through the "cattle cars" and the soldiers with their own kitchen facility. As we walked through the soldiers' cars they looked at us quizzically as if to ask who we were and why were we traveling first class? We were wearing our undress blues with no insignia and I wonder if they even realized we were navy personnel. This was the routine until the soldiers' cars were split off and we continued on to Yuma, Arizona. In the dining car we were seated at tables with white tablecloths and silver service. Our food was presented to us by very proficient colored waiters and every meal we had on that trip was excellent.

Before we reached Yuma we crossed the Great Western Desert. The train had halted for some reason and some of the guys left the train to get some prickly pear cactus. These Chicago boys had never seen cacti and I laughed when they came back to the train with spines in their fingers. I got off the train to stretch my legs, but I wouldn't venture out near the rocks where they went because of the danger of rattlesnakes, Gila monsters, and scorpions.

Yuma, on the Arizona side of the Mexican border, was protected by the U.S. Army and they made their presence known as the train halted there before branching off on a track that crossed the Colorado River. It then continued on through the Imperial Valley of California below sea level, and then up and over the Laguna Mountains to an elevation of 4,140 feet. Parts of the track paralleled the Mexican border, and part was actually in Mexico. The train wound around tight curves and precipices where the drop-off averaged 1,000 feet. By this time it was night and many of our guys didn't realize the dangerous terrain we were in. After we passed over the Tecate Divide we continued on to the little village of Campo on the U.S. side of the border where there was a small army base. It was strategically located there to protect the railroad and highway supply route into San Diego.

During our trip over the mountains I had been standing with two other fellows at the end of our car with the top half of the exit door open, which was a window. When we finally left to return to our seats the car jerked and the window slammed shut and broke. Sam immediately blamed me and told a trainman who happened to come through that I was the culprit and should be held accountable. The trainman looked at him as if he was crazy, said something, and went about his business.

It was night when we arrived in San Diego at the destroyer base. The base was all lit up and there was a lot of activity—it was a very busy place. We were met by guides who ushered us into our barracks, and gave us instructions for the next day. Our gear showed up on time and our entry into our new quarters went smooth as clockwork. The navy had transferred us with precise efficiency.

The next day we fell into navy routine and did our calisthenics on a dock before breakfast. The instructor stood before a Grumman torpedo bomber that was permanently displayed. It had taken part in the battle of Midway and had so many bullet holes in it that I don't know how the pilot could have flown it back to his carrier. After breakfast we reported to our classroom where our chief torpedoman and a second class torpedoman were waiting for us. The chief introduced himself and his assistant torpedoman, gave us a short introduction and class started. When we broke for lunch Sam had to inform the chief of the glass breakage on the train. I don't remember what the chief said to him but I do remember that he put him down once and for all. This was not going to be like Great Lakes.

Our chief was a kindly no-nonsense veteran of thirty years who had been called back into the navy at the onset of the war. He and his assistant were very competent and excellent instructors.

As usual the training was intense with no notes—everything was memorized. Every third night was a duty night—then came two liberty nights.

Our training at the destroyer base emphasized routine service of torpedoes, torpedo mounts, and depth charges. All of this equipment had to be serviced at regular intervals. Each torpedo came with a logbook that had a corresponding serial number to the torpedo. Any torpedoman who serviced that equipment had to sign and date the logbook and detail the service completed. To miss a required service period, or sign off on service not done, or not properly performed, was a very serious offence punishable by court martial. We were therefore intensely trained by doing the hands-on service work in the torpedo workshop under the supervision of a chief petty officer. We also received intense training in charging the air flask of the torpedo with high air pressure. This was a dangerous operation and required certain safety precautions.

We also went out for one-day cruises on a training destroyer to view the firing of torpedoes equipped with an exercise head. The exercise head was a hollow head filled with water, (painted bright yellow with orange stripes), to replace the warhead for torpedo firing practice. At the end of the firing run the water was automatically pumped out of the head, and the buoyant torpedo then came to the surface and was recovered to be used again with either a war head or exercise head as need required.

The training destroyer was an old World War I four-piper. (It was called that because it had four stacks.) It had been modified for training by relocating the torpedo mounts from the sides of the ship to the center. This configuration was then the same as the newer destroyers. It was also modernized with radar and a torpedo director for practice in torpedo fire control. We also received a lot of training in torpedo fire control. This type of training was very important, and these old greyhounds were suitable for the job.

Towards the end of the course I passed my examination for Seaman 1/C, and upon graduation, Torpedoman 3/C. I was now a petty officer in the U.S. Navy, given a choice of duty stations, and chose destroyers. I was assigned to the USS *Barton* DD 599 and transferred to NOB (Naval Operating Base) Norfolk, Virginia under delayed orders of ten days.

Since we had relatives in San Diego, my mother had arrived in town two weeks prior to my graduation to visit our relatives and me. Because I had ten days leave, she decided to return home with me to Chicago on the same train. The catch was that I had a first class train ticket issued by the navy and she had a chair car ticket. We took the same train together from San Diego to Los Angeles where we transferred trains for the long trip to Chicago.

There were scads of people in the Los Angeles station, mostly servicemen, and in the confusion Mother gave me her money to hold. As we went to the train we became separated because I had a first class ticket—we figured that we would be on the same train, not realizing that there were two sections. (One train for first class and one for chair car passengers) I had forgotten that I had her money, and while I was living it up in the Pullman section with the officers and eating in the dining car, Mother was without enough money to eat in the diner of her train. So, being a resourceful woman, she took what money she had and accepted an invitation to play poker with some Marines. She was able to parlay her meager funds enough so that she too could eat in her dining car.

When the two trains arrived in Chicago, and Dad met us at the station, she told us this story and exclaimed that she felt guilty for taking money from the Marines. I laughed and said that any man dumb enough to play poker with a woman deserves to get separated from his money.

At Norfolk I found myself taking more instruction in torpedo fire control, the method by which torpedoes are set for guidance so that they will reach their target. To accomplish this, a torpedo director on the bridge had a set of dials for entering all needed information for scoring a hit on a moving target. These things were the forerunners of the modern-day computer, except that they were run by mechanical means. Target angle, range, course, and speed could be obtained from radar and fed into the director to increase accuracy.

In December, just before Christmas, a group of us were transferred to Boston and housed in the Frazier Barracks along with men from other naval stations. We were all assembled to form the crew of the new *Barton* DD 722 and to await the arrival of our ship.

Boston was a navy town with huge facilities for servicing warships. With so many of the population working in the yards, the civilian population had developed a liking for the sailors. I at once developed a liking for the town and its citizens, many of whom were friendly, fun-loving Italians. There was no sign of the hostility we experienced from many of the citizens of Norfolk, or the holy attitude of the San Diego city fathers who, under pressure from the churches, prevented sailors younger than twenty-one years of age from having a drink, or even a beer. We were old enough to die for our country, but heaven forbid if we were discovered having a drink in a public establishment—the owner/manager would suffer dire legal consequences for such an audacious violation of public law. That was absolutely *verboten*!

Late in December a skeleton crew with civilian engineers aboard brought the new *Barton* down to Boston from Bath, Maine, where she was built. I didn't know it at the time but the *Barton* DD 599 had been sunk while in action against the Japanese at Savo Island in the Solomons, 12-13 November 1942—someone had put the wrong hull number on my orders.

The commissioning ceremonies for our new ship occurred 30 December 1943 on a gray, cold, windy, morning. I remember standing at attention listening to what our new commanding officer, Commander Joe Callahan had to say—fortunately, he was not long-winded. When he was finished the long thin seven star commission pennant was raised and the ship was officially in commission in the U.S. Navy. At that moment the colors were also raised, and I would forever be known as a plank owner because I was a member of the original crew that put her in commission. We were then released to receive our compartment and bunk assignments. We returned to the barracks, packed our gear, and returned to the ship to stow our gear and settle in as full time seagoing sailors.

She was a beautiful ship of the new *Allen M. Sumner* class—a new design having more fire power than any destroyer ever built to that date. She displaced 2,651 tons (standard), with a length of 376 feet, 6 inches; and a beam of forty feet, ten inches. She developed 60,000shp (shaft horsepower) at 36.5 knots. Her fuel bunkerage was 504 tons with a range of 3,300nm (nautical miles) at twenty knots. She mounted six 5-inch 38 caliber dual-purpose guns in three double mounts, two forward and one aft as her main battery. Her secondary battery consisted of twelve Bofor 40mm dual-purpose guns in two quad and two double mounts, and eleven 20mm antiaircraft guns for closer range targets. Ten 21-inch torpedoes were located in two center mounts of five torpedoes each. Our ASW (anti submarine warfare) armament consisted of six K-guns of three each, port and starboard, for propelling depth charges plus two racks of charges on the fantail. She had the latest radar and other electronic gear.

About one-third of the entire complement of officers and men had never had sea duty and we spent the first few days aboard ship receiving our watch, cleaning, and battle stations. I was given responsibility for the number two torpedo mount. During the first week we received our ten torpedoes, and within four hours had them loaded in the torpedo tubes. Our next job was to give both the torpedoes and mounts their first routine checks to make certain that they were battle ready. We loaded our complement of depth charges, installed their detonators, checked the K-guns for firing, and declared them to be battle ready. It all went smooth as clockwork—our training in torpedo school had been so complete that I felt like I had been doing it for years.

Our captain, Comdr. Joe Callahan, started getting everyone acquainted with our new ship by taking us out for one-day cruises. He began drilling the crew for general quarters (all hands man their battle stations). The first time the crew was called to general quarters the captain declared that we were too slow in responding to the command, and that we would have to constantly drill until we improved our time. It wasn't long before we improved to his satisfaction.

We of the deck force were issued personal foul weather gear. It consisted of heavy water-repellant lined material that was very warm and comfortable. The pants were proper fitting overalls of the Farmer Brown design that came up over the chest. The jacket had knitted cuffs and neck and buttoned with special clips that could be released easily. The cap was similar to an aviator's helmet and made of the same material; it buttoned under the chin and had a skirt on the back to prevent water from going into the jacket. The mittens had an index finger. I was never cold regardless of the weather and heavy seas.

Plate 4. USS *Barton* DD 722, 28 December 1943 off Rockland, Me. (Official U.S. Navy photograph.)

Plate 5. USS *Barton* DD 722, 14 January 1944, off New York. (Official U.S. Navy photograph.)

Soon we were going out for one week, and finally longer cruises while constantly drilling until I felt that I could do it in my sleep, which I finally did one night during the invasion of Normandy.

Every new vessel has to complete a shakedown cruise to prove that the ship and crew are battle ready to join the fleet. We were ordered to Bermuda for our shakedown cruise—we thought we were sailors until we sailed past Cape Hatteras, North Carolina. This area of the Atlantic is well known to salt sailors as being always rough, and over the years has claimed more than its share of capsized ships. Our ship rolled, while the bow would come up to dig into a huge wave with water coming over the bow and swamping the open bridge. It would hang in that position for a moment or two exposing the sound stack on the keel about a third of the way back from the bow. With about a fourth of the ship hanging out of the water it would then come crashing down to dig into another wave again as the stern came out of the water exposing the rudders and screws. We quickly learned that to open a watertight door leading out onto the deck; you had to wait for the ship to roll to its center position before opening the door. To open the door as the ship was rolling away from you was to chance being thrown overboard. To try opening the door as the ship was rolling towards you was almost impossible because the steel door was extremely heavy, and if the timing was off, the door would slam shut and throw you back into the compartment to result in possible injury. We had to learn how to go up or down a ladder with the ship rolling, heaving and bouncing up and down, all at the same time. To try it without holding firmly to the grab rails usually resulted in a fall and a broken leg or two. We quickly learned to strap ourselves into our bunks so as not to be thrown out on the deck. Since one of my battle stations was at the port K-guns on the main deck, water coming over the side would freeze on my foul weather clothes—ice would shatter when I bent my arms or moved my legs. I personally learned never to wear a kapok life jacket without being securely lashed to the ship—a large wave coming over the side could wash me overboard because of the buoyancy of the life jacket.

Eating in the mess hall was another experience. The mess hall was located amidships directly aft of the number two ammunition hoist for the number two 5-inch gun mount, and below the bridge and forward deck house. It was "U" shaped with the scullery located in the "U." The galley was located on the main deck with the entrance and serving window on the port side. We picked up our food at the galley window and then went down the ladder (stairs) to the mess hall holding on to the tray with one hand, and grab handles with the other in order not to fall down the ladder. This was quite a trick when the ship was lurching in all directions. Coffee, milk, cups, bowls, and silverware were all available in the mess hall.

The tables in the mess hall were all bolted to the deck and all had ridges around the perimeter so that trays and silverware wouldn't slide off when the ship was pitching and rolling. The benches we sat on were not bolted to the deck and required some cooperation when a sailor decided to leave. The sailors sitting on the end of the bench would wrap their legs around the stanchions supporting the tables. When they were ready to leave, they would warn everyone to grab hold of the table, and someone else would take their position to offer balance and keep the bench from taking off into space with sailors and food. Despite careful attention to glass cereal bowls and coffee mugs, breakage was heavy in rough weather.

We entered the harbor of Bermuda in the evening and awoke to a tropical paradise in the morning. Bermuda is a British possession, and the naval base was one of the bases received from the British on a ninety-nine year lease in return for fifty overaged U.S. destroyers in 1940. It was strategically located in the Atlantic as a base for our destroyers to harass German submarines operating there.

Liberty was immediately granted for one third of the crew. I was not one of them and had to wait several days for my turn. We spent many days patrolling in the area surrounding the islands looking for German submarines. One day I went ashore with my buddy Jim Dudly. Liberty was from noon to 1700. Motor vehicles were not allowed on the islands at that time except for a few jeeps of the navy shore patrol. We found the British subjects to be very friendly. I was fascinated with the quaint white coral houses with their red tile roofs, and the little shops. Jim purchased some pieces of china for his mother, and I purchased some perfume for mine, all duty free.

A few days later I was able to go ashore again, this time with Blackman, another torpedoman. One of our first stops was a quaint little bar. We were sitting at the bar having a nice conversation with the bartender when a shore patrolman stuck his head in the door and called, *anyone in here from the Barton?* When we answered *yes* he yelled, *come on your ship is leaving!* We had hardly had two sips from our drinks, Blackman downed his Zombie, and I downed my Tom Collins in one gulp. The bartender's mouth fell open and we took off piling into the SP Jeep. We were raced back to our ship and scrambled up the gangway just as the special sea detail was singling up all lines. The gangway was immediately landed, lines were cast off, and the ship got under way. As we were standing out of the harbor I took my last look at Bermuda.

While we were ashore on liberty, six or seven marines came aboard as passengers. They were being transferred back to Virginia. A condition three watch was set and I drew the 2000 to 2400 watch at the port K-guns. A condition three watch meant that all hands were to be on watch for four hours and off for eight. The condition three watch (wartime cruising) was usually set when we were in a green zone with one third of battle stations 100% manned. A green zone was a location that was not a battle zone, but was subject to possible attack by enemy submarines, surface crafts, or aircraft. A battle zone was designated as a red zone because it was subject to enemy action. A condition two watch was really a modified general quarters and was usually set in a red zone when enemy action was possible. In this condition all of the crew were at battle stations with half of the crew resting while the other half were alert. Condition one, or general quarters (GQ), was set for possible battle action with all hands manning their battle stations. Even in a green zone the crew was routinely called to GQ one hour before sunrise, and one hour before sunset, because these were the usual times for enemy submarines to attack.

Destroyers of that day carried forty-two depth charges, each weighing 340 pounds. These were the Mark 9 teardrop design containing 270 pounds of TNT—the other seventy pounds being in the metal shell and exploder mechanism. Eighteen of these charges were in two racks on the fantail and were rolled off the rack one at a time. The other twenty-four depth charges were stored in racks of four each with one charge loaded in the arbor, and three in the reserve rack of each K-gun ready to be fired, but not with the depth set. The six K-guns were located three on the port, and three on the starboard side of the ship, between the quarterdeck and the fantail.

The K-gun holding the arbor with one depth charge was much like a mortar with a simple breach mechanism. When a cartridge of about five inches in diameter containing black powder was inserted into the breech, the arbor and depth charge was ready to be fired from the ship—the charge could then be fired from the bridge, or by the torpedomen on station. The torpedomen on station would set the depth at which the charges were to explode after receiving instructions from the bridge. They would then inform the bridge that the K-guns and the racks were ready for action.

Depth charge patterns were determined by CIC calculations of the depth, speed, and course of the enemy submarine, and the speed and course of our ship. This was extremely important because if the charges were set for too shallow a detonation for the speed of our ship, we could sink our own ship. Enemy submariners were deathly afraid of destroyers, and with good reason. With our sonar gear we could locate submarines and kill them.

We were on a westerly course bound for the mainland when the captain ordered an engineering check, which was a test demanded by the shakedown routine. The ship increased speed to over thirty-two knots and all hands topside were warned to get off of main decks. At that point the ship was thrown into reverse at maximum speed. The tremendous force of water coming over the fantail bent the heavy steel blast shield plates of the three 20mm guns on the stern back against the guns like so much cardboard. After the ship attained flank speed in reverse it was again reversed to forward speed, and the test was completed. I have been told that U.S. destroyers were the only ships of their kind in the world that could do this maneuver.

The following day as we came closer to the mainland our ping jockey (soundman) detected a submarine contact. I was on watch at the port K-guns when GQ was sounded. The ship immediately increased speed and we were directed to prepare to fire depth charges. We made three passes dropping and firing depth charges over the contact at each pass. At that point the contact was lost, and while we kept searching, no contact was ever made again. There was some debris on the water, but this was not sufficient evidence to indicate a kill of a submarine. Years later sport divers discovered the remains of an unidentified German submarine on the ocean floor in the general area where we depth charged a submarine contact. Neither our navy, nor the German navy, had any record of a German submarine being sunk in that area during World War II. Did we sink it? All kinds of theories abound, but I believe we will never know. The nature of anti-submarine warfare was such that attacking surface vessels many times had a difficult, if not impossible task of determining the outcome of their attack—enemy submarines could be sunk, or damaged to the point where they would limp away and sink, never to be heard from again. These situations were simply listed as "U XXX overdue and presumed to be lost." Such was the fate of many a submarine crew. I do believe, however, that with our modern technology of diving and treasure hunting, more German submarine wrecks will be discovered as time goes on.

A few days later we sailed through torpedo alley (so named because of the number of merchant vessels sunk by German submarines in that area) into Chesapeake Bay. We proceeded directly to Portsmouth, Virginia, which was the navy repair yard for Norfolk OB. (Operating Base) We moored to a dock opposite the machine shops. The next day civilian engineers and workers came aboard, removed the plates from our main deck to expose our starboard reduction gears in the number two engineering space, removed and transported them to the machine shop abreast of where we were tied up. It seems that our starboard reduction gears were damaged during the test when we went from flank speed ahead to flank speed reverse.

While we were tied up in the yard our captain took the opportunity for further training of the crew. I was part of a group that was sent to fire fighting school. It was a several-day course involving classroom lectures and practical training. The school had a mockup of a destroyer engine room and other shipboard structures. Fuel jets were located in the appropriate areas so that engineering and other spaces could be ignited. Under supervision we then went into the blazing inferno and extinguished the fires. It was all very instructive, interesting, and practical. They also taught us about the dangers of combustible materials such as gasoline and how to minimize the risk of fire or explosion when handling them.

The first day in the yard an interesting situation occurred. The noon whistle sounded, a door to the machine shop opposite our gangway opened, and out stepped the most stunning blonde we had ever seen. She wore a red sweater, black skirt, nylons, and black high heels. She had a figure and poise that would have put Marilyn

Monroe to shame. She walked down the pier a short distance and disappeared through a door, probably to a cafeteria. Every day at noon she appeared, walked down the pier and entered the same door. From the first day of her appearance, and every day thereafter, all guns and directors, and anything with optics on it was focused on the exit door at five minutes before noon, and remained trained on her coming and going. Because I was a right arm rate I frequently stood a gangway watch with the OOD (Officer of the Deck).

Right arm rates were called right arm rates because the rate was worn on the right sleeve. All other rates were worn on the left sleeve. Right arm rates were torpedoman, gunner's mate, fire controlman, coxswain, boatswain, and quartermaster. One reason for the right arm designation was that we were all trained in small arms—when on a gangway watch we always carried a service .45, as did the OOD. Nowadays all rates are left arm rates for some reason I'm not aware of. A rating is a name given to an occupation in the navy such as torpedoman, which requires basically related aptitudes such as training, experience, knowledge, and skills. The higher the rate, the higher the pay grades. Rate refers to a petty officer rank above seaman, but not a commissioned officer. During World War II there were four grades of petty officers, starting with third class, the lowest, and ending with chief, the highest. Each rating has its own specialty mark which is worn on the appropriate sleeve by all men properly qualified.

One day I had just relieved the 0800 to 1200 watch when flag officer Captain W. L. Freseman, our commodore, Lieutenant Commander Joe Callahan, our captain, and two other officers had just started up the gangway when the noon whistle sounded. Right on time our blonde lady stepped out of her door—all of our officers stopped right in the middle of the gangway, watched her until she entered the mystery door, and then continued up the gangway while we proceeded with the naval formality of welcoming them aboard. I'm proud to say that our officers could put naval routines second to more essential developments—important things first. Sadly we never discovered who the blonde was or how we could get to meet her. She will always remain one of the great mysteries of World War II.

While we were in the yard the newly formed 60th Destroyer Division was created of the destroyers *Walke* DD 723, *Laffey* DD 724, *O'Brien* DD 725, *Meredith* DD 726, and Flagship *Barton* DD 722, flying the pennant of Capt. W. T. Freseman, COMDESRON 60. In World War II destroyer divisions were usually composed of four to six ships with the division under the command of a four-striper captain known as a commodore. The ranks of commodore and above were known as flag officers because each had the privilege of flying their personal flag on the ship they chose as their headquarters. The ship they chose then became known as the flagship of the division. Commodore Freseman's staff included Lt. Commander Robert B. Montgomery, USNR (the famous movie actor), another officer whose rank and name I can't remember, and a yeoman. Commodore Freseman was responsible for the disposition, operation, supply, and battle orders of the entire division in accordance with his orders from a senior officer above him.

Following the completion of our repair work, we were ordered to sea where we conducted sea trials testing our newly repaired reduction gears. We also engaged in more gunnery practice.

We spent some time on patrol in the North Atlantic searching for German submarines, but found none. I think they were probably operating more in the vicinity of Iceland. By this time in 1944 the Kriegsmarine had fallen on hard times. Allied innovations and improvements in ASW (antisubmarine warfare) had improved to the point that U-boat losses had increased at an alarming rate. Convoy tactics had improved substantially making it much more difficult for the U-boats to pick off merchantmen. Improvements in ASDIC (submarine detection device) made location of target submarines more accurate for depth charging. Standard Mark 9 depth charges were improved along with the British introduction of Hedgehogs, and the U.S. Navy's Squid. The Hedgehog was fitted on the bow of the escort vessel and was composed of twenty-four bombs filled with 321 pounds of Torpex and fired as the U-boat was identified in the ASDIC beam. It was armed as it attained a shallow depth and exploded on contact. The Squid was even more accurate than the Hedgehog. It was a three-barreled mortar system mounted on the bow that shot 100-pound depth charges ahead or abeam with their firing mechanisms set automatically during the final seconds of the attack. It was operated in conjunction with the improved ASDIC transmitter which provided a more improved and accurate depth identification system.

In addition to these improvements, air power was introduced into the ASW battle. PBY's were twin-engine long-range amphibian bombers built by Convair that were well fitted for the job. They could carry a heavy load of depth charges, could spot a submerged or surfaced submarine easily despite the condition of the sea, and could blow it out of the water before it had a chance to take evasive action. The PBY carried a very bright searchlight that was used at night to illuminate a surfaced submarine charging its batteries. Before the submarine could react, the PBY would drop its bombs with accuracy because it could fly slowly and at a low altitude. Submarines had almost no chance to react quickly enough to use their antiaircraft guns against the aircraft and were almost always killed by this method.[1]

Small Jeep carriers, also known as escort carriers, proved very effective as an ASW weapon. These were built by the Kaiser Ship Yards and converted to carriers while still under construction. They were able to carry enough torpedo bombers and fighter aircraft to be

---

[1] For more detail on ASW armament please consult Hughes and Costelllo, *The Battle of the Atlantic*.

lethal to submarines. One hunter-killer group comprised of the Jeep carrier *Guadalcanal* and her five escort destroyers captured *U-505*, a German submarine, intact, in July of 1944. No American naval vessel since 1815 had captured and boarded an enemy man-of-war. The captain of the *Guadalcanal*, his crew, and the crews of the escort destroyers had much to be proud of! They also captured the German ENIGMA code machine complete with all of the rotors and code books.

Ultra, (British Intelligence) was reading German signals in real time and rerouting convoys away from known wolf packs, (a group of submarines operating as a unit) and sinking their "milch cows" (refueling oilers). All of these advances in antisubmarine warfare had a devastating effect on German submarine operations. By 1944 German U-boat losses had increased to the point where all of their aces had perished and many of their newly commissioned U-boats never completed their first cruise. While they had no trouble recruiting for their U-boat fleet, they were having a problem of morale among the existing crews because so many boats were not returning from their missions. Their "happy days" of 1940-41 were long gone.

By now we were entering the middle of April when we were ordered to Norfolk OB to refuel and take on stores. We moored to a dock that was loaded with supplies for our ship and we spent a couple of days loading. It was quite evident that we were preparing for a long trip, and by deduction we figured we were on our way to Europe. Our next stop was a mooring at a different dock at Norfolk OB where we nested with the other ships of our division. We were there for about three days during which we had liberty. While there we discovered that one of the crewmembers on—I think it was the *Walke*—was the actor who portrayed the part of the Lone Ranger on radio. Caesar Romero (the Hollywood actor) was also a crewmember of one of the other ships—which one I don't remember. We also had celebrities of a different kind.

Since we were the flagship of the division we were tied up to the dock. The *Walke* was tied up to us on our starboard side, and the other ships tied up to the *Walke* in proper order. I was doing some work on my torpedo mount when I saw an officer walking down the dock with two bimbos. They came over the gangway onto the quarterdeck of our ship and crossed over the starboard gangway to the *Walke*. The next thing we heard was the word passed on the *Walke* for two of their crewmembers to report to the quarterdeck. By this time all hands topside figured that something was up with these two crewmen of the *Walke*, and the two women who looked like a couple of old time dolls of the evening who had accrued plenty of miles and experience. When the two crewmen showed up these two old broads started screaming at them in language that would make a sailor blush. The officer quieted them down, asked the two crewmen a few questions, and decided in favor of the sailors, whereupon these two soiled doves from some den of iniquity started in on the officer—big mistake. It sounded like the big flap was over money, and the officer told these two purveyors of joy that they had it coming and that they had probably rolled their share of sailors. He then ordered them off of the ship and escorted them to the gate. We who were spectators to all of this had a good laugh over the incident—to think that two of our navy's trusted sailors would take advantage of damsels in distress.

The next day we were ordered to New York where we docked at a downtown pier usually reserved for large ocean liners. We were scheduled to be there a couple of days and I was ordered to do some maintenance on the number two torpedo mount. A seaman by the name of Ryner had been transferred from the destroyer *Nelson* (just to get rid of him) because he was such a recalcitrant character who was always in trouble, wouldn't take orders, and was continually bragging about it. For some reason he was assigned to me for work on our equipment. He had been bragging that no one on the *Nelson* could make him work, and he wasn't about to change on the *Barton*.

He showed up for work after lunch, sat down on an overturned bucket, and proceeded to tell me how tough he was and that I couldn't make him work either. He watched me work, all the while attempting to antagonize me with more threats. The word soon spread through the ship about what was happening, and everyone in the deck force was waiting to see what I was going to do. While I was working, and he was sitting on his can mouthing off, I was thinking about what I would do to teach him a lesson and perhaps straighten him out. It finally became 1700 and time for me to secure the mount. I told Ryner, "you're a punk and I'll make you a proposition. We'll go down on the quarterdeck and I'll let you get any kind of a hold on me you want. If I can't break it I'll take orders from you. If I break it, you take orders from me." He said "you can't whip me, let's go." We went down to the quarterdeck and I allowed him to get a "full Nelson" hold on me—which is supposed to be nearly unbreakable.

At that moment the OOD suddenly had business on the other side of the ship, because as a petty officer I wasn't supposed to fight. A bunch of the crew had gathered around to watch the match, and before they could get comfortable I flipped Ryner—he landed on the steel deck visibly shaken with the fight taken out of him. I grabbed him, hauled him to his feet, and said in a very loud voice so that everyone topside could hear it, "from now on you work for me and when I yell shit you better squat and strain or there will be more of this." I never had any more guff from him after that! Actually, he didn't know how lucky he was, because if I had lost my temper, I could have broken several bones in his body in a split second—I was sufficiently trained in the art of jujitsu to do it.

That evening I went ashore with three of the torpedomen from our gang. Our first stop was a cocktail lounge not too far from the pier where we were tied up. It was a nice quiet classy place decorated with plush carpets, nice round tables, and overstuffed chairs. The four of us were sitting at a table sipping our cocktails and chatting in low tones when four girls walked in and sat down at the table next to us. One girl was just at my back and she began talking to me. I swung my chair around so that I could look at her and as we were carrying on a nice quiet conversation the bartender came over and said "we don't allow sailors to talk to our lady customers in here." I of course protested politely and informed him that I was being a gentleman and that if the lady wished to talk to me I would talk to her. At that moment three of our officers walked in and sat down. They ordered their drinks and two bouncers appeared from the back room to order us out. From that moment things went from bad to worse with tables and chairs going in all directions. We couldn't get any more drinks and we finally left as the shore patrol was entering the place. The next morning I discovered that our engineering officer somehow lost his hat in a scuffle after we left. I razzed him about going where the enlisted men go. I'm not certain but I think he slugged one of the bouncers—there was evidence on his face and hands. I guess he wasn't about to take any guff from those goons.

Our stay in New York was very short, and the next day all liberty was cancelled and we were ordered to make ready to put to sea.

Chapter 7

OPERATION NEPTUNE:
THE INVASION OF FRANCE

6 June 1944 to 25 June 1944

We Depart New York City

The end of April, we departed from New York City to help escort a convoy of merchant ships to Great Britain. Our speed of eleven knots dictated by the speed of the slowest merchantman, and our zigzag course, required us to take about twelve days to complete the crossing. We were about halfway to the Azores when we received an ALNAV from COMDESLANT, (Commander Destroyers Atlantic Fleet) directed to DESLANT, (all destroyers of the Atlantic fleet) concerning a new weapon being used by German submarines. It was an acoustic torpedo which would be directed to the target ship by the noise of its propellers. This was serious because it meant that a submarine captain now had more flexibility in positioning his vessel for attack, and he was now much more dangerous, and more difficult for a surface anti-submarine ship to locate. The torpedo, once fired, could now change course to search out the propeller noise of a ship and hit it from an angle not indicating the true target angle of the submarine.

I happened to have the afternoon watch on the fantail when this information was passed to all torpedomen aboard ship. The two depth charge roller racks on the fantail contained nine 270-pound charges each for a total of 2.43 tons of TNT. There were also three 20mm gun mounts along with their ammunition. I was sitting on the 20mm ammunition box digesting the ALNAV and thinking that if a torpedo were to hit the propellers, I would make a spectacular exit into oblivion, when a ship-fitter and a seaman showed up with some metal junk and a long metal line. He also had an ALNAV explaining how to tow a noisemaker that would attract the acoustic torpedo to it instead of the propellers. His metal junk turned out to be heavy steel plates fashioned in such a way as to cause it to twirl and clank together making underwater noise to attract the torpedo. They attached about 125 yards of metal line containing the noisemaker to a cleat on the deck, threw it over the stern, and we all hoped for the best. Fortunately we never had to test it.

We went by way of the Azores to avoid German submarines. There was a U.S. Navy air base there where PBY Catalina bombers flew antisubmarine patrols. These aircraft, equipped with the newly developed MAD (Magnetic Anomaly Detectors), could detect a submerged submarine and attack it with rocket propelled retro-bombs—they were called Madcats and were death to German submarines. We felt quite secure when we came in range of their patrol radius.

It was night when we entered the harbor at Plymouth in southern England, and the fog was the thickest I had ever seen. The next morning when the weather cleared I was amazed at the number of ships jammed in the harbor. The night before it seemed we were the only ship moored. Now I wondered how the harbor pilot had managed to get us in without us ramming another vessel.

I went ashore on a five-hour liberty with a fellow torpedoman, Jim Dudly, just before noon. We were advised that because food was so short in Great Britain we were not to visit any restaurants. We walked up a narrow quaint street from the dock where our whaleboat had deposited us, gawking at the side by side houses, and wondering what all of the fuss was about concerning the bombing of Britain. We rounded a corner and there it was, building after building which at first glance seemed to be unscathed by war. These were buildings which I had observed through the high powered optics of our main battery director that morning; however, they didn't seem damaged at that distance. Up close we could see that they were just shells of buildings that were bombed out by German bombers and completely gutted during the blitz of 1940.

We wandered around the town viewing quaint English shops, all the while marveling at the people going about their business, seemingly oblivious of the war and what they had been through. Finally we stumbled upon a USO which was sponsored by the U.S. government. We went in and discovered we could buy sandwiches and milk, and relax in a friendly "homey" atmosphere. Since this was an organization sponsored by our government we weren't depriving the local citizens of scarce food. I had a ham, cheese, lettuce and tomato sandwich on white bread and a glass of milk. The very polite English ladies working there made the sandwich to order and made us feel comfortable. We paid in U.S. dollars; this was the only thing we could buy. Goods of any kind, thanks to the efficiency of the German submarines, was rationed to the English citizens, and was therefore unavailable to American servicemen. Security was tight; we couldn't even have a camera in our possession. Even though we couldn't do anything but sightsee and have a sandwich, it was a pleasure to get off the ship for a few hours.

During the first week of May, 1944, transport ships started moving troops and equipment from Northern Ireland, Scotland, and other parts of Britain to Plymouth, Torquay, Weymouth, Bournemouth, Southampton, Portsmouth, Eastbourne and other locations in southern England. It took about a month to assemble almost a million men and their equipment at the embarkation points.

While in the harbor of Plymouth we refueled, took on stores, and then embarked for Belfast, Northern Ireland. We sailed northward through the Irish Sea to rendezvous with a large passenger liner which was transporting U.S. troops. We escorted the troop ship south through the Irish Sea, around the southern tip of England to Weymouth on the English Channel.

During the next few days all hands were confined to the ship for loading of stores, refueling, and last-minute checking of equipment. The word came down from our executive officer, Lieutenant Commander Sanderson, who told us that we were about to take part in the invasion of France. Security was tight and we were advised that our mail had not left England and would continue to be held for some time for security reasons. We were not given a date for the invasion, but were ordered to be ready to embark at a moment's notice.

Years later I learned that some pin-headed general had bragged about movement of equipment and supplies at a cocktail party, and had also written his wife about what he knew so that she could brag to the girls back home about how important her husband was. When Eisenhower heard of it he naturally exploded, and relieved the general of his command. He demoted him and sent him back to the states with a severe reprimand to command a desk. With German spies all over the place, both in England and the U.S., this was a severe and serious breach of security. When I look back on the situation, and consider what was involved in assembling that huge invasion force, I still wonder how it was possible to do it right under the noses of the Germans without them becoming aware of what was happening.

June 3, 1944, the Western Naval Task Force left Belfast in pre-dawn hours and sailed south through the Irish Sea to the vicinity of the Isle of Wight which was the assembly area for all task forces taking part in "Operation Neptune" (the invasion of Normandy in France), and had the code name "Piccadilly Circus." The Western

Task Force was made up of the battleships *Texas*, *Nevada*, and *Arkansas*, seven cruisers, and twenty-one destroyers. We joined the Western Task Force in the wee hours of 4 June. "Operation Neptune" was the code name assigned to the Normandy invasion as part of "Operation Overlord," which was the entire plan for the ultimate defeat of Nazi Germany.

The British Eastern Task Force had sailed down from seaports in the north, through the Dover Strait, escaping detection by the Germans who were anticipating the main invasion thrust to be near the French town of Calais at the narrowest part of the English Channel. (See map, Plate 6.) The merging of the two task forces formed the largest naval invasion force ever assembled for battle in the history of the world at that time. Included in this armada were warships from many countries including Australia, Belgium, Greece, Holland, New Zealand, Norway, Poland, and South Africa. It was truly an international force.

Task Force Western was composed of 931 ships, including everything from warships to transports and support vessels of all kinds. Task Force Eastern included 1,796 ships of all kinds including warships, transports, support vessels, and ships from most of the nations mentioned above. Not included in the above ship count were 2,606 Higgins landing boats which were carried on board transport vessels. Their number brought the total count of vessels of all sizes in the armada to 5,333.

Minesweepers had begun clearing mines from the proposed invasion route, 31 May. There were almost 250 vessels engaged in this monumental task. They cleared quarter-mile wide channels to Utah, Omaha, Gold, Juno, and Sword beaches, marking the channels with lighted dan buoys every mile, and then cleared the anchorage areas where the battleships, cruisers, destroyers, and transports would take up their fire support positions. We were advised that the English Channel was so loaded with mines of every description that on D-Day we were to anchor and sacrifice

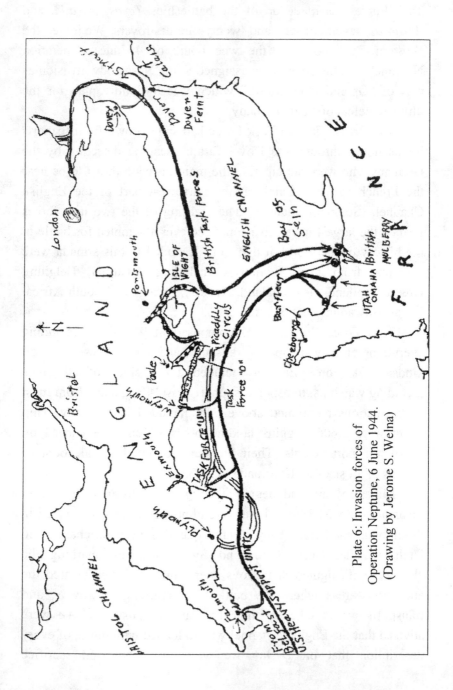

Plate 6: Invasion forces of
Operation Neptune, 6 June 1944.
(Drawing by Jerome S. Welna)

maneuverability until the minesweepers could enlarge the cleared areas. Many of the minesweepers were actually converted heavily armed refitted destroyers. On D-Day, 6 June, they were still at work in the Utah/Omaha sectors, and were still sweeping nineteen days later. This was necessary because the Germans actually increased their mine-laying during the first few days of the battle using aircraft until the American and British air forces put a stop to it.

Operation Neptune was commanded by Allied Naval Commander Chief Expeditionary Force Admiral Sir Bertram H. Ramsay, RN. His command was composed of five task forces: three British under Rear Admiral Sir Phillip L. Vian, RN, and two American under Rear Admiral A.G. Kirk, Commander Western Task Force. The British Eastern Task Force was divided into three forces designated Gold, Juno, and Sword beaches for which they would provide fire support. The British 5th Division would take Gold, the Canadian 3rd Juno, and the British 3rd Sword. The Western Task Force was divided into two groups designated Task Force "O" for Omaha, and "U" for Utah—the two beaches for which they would provide fire support. The American 1st Division would take Omaha, and the 4th Division would take Utah.

The following pages show the command structure and organization of the U.S. Navy Fire Support Groups complete with the destroyers and destroyer escorts that served with the Western Task Force.

COMPOSITION OF WESTERN TASK FORCE
Rear Admiral A.G. Kirk, Commanding
USS *Augusta* (Flagship)

Rear Admiral C.F. Bryant, Commanding
Fire-Support Group "O"
  Battleship *Texas* (Flagship)
  Battleship *Arkansas*
  Light Cruiser *Glasgow*, RN
  Light Cruiser *Montcalm*, RN
  Light Cruiser *George Leggues*, Fr.
  Three British Destroyers

Rear Admiral M.L. Deyo, Commanding
Fire-Support Group "U"
  Battleship *Nevada*
  Battleship *Erebus*, RN Reserve Fire-Support Group
  Heavy Cruiser *Tuscaloosa* (Flagship)
  Heavy Cruiser *Quincy*
  Heavy Cruiser *Hawkins*
  Two British Light Cruisers
  Dutch Gunboat *Samba*

Reserve Fire-Support Group
USS *Augusta* (flagship)
British Light Cruiser *Bellona*
Four destroyer divisions, 60,19,33,18
(Seventeen destroyers total)

OPERATION NEPTUNE
U.S. Destroyers Battle Organization
6 June, 1944

FIRE SUPPORT GROUP "O"
DESRON 18

Ship's Name

Frankford	Lt. Comdr. J.L. Semmes, flying the pennant of Capt. H. Sanders, COMDESRON 18
Baldwin	Lt. Comdr. F.S. Powell, Jr., flying the pennant of Comdr. W. Marshall, COMDESRON 36

Carmic	Comdr. R.O. Beer
Harding	Comdr. G.G. Palmer
Doyle	Comdr. J.G. Marshall
Saterlee	Lt. Comdr. R.W. Leach
McCook	Lt. Comdr. R.L. Ramey
Thompson	Lt. Comdr. A.L. Gebelin

FIRE SUPPORT GROUP 'U'
DESDIV 34

Butler	Comdr. M.D. Matthews, flying the pennant of Comdr. W. L. Benson, COMDESDIV 34
Gherardi	Comdr. N.R. Curtin
Herndon	Comdr. G.A. Moore
Shubrick	Lt. Comdr. W.L. Blenman

COMDESDIV 20

Hobson	Lt. Comdr. K. Loveland, flying the pennant of Comdr. I.W. Nilon, COMDESDIV 20
Forrest	Comdr. K.P. Leits
Fitch	Comdr. K.C. Walpole
Corry	Lt. Comdr. G.D. Hoffman

RESERVE FIRE SUPPORT GROUP
DESDIV 60

Barton	Comdr. J.W. Callahan, flying the pennant of Capt. W.L. Freseman, COMDESRON 60
Walke	Comdr. C.J. Zahm
Laffey	Comdr. F.J. Becton
O'Brien	Comdr. W.W. Outerbridge
Meredith	Comdr. G. Knuepfer

DESDIV 33

Jeffers	Lt. Comdr. H.Q. Murray, flying the pennant of Capt. A.C. Murdaugh, COMDESRON 33
Nelson	Lt. Comdr. T.D. McGrath
Murphy	Comdr. R.A. Wolverton
Glennon	Comdr. C.A. Johnson
Plunkett	Comdr. W. Outerson

DESDIV 19

Ellyson	Comdr. E.W. Longton, flying the pennant of Capt. A.F. Converse, COMDESRON 10
Hambleton	Comdr. H.A. Renken
Rodman	Comdr. J.F. Foley
Emmons	Comdr. E.B. Billing

DESDIV 18

Somers	Comdr. W.C. Hughes,
	Also acting COMDESDIV 18
Davis	Comdr. W.A. Dunn
Jouett	Comdr. J. C. Parham, Jr.

U.S. Destroyer Escorts

Amesbury	Lt. Comdr. A.B. Wilbur, USNR
	Flying the pennant of
	Comdr. A.B. Adams, Jr., COMCORTDIV 19
Borum	Lt. Comdr. J.K. Davis, USNR
Maloy	Lt. Comdr. F.D. Kellogg, USNR
Rich	Lt. Comdr. E.A. Michel, Jr. USNR
Bates	Lt. Comdr. H.A. Wilmerding, Jr. USNR
Blessman	Lt. Comdr. J.A. Cillis, USNR

We weighed anchor on 3 June 1944 and proceeded into the English Channel where we took up a position, along with other destroyers of our division, as a radar picket ship. Our job was to intercept any German surface craft or submarines that might venture into the area and sound the alarm of the assembly of the invasion force.

During this time our air force was extremely active in ridding the skies of German aircraft over both the English Channel and the Normandy coast. We were instructed not to fire on any aircraft because they would probably be our own. We were also advised of the German V-2 rockets (flying bombs) and instructed not to fire on them. The English had that responsibility because they were aimed at London anyway. We operated under radio silence, and could not use blinker signal lights. D-Day (invasion date) was set for 5 June

1944. The evening of 3 June the weather which had been beautiful, sunny and warm started to deteriorate.

In his book, *Crusade in Europe*, General Eisenhower discusses the weather problems he and his staff dealt with in executing the invasion of France. Because the weather so dramatically affected the entire invasion force, I have abstracted the proceedings of the staff meetings held during this critical time:

Since the end of May, Eisenhower and his staff had been holding two weather briefings daily at 0930 and 1600. Group Captain J. M. Stagg, a wily Scot from the Royal Air Force (RAF), with a reputation for being knowledgeable and clever, was Eisenhower's weather prognosticator. I use this term because, as anyone who has had experience with the weather in that part of the world knows, predicting it with any degree of reliability is almost impossible.

What was supposed to be the final weather briefing was set for Sunday, 4 June, at 0400. Stagg reportedly informed Eisenhower that a high-pressure system was moving out, and a low one was coming in. Worse yet, the ceiling for air operations would be zero to 500 feet, and forecasting more than twenty-four hours in advance was undependable because the situation was deteriorating so rapidly.

The wind had picked up to Force-5, drizzle had turned to heavy rain, and the sea became increasingly rough. As destroyer sailors we didn't think anything of it. This was just foul weather typical of the North Atlantic and the English Channel. It didn't occur to us that those poor soldiers in the landing crafts were landlubbers who had no experience with the sea, and were subject to seasickness.

Unbeknown to us, Eisenhower was faced with a big problem back at Supreme Headquarters Allied Expeditionary Force (SHAEF). We now know that at 0400, 4 June, Eisenhower met with the SHAEF staff which included General Bernard Law Montgomery, Commander British Eighth Army, Air Marshal Tedder and Air Vice Marshal Sir Trafford Leigh-Mallory, Admiral

Bertram Ramsay, RN, Commander in Chief, General Kenneth Strong of SHAEF G-2, and General Walter B. Smith, Eisenhower's chief of staff, and other high ranking officers.

Eisenhower needed reasonably good flying weather for air cover, and good moonlight the night before the bomber runs, glider operations, and airborne drops. Without air cover Neptune was almost impossible. He needed calm seas for adequate control of landing craft. Heavy seas would reduce the accuracy of naval bombardment. Poor visibility with fog would create a traffic problem with hundreds of landing craft attempting to reach the beaches on schedule. He needed three to four hours before high tide to permit landing craft to maneuver around beach defenses located in the high and low tidal areas and so designed as to impede landing craft. (These defenses will be explained in detail later.) If Neptune were postponed more than a day or two it would not be until 19 June when suitable tide conditions would occur again. In the meantime the Germans would certainly learn of the Allied invasion plans. To further add to the problem, German General Erwin Rommel had been named Tactical Commander for the Western Front in December of 1943, was charged with analyzing existing defenses, and had identified all of the possible invasion locations. He was feverishly increasing the defenses of these areas, especially the Omaha and Utah beaches. To allow him more weeks to prepare would simply increase the risk to Operation Neptune and add more casualties.

Eisenhower asked his subordinates for their opinions: should the operation continue or should it be postponed? Tedder and Leigh-Mallory wanted a postponement. Montgomery wanted to go. Ramsay said the navy could handle the weather, but warned of the problems with the landing craft in heavy weather—many might flounder or capsize in the high surf. There was also the probability that navy Shore Fire Control Parties (SFCP) put ashore would have problems with visibility and radio communications when attempting to direct naval gunfire. He also warned that no further postponement to the seventh could be made because part of the landing fleet would have to be refueled. Smith thought it was a good gamble.

Eisenhower retired for a couple of hours trying to reach the most important decision of his life. On 4 June 1944 at 0600 he issued the order to hold off for one day. He would hope to cross the channel 5 June, for an invasion 6 June 1944.

Along with the other ships of the destroyer screen we turned around to cover the retirement of the landing vessels back to their respective ports. We also had to cover the battleships and other large ships of the invasion force. Since torpedomen man all antisubmarine weapons except sonar, we were compelled to remain at our battle stations near the K-guns and depth charge racks.

We now know that on the night of 4 June, Eisenhower met with the SHAEF staff and other high ranking officers. The weather was terrible! It was so bad that most of the high ranking officers of the German army went home because they felt that there was no possibility of an invasion in such inclement weather.

At 2130, 4 June, Stagg arrived at the routine weather briefing with a late weather report. He informed the group that he anticipated a break in the storm, and that the heavy rain would stop before daybreak. He predicted thirty-six hours, more or less, of clear weather. Winds would moderate and although there would be scattered clouds, air activity should be able to resume 5 and 6 June. Eisenhower asked for input from his staff—should we go, or call it off? Smith, one of Eisenhower's most trusted generals, said "it's a 'helluva' gamble but it's the best possible gamble." The ever cautious Leigh-Mallory suggested postponement to 19 June. Tedder agreed and wanted a postponement. Eisenhower asked Monty—do you see any reason for not going on the fifth? Monty replied "I would say go!" Eisenhower is reported to have left the room, went to a window where he could watch the pounding rain, and returned a few minutes later. At this point he must have been the loneliest man in the world. His staff was divided; Eisenhower, and only Eisenhower, could make the decision. On his shoulders rested the fate of almost a million men, and the future of a free world. He was pacing the floor when he suddenly asked, "The question is, just how long can you hang this operation on the end of a limb and let it hang there?" No one answered! At 2145 hours Eisenhower gave the order to go.

By 2300 hours, 4 June, all vessels had received orders to resume sailing, and convoys began forming up again. We of the torpedo gang were dressed in our foul weather gear. The rain, choppy sea, and wind weren't bothering us, but we were tired and still wondering what in hell the problem was.

On 5 June, 0330, the weather was still terrible. Stagg conducted his last weather briefing at 0400 hours. The weather was still awful, but he predicted that the storm should break before dawn; however, good weather was only likely through Tuesday the sixth. Wednesday the seventh could be rough again. The danger was that the first assault troops could get ashore, but the follow-up units could not. Eisenhower again asked for opinions. Monty still wanted to go as did Smith. Ramsay was concerned about spotting for naval gunfire, but thought the risk worth taking. Leigh-Mallory still thought that air conditions were below acceptable minimum. The ships were sailing into the Channel, and it was still not too late to call the operation off. If they were to be called back it would have to be now; again, Eisenhower was the only man who could do it. Years later Eisenhower recounted what he had been thinking at the moment.

If Stagg were wrong, at best the AEF (American Expeditionary Force) would be landing seasick men without air cover and accurate naval bombardment. To postpone again would be dangerous, and the Germans would have more time to learn the secret of Neptune.

That must have been a terrible time for the senior commander. He couldn't keep seasick men locked up in their landing crafts much longer. He wanted to do the best he could do for his country, but he didn't want unnecessary casualties. The responsibility for the outcome was entirely his.

We in the torpedo crew spent the night at our battle stations at the K-guns and the depth charge racks on the ready for a possible submarine attack. We were all exhausted from lack of sleep. I wrapped my arm around the breather pipe which extended from the emergency diesel generator located below our port K-guns and promptly fell asleep standing up—sometime later an officer came by and woke me up. After that, we were allowed to split the group and allow half of the men to sleep on the deck at their battle stations with the other half awake and alert.

We crossed the channel at five knots. At that speed we were sitting ducks for a submarine or *Schnellboot* attack. (Motor torpedo boats, or E-Boats as we called them, stationed in Cherbourg and Le Havre.) These E-Boats could be lethal. On 28 April an American convoy of eight LCTs (Landing Craft Tank) escorted by HMS *Azales* was attacked at 0200 hours while conducting an invasion exercise off the Dorset coast. Within twenty minutes three LCTs were torpedoed and sunk with 749 men killed—only nine men survived. Fortunately we made no submarine or E-Boat contacts on 5 or 6 June, probably due to the rough seas. E-Boats preferred to make their forays at night when it would be more difficult for destroyers to identify and kill them.

We were cold, wet, tired, and facing a long day of battle when shortly after midnight mess cooks came around with huge buckets of hot vegetable soup that we really appreciated. It was served in large coffee mugs so that we could consume it easily while at our battle stations. I don't believe I ever enjoyed soup more than I did that night.

Just before dawn on 6 June an LCI (Landing Craft Infantry) hit a mine and was sinking. We launched our whaleboat, which made three or four trips to the sinking craft, and rescued thirty infantrymen including one sergeant. The other thirty soldiers, their lieutenant, and the LCI crewmen were taken off by one of the other destroyers. By the time we had all men aboard and the whaleboat out of the water it was gray light, and we proceeded to our battle station just off Pointe du Hoc. One navy crewman of the sinking LCI was confirmed killed in the explosion—there may have been more (and probably were) that I am not aware of.

Pointe du Hoc is a spectacular promontory at the western end of the Omaha sector, and about four miles west of the Vierville draw, right on the sea. It was chosen as a target for the 2nd Battalion of the United States Army Rangers because of its strategic location. Its 136 foot cliffs provided a perfect location for heavy artillery to command both the Omaha and Utah sectors. It was code-named "Maisey." Pointe du Hoc was labeled "Target No. One" out of 300 German installations in the First U.S. Army sector because of its six 155mm guns with a range in excess of 25,000 yards. Our entire Western Task Force was within range of these guns on D-Day, most of which were housed in reinforced concrete bunkers thirty-five feet thick, with an infantry garrison protecting them from ground assault. Prior to D-Day both the U.S. and British air forces attempted to destroy these gun emplacements by bombing—with no success. Now it was up to the U.S. Navy and the Rangers to take them out.

Our ship was on station 2,500 yards off Pointe du Hoc at first light, which was about 0520 hours. General quarters was sounded and I assumed my battle station on the bridge. My close friend Jim Dudly had already taken his position on the bridge. As I strapped my telephone headset on we both said that we were going to make history this day.

The fog hadn't cleared and we couldn't see the shoreline. As it became lighter the shoreline came into view, and before long I could see the cliffs of Pointe du Hoc clearly. We looked north at the armada of ships of all types anchored between us at the very head of the invasion force, to the battleships 25,000 yards out from our position near the shoreline. We agreed that we would never see such a sight as this again. We also agreed that we should keep our heads down because we were close enough to the shore to be hit by machine gun fire when the shooting started. The naval bombardment was to commence at sunrise, which was 0558 hours. We waited patiently and we spoke in subdued voices lest the enemy should hear us.

Our captain and two other officers were busy reviewing a huge aerial photograph of the sector we were assaulting. This reconnaissance photo was at least ten feet long and over two feet wide and was displayed in the pilot house on a special stand built just for the occasion. It had been created just a few days prior to the invasion date and showed numerous targets we were required to take out. While everyone thought at the time that we knew where all of the important targets were, we soon learned that there were whole panzer divisions and heavy field batteries so well camouflaged that they didn't show up on the photo-map. This was later declared to be a serious intelligence blunder which resulted in excess casualties.

The fleet had orders not to fire until H-Hour minus forty minutes (0550) unless fired upon before that time. At 0535 hours a German battery of four 210mm (8.27-inch) guns at Utah Beach opened fire on the battleship *Nevada*. The *Nevada* immediately answered with her ten 14-inch guns. During the duel the *Nevada* was straddled twenty-seven times. At the same time the entire fleet commenced firing. The noise was unbelievably loud. In all of the battles I've been in this was one of the most impressive shows of power I have ever seen. The sky was overcast with a humid atmospheric condition which caused the sound waves from the big guns to bounce off the cloud cover and exacerbate the noise.

Our main battery of six 5-inch guns had commenced firing simultaneously with the rest of the fleet. Each time a salvo was fired the entire ship would shake. The soldiers that we had taken aboard were wild-eyed. They hadn't been briefed as to what to expect from the firing of our main battery, and it didn't take them long to figure out that they were aboard a ship loaded with ammunition and other explosives, and that one hit from a German shore battery would cause considerable damage and casualties. Unlike fighting on land there were no holes to hide in. The soldiers were assigned the task of passing ammunition from the magazines on deck to the 40mm gun mounts. They seemed to be in awe of the cool way our officers and sailors conducted themselves in battle, and I think they felt secure in our expertise and the way in which we went about discharging our duties. As a result they assumed their work with cheerfulness and vigor, and in the days that passed we got to know them well and almost made sailors out of them.

From my vantage point on the bridge I could see the battleships firing their main batteries. Each time the guns fired I could follow their trajectories until the shells disappeared to explode on land. Shells from the battleship *Texas* were passing directly overhead, and I was confident that one wouldn't fall short and land on us. The *Texas* mounted five double turrets of 14-inch guns as their main battery. The *Nevada* mounted two triple turrets and two double turrets of 14-inch guns as her main battery. When the triple turrets fired I could see the center gun firing a split second ahead of the two outside guns. The impact of these shells exploding on land was spectacular. They would create a hole large enough to drop a large truck in, and yet they wouldn't always destroy a gun casemated in thirty-five feet of reinforced concrete; however, German prisoners described the tremendous noise, concussion, dust, gas, and concrete fragments from the exploding projectiles, as almost maddening and terribly demoralizing. My buddy Les Cline described many of the prisoners taken from the bunkers to be in complete shock and no longer capable of functioning as fighting men.

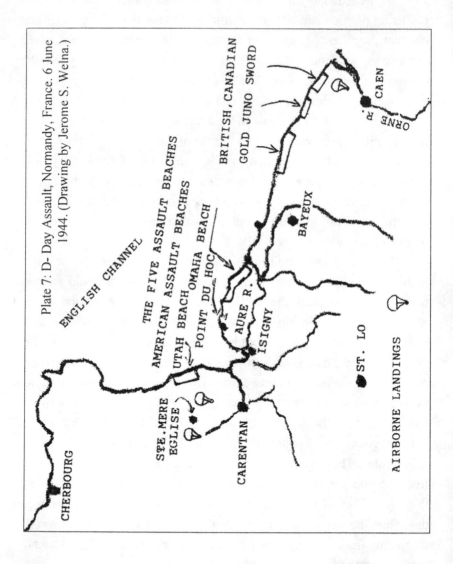

Plate 7: D- Day Assault, Normandy, France. 6 June 1944. (Drawing by Jerome S. Welna.)

At about 0537 the Norwegian destroyer *Svenner* was covering the British assault at Sword Beach when six German E-boats operating out of Le Havre suddenly appeared and fired a spread of torpedoes. One struck the *Svenner* amidships. The explosion must have detonated a magazine because men who witnessed the incident said that the burst of fire and smoke shot high into the air. The ship sank in less than five minutes—it broke in two as the ends folded together like a jackknife. I can't remember the number of casualties, but I do know that the dead and missing number was very high with few survivors. The *Svenner* was the only Allied war ship sunk by the German Navy that day. The British battleship HMS *Warspite* attacked the E-boats sinking one of them—the others retired to Le Havre. And so ended the only feeble attempt of the Kriegsmarine to attack allied ships on D-Day.

At about 0635 we received a radio message from the USS *Anchon*[1] transmitted over the TBS frequency (talk between ships) advising that the USS *Corry*, DD 463, was under fire from German shore batteries and had hit a mine. She was operating about 4,000 yards off Utah Beach in the company of destroyers USS *Fitch*, DD 462 and Flag destroyer USS *Hobson*, DD 464. Destroyers *Hobson* and *Fitch* were able to avoid the heavy German fire by escaping into a smoke screen laid down by allied aircraft, but the aircraft which attempted to screen the *Corry* was shot down, leaving her exposed to all of the big German defense guns. *Corry* continued firing on these guns while taking evasive action when she struck the mine. She had gone dead in the water at 0633, and by 0639 her main deck was awash and she was sinking. Admiral Deyo, aboard *Anchon*, immediately ordered destroyers *Fitch* and *Hobson* to aid the *Corry* and pick up her survivors. German guns were still firing on her and her wounded men floundering in the fifty-four-degree water as the

---

[1] The *Anchon* was a command ship serving as a headquarters and communication center for all US forces of "Operation Neptune."

Fitch and *Hobson* were firing on the German batteries, while at the same time lowering cargo nets and boats on the other side of their ships to pick up survivors. German shells exploding in the water were creating more wounded. One man in the water was offered a rescue line but declined the help because he had no hands or arms with which to grab the line. A moment later he had slipped beneath the waves and was gone. While this entire rescue work was occurring, the *Butler* DD 636 and PT *199* joined the operation. The last of *Corry's* 260 officers and men, including thirty-three wounded, were picked up by 0900. Twenty-one men and one officer were killed in the action.

When German Field Marshall Erwin Rommel (also known as the Desert Fox) was put in charge of defenses of the so-called "Atlantic Wall" 15 January 1944, his new command included the 15th and 17th armies under Army Group B stretching from Holland to the Loire River in southern Brittany in France. In his first briefing he informed his generals that *if the expected assault on the "Atlantic Wall" were to be repulsed it must be on the beaches of Normandy.*

At a meeting with Hitler, Field Marshal Keitel, Colonel General Jodl, and other members of the German General Staff, 20 March 1944, the discussion was concerned with the defenses of the "Atlantic Wall" and the expected Allied invasion. Hitler reportedly gave a long dissertation concerning the Calais area and his expected invasion at that location. Field Marshal Erwin Rommel was also in attendance at that meeting, and had previously identified five beaches along the Normandy coast where the impending invasion was most likely to occur. Hitler charged that he knew more than his generals about conducting military operations; and, he and his General Staff disagreed with Rommel and refused to accept his plan, which resulted in a disproportionate number of divisions being located at Calais east of the Somme in anticipation of the expected invasion there. In addition, disbursement of German troops and

Panzer units throughout Army Group B were located within range of navy guns, and were situated so that they were also subject to air attack. To further complicate the defense of the "Atlantic Wall," Hitler gave orders that no divisions could be moved without his permission. Rommel was right, and all of this worked in our favor in conducting the invasion, and the army punching through the thinly defended "Atlantic Wall" in just one day.

One reason for Hitler's decision may have been the fact that Calais is the closest location in the mainland (Belgium) to the British Isles. Secondly, the British had created an imitation army buildup across the channel from Calais that was constructed of fake plastic tanks, trucks, and other motorized vehicles that gave the impression of an invasion mobilization. To further support the charade, Eisenhower named General George C. Patton as commander of the fictitious paper army, complete with all necessary paperwork to give it the impression of authenticity.

On 17 May, or just prior to the invasion of 6 June 1944, General Bayerlein, a close confident of the disillusioned Rommel, had the following conversation with the Field Marshall. General Bayerlein quotes from Rommel's remarks:

Our friends from the East cannot imagine what they're in for here. It's not a matter of fanatical hordes to be driven forward in masses against our line, with no regard for casualties and little recourse to tactical craft; here we are facing an enemy who applies all his native intelligence to the use of his many technical resources, who spares no expenditure of material and whose every operation goes its course as though it had been the subject of repeated rehearsal. Dash and doggedness alone no longer make a soldier, Bayerlein; he must have sufficient intelligence to enable him to get the most out of his fighting machine.

And that's something these people can do, we found that out in Africa.[2]

To confine the assault to the beaches, Rommel ordered defenses to begin out in the ocean. The mine was his favorite weapon; and consequently the Germans heavily mined the English Channel in the vicinity of all possible troop landing beaches. The heavy German shore defense system started at about 250 yards off shore from the high waterline and was only visible at low tide. In planning their defenses the Germans assumed that landings would occur at high tide, and the submerged mined traps would destroy the landing crafts well before they reached an unloading position at the beach; however, the assault forces went in at low tide so that navy and coast guard coxswains could maneuver around the exposed obstacles which were supposed to have been blown by special demolition navy and army engineers just prior to the landings. Destruction of these obstacles didn't occur until later in the day after the first wave or two of assault troops went in, due to the high surf and heavy mortality of the demolition teams. The high surf and rough water made it difficult for the coxswains to avoid the obstacles even though they could see them. The fast current and rough water would push the Higgins boats (landing craft) towards the mined obstacles and the soldiers would lean out of the boat and push it away to safety as the coxswain would apply power.

The one advantage of the weather was that the Germans were taken completely by surprise because they figured we could never pull off an invasion in such heavy seas and foul weather. The German high command had taken a few days off for rest and relaxation. Even Field Marshal Rommel had gone to Berlin for a conference with Hitler, and then home to celebrate his wife's birthday which happened to be the date of our landings, 6 June 1944. That morning there was much confusion and indecision at

---

[2] Source, Liddell-Hart, *The Rommel Papers*, p.467.

headquarters and it took the Supreme German high command three days to determine that this was indeed the long expected invasion, and the main thrust, and not just a diversionary tactic. The German high command had been certain that the main thrust would occur at Calais, the narrowest part of the English Channel. They had their heaviest fortifications and troop concentrations in this area, and, during the first three days of the battle, still believing that the main thrust would come at Calais, refused to move their troops into the Normandy area. All of our combined forces made the best use of those three days to further secure established beachheads.

In the Omaha sector the morning tide ran at twenty-two feet, and the afternoon tide at twenty-three feet on D-Day. At high tide all of the beach obstacles were submerged and not visible. British intelligence had identified these defenses but SHAEF had refrained from ordering them destroyed during pre-invasion preparations so as to maintain the element of surprise.

Navy coxswains bringing their invasion boats in first encountered "Belgium Gates"—steel uprights ten feet high (at low tide) with waterproof teller mines attached at the top. If they successfully maneuvered past these they next encountered concrete poles about twenty-five to thirty yards further inshore which were angled towards the open sea and also mined. Seventy five yards further inshore were the mined "hedgehogs": six-foot-high steel bar structures (modified tank traps) intended to rip the bottom out off landing boats. And finally, about twenty-five yards from shore were steel and wood ramps with their high sides pointed shoreward and mined. All obstacles were mined with about twelve pounds of TNT, and many with old captured French artillery shells set to detonate.

Swimming tanks (called "Hobart's Funnies" by the British soldiers) were the idea of British General Percy Hobart. They were designed to swim as far as eight miles to the beach from deepwater embarkation from an LCT (Landing Craft Tank). They were officially designated as DD tanks because of their duplex drive that drove twin propellers off the main engine. They sported an inflatable air-filled canvas screen which surrounded the tank on all sides and bottom.

The DD tanks were to precede the infantry by about five minutes. Thirty-two were launched into the heavy seas according to plan and twenty-seven promptly went to the bottom with most of their crews. Of the five that reached the beach, three were knocked out by German 88's almost immediately.

Higgins boats couldn't go all the way to the beach because they would hang up on the sand reefs preceding deepwater trenches created by the recent rough weather which had rearranged the ocean bottom; consequently, coxswains were forced to drop their ramps prematurely. When the men stepped off the ramps they went into water over their heads. They were loaded with equipment and were top-heavy. They wore a life belt around their waist that inflated on impact from two CO-2 bottles in the belt. The result was that their head went down into the water, their waist went up to float on the surface, and they died of drowning.

For years I have thought about this tragic event, and as one who has had over forty years experience swimming and scuba diving in oceans of the world with high surf, rip tides, and fast currents, I feel that army trainers had no idea of the problems that our forces would experience in the rough surf. Had they had knowledge of the sea, they would have equipped these men with different floatation devices and trained them to disembark from a landing craft in rough seas. As a result of this oversight, and lack of training, hundreds of men were lost unnecessarily.

Fire from the heavy German batteries was concentrated on the landing craft as they negotiated their way through the mined obstacles and surf. Some landing craft suffered direct hits resulting in 100% casualties. As the Higgins boats dropped their ramps to unload the soldiers, they were raked with machine gun fire which again resulted in heavy casualties. Some men jumped over the side before the ramp dropped, hoping to escape before being hit by the machine gun fire, only to sink below the surface of the water and drown as described above. The slaughter was unimaginable, and yet the men had only one chance of survival—to head for the beach and hope to reach the safety of the base of the bluffs. The 116th RCT of the 1st Division was the only outfit in the first wave with combat experience. Survivors whom I talked with all said that they had been in the North African invasion in 1942, and the Sicily operation in 1943, but nothing prepared them for what they experienced D-Day at Omaha Beach.

The surviving soldiers who made it to land had to cross about thirty-five yards of shingle, go over a nine-foot-high concrete sea wall, and then cut through barbed wire, all of which was constructed at the high water line of the beach. Finally they had to cross 150 to 300 yards of open beach, heavily mined, and with tank traps, to reach the shelter of the bluffs, while facing murderous machine gun fire raking the beach. There was no cover for the invading troops until they reached the base of the 100-foot-high steep bluffs, except on the extreme end of Omaha Beach where there were two old fishing villages, Les Moulins and Hamel-au-Pretre. These villages consisted of a few old Norman stone houses, some of which were fortified by the Germans, or used as command or observation posts. The draw from these villages led up to the village of St. Laurent-sur-Mer to the south which is on the Colleville-Vierville road that parallels the beach.

Omaha Beach is a crescent shaped beach with 100-foot-high bluffs and five exits, or draws, leading down to the beach. The terrain was a defender's delight and provided ample positions for enfilading guns of all calibers that were placed so as to remain from view from the sea. Machine guns were positioned near the base of the cliffs and covered the beach entrances to the draws. Eighty-five of these were known to be in position where they could rake every inch of the beach with their cones of fire. Concrete bunkers housed

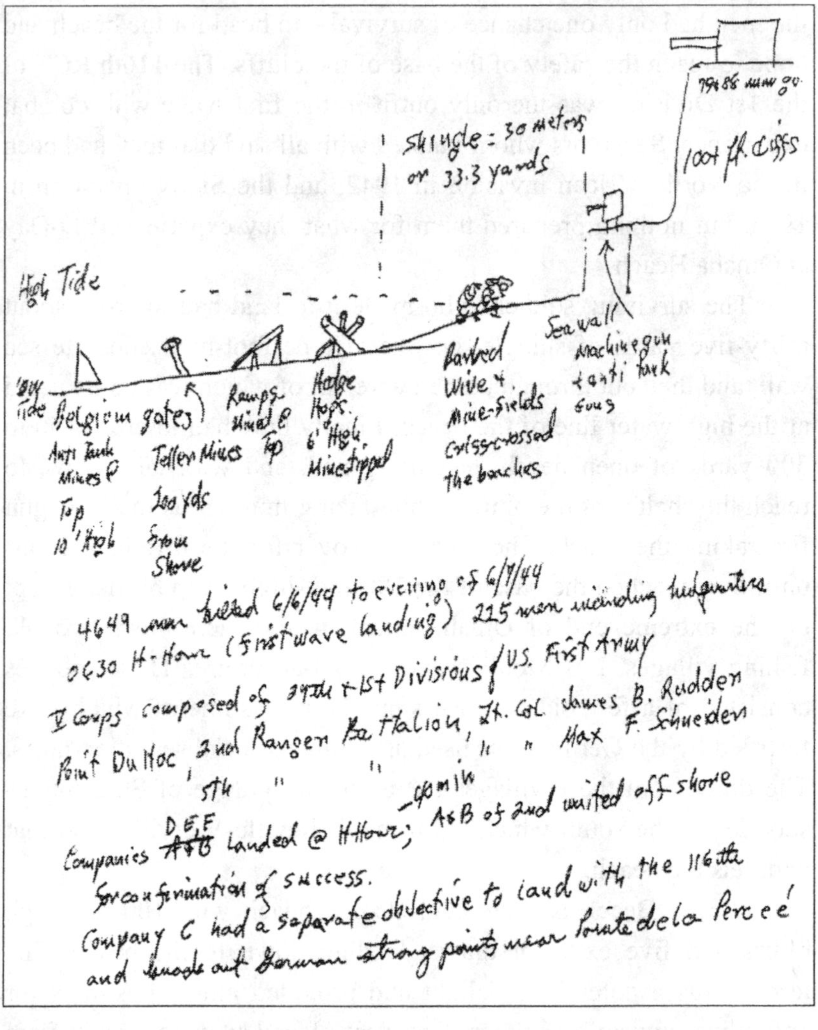

Plate 8: The Defenses of Omaha Beach.
(From the personal notes of Jerome S. Welna.)

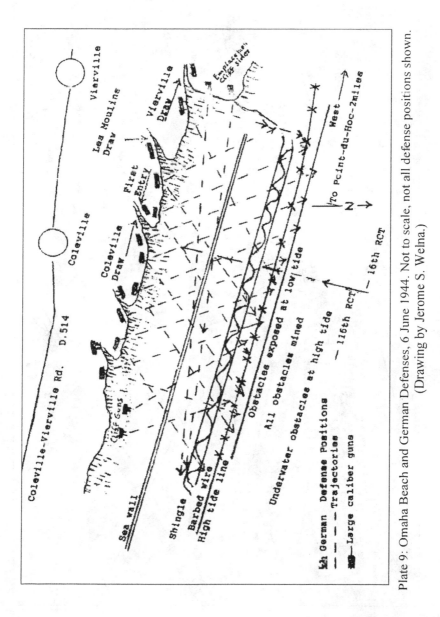

Plate 9: Omaha Beach and German Defenses, 6 June 1944. Not to scale, not all defense positions shown. (Drawing by Jerome S. Welna.)

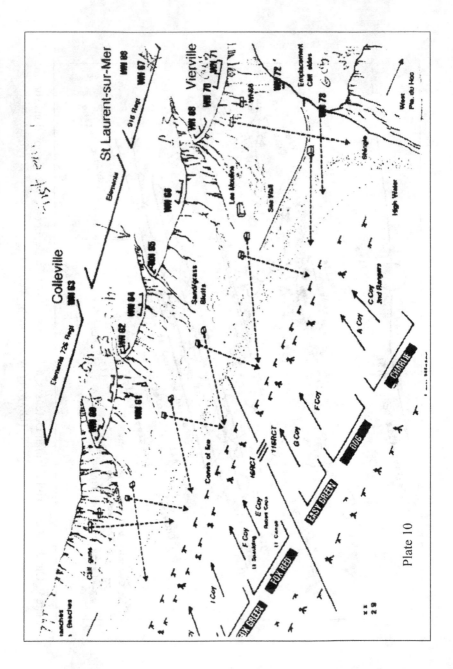

Plate 10

Preceding page, Plate 10: Omaha Beach defenses, 6 June 1944. (Source: Tim Kilvert-Jones, *Omaha Beach*, p. 65. Map by Anita Karl and James Kemp.) Five exits from the beach formed the strong points around which the battle was fought.

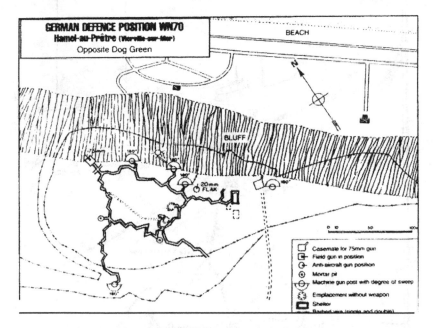

Plate 11: German Defense Positions, 6 June 1944.
(Source: Tim Kilvert-Jones, *Omaha Beach*, p. 66. Map by Anita Karl and James Kemp.)

Omaha Beach was the most heavily fortified, with defense positions, of the five invasion beaches. These defense positions were provided with one or more 75mm, 80mm, and 4-6 machine gun emplacements, as indicated on the diagram. Forward artillery directors were located at indicated positions WN 60, 62, 72, 73 and 74 and were able to direct accurate fire on the assault troops landing on the beach. The German defenders' big problem was the U.S. Navy. Their placements of reserve ammunition were located too far in the rear and had to be brought up by trucks. Navy destroyers firing 5-inch ammunition controlled the roads and prevented most vehicles of any kind from advancing to the front for resupply. This is exactly what German Field Marshal Rommel warned about, however, superior commanders paid no attention to him. For more on his remarks concerning the subject please refer to page 141.

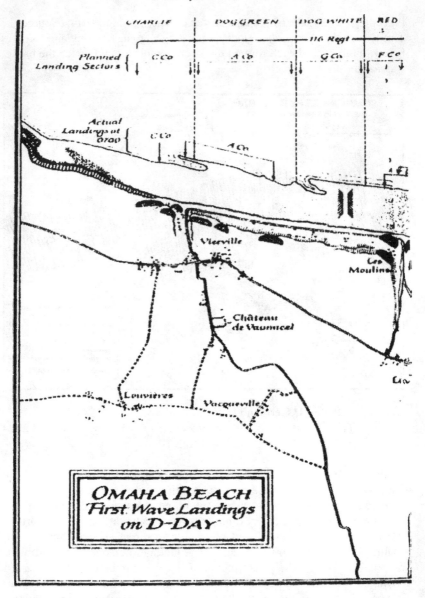

Plate 12: Omaha Beach, First Wave Landings on D-Day.

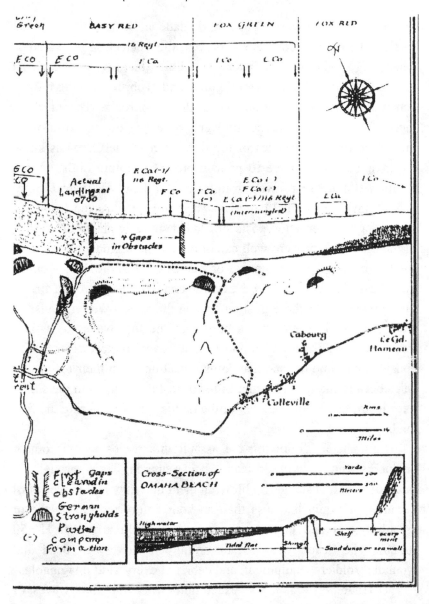

(Source: Stephen E. Ambrose, *D-Day*, p. 332-3.
Map by Anita Karl and James Kemp.)

88mm guns which were sighted in defilade and equipped with blast shields of steel and concrete to prevent their detection by warships when they fired down the beach. In addition, there were placements of 75mm, 50, 50mm, 37mm guns, and Tobruks (topless open concrete weapons pits equipped with 32cm rockets or machine guns). Tobruks and flame-throwers were positioned to provide protection to the entrances of the draws where the Germans knew the invaders would have to pass in order to capture high ground. Positioned in the rear, away from the rim of the bluffs were 155mm and 88mm conventional batteries. Their fire was directed from five separate gun observation posts situated at strategic places on the rim of the bluffs. They were well camouflaged and unknown to us until spotted by our spotter planes, or our SFCP. (Shore Fire Control Party) The SFCP were U.S. Navy personnel trained to direct fire of the warships from shore positions when the targets were not visible from shipboard. They went ashore with the first waves of assault troops to begin directing support fire; however, in most cases it took considerable time to establish communications with their respective ships because they were either killed or lost their radios in the surf. I have heard that eighty percent of the radios were lost during the first landing.

Immediately following the assault infantry came the combat engineers who, working in teams, began creating lanes through the maze of mined obstacles by blowing them up. They had to work fast because they only had less than an hour before the next wave of assault troops and command companies would arrive at H-+50 (0720). The beach was fast becoming cluttered with dead and wounded soldiers, equipment, and debris of every kind imaginable.

H-Hour was 0630, the exact time when the first waves of assault troops of V Corps were to hit the beach. The objective of V Corps was to secure the beachhead between Port-en-Bessin on the east and the River Vire on the west. V Corps was composed of the

116th RCT (Regimental Combat Team), 29th Division; 16th RCT, 1st Division; and Co C, 2nd Ranger Battalion.

At 0730 the command group of the 116th began to come in. It included the assistant commander of the 29th Division, Brig. Gen. Norman Cota, and Col. Charles Canham, Regimental Commander. Dead soldiers were floating everywhere and the sea was red with blood. Somehow General Cota made it from his LCVP (Landing Craft Vehicle and Personnel) along with Colonel Canham to the sea wall where men were huddled to escape machine gun fire. General Cota immediately appraised the situation and abandoned the battle plan, which was to open the Vierville draw. He knew it would never work. He ordered the barbed wire obstacle between his men and the cliffs to be blown with a bangalore torpedo (a long tube packed with explosives designed to blow apart and cut through wire obstacles).

The first man through the gap was shot dead in his tracks. Cota then rushed through and ran for the base of the bluffs with his men following. They all made it! They worked their way up the bluff through the German lines wiping out machine gun nests, German soldiers, and suffering casualties as they went. They reached the high ground around 0900, at about the same time that Canham was approaching Vierville with his men. They held a quick battle conference and decided that Canham would advance to the Les Moulins draw and attack it from the rear, while Cota would attack the Vierville draw from the rear, and they would unplug both draws so that mechanized units could be brought up to the high ground to outflank the German defenders.

The main assault at Omaha Beach had been in progress for about an hour when I suddenly realized that things were not going well. The strong ocean currents were carrying large numbers of dead soldiers by us. We were suddenly floating in a sea of dead soldiers, pieces of equipment, boxes of rations, and every other thing imaginable. As it developed, Omaha Beach with its heavy defenses turned out to be a killing field. It so happened that everything that could go wrong did go wrong. Omaha Beach, in battle briefings, had been guaranteed to be an easy landing—it didn't work out that way. Omaha Beach, in terms of casualties, turned out to be the most costly of all the five beaches assaulted on D-Day, and thus it earned the name of "Bloody Omaha."

Meanwhile, General Bradley and other commanding officers aboard the *Anchon*, anchored about eleven miles offshore, knew that things were not going well at Omaha, and Admiral Arthur Cook and General Thomas Handy were dispatched to tour the beach to appraise the situation.

They hitched a ride on the destroyer *Harding* DD 625 for a tour of the battlefront. When they completed their inspection they proclaimed the operation a complete disaster, and notified the high command aboard the *Anchon* of such. Rear Admiral Carleton F. Bryant received the message and immediately sent a message to all destroyers of Bombardment Force "O" over the TBS radio (Talk Between Ships). It was an uncoded voice message in plain English which indicated the urgency of the situation. It read: *Get on them men, get on them. We must knock out those guns. They are raising hell with the men on the beach, and we can't have any more of that. We must stop it.*

The results of this order were dramatic! Every destroyer captain responded immediately. Even though communications were lacking between some SFCPs and the destroyers, the captains and gunnery officers were quick to improvise in locating targets. Some destroyer captains went so far as to run their ships into very shallow water so as to be able to knock out the casemented enfilading guns. Since these guns were protected under thirty-five feet of reinforced concrete, and heavy shell fire would bounce off of them, destroyer gunnery officers had to fire directly into the gun slits in order to silence them. When soldiers on the beach saw the determination of the navy in helping them, a silent cooperation developed and they pointed at targets, such as machine gun emplacements, with their rifles. Destroyer gunnery officers would then follow up by placing 5-inch rounds in the indicated spot. Tank commanders would fire a round at a target that could not be seen by the destroyer gunnery officer so that he could use it as a point of aim and fire at the same spot. Innovative infantrymen and tank commanders were directing destroyer fire. The results were quite remarkable and dramatic.

We were not affected by Admiral Bryant's order of 0900 because we were not part of Bombardment Group "O"; however, we were positioned just west of Omaha Beach about 1,000 yards off Pointe du Hoc, which placed us within easy firing range of the Vierville draw, and we did receive orders to lend fire support to the area. We had been aiding the Rangers at Pointe du Hoc with support fire when a lull occurred in the action. At about that time we received a message from someone that there was an old Norman house on the beach containing a German command position that was apparently directing fire down on the beach. We immediately took it under fire and put it out of action with our 5-inch guns.

It was now mid morning and landing craft of all types were crowding up onto the beach to unload their cargoes. They were depositing everything from troops to tanks, jeeps, bulldozers, Gasoline, ammunition, food, and everything imaginable. The beach was cluttered to the point that putting supplies somewhere was a problem. Beach masters (Navy Seabee officers) provided order and directed traffic on the beach much as a traffic cop on Main Street, U.S.A. They determined where everything would be put so that it could be located and supplied to the troops on the battle line as needed. They were extremely important and did a magnificent job in eliminating unnecessary confusion and in providing a steady flow of supplies to the troops on the battle line in spite of shell and machine gun fire raining down on the beach. On the beach there were landing craft on fire, dead and wounded soldiers and sailors, smoke, explosions now and then, and yet the work of resupply continued as if everything happening was every day routine.

Battleships and cruisers were pouring fire into railroads, bridges, and crossroads, well behind German lines, and concentrations of German troops attempting to move up to the front to counterattack. The air force was doing the same thing in areas further inland out of range of navy guns. This combined action made it impossible for German generals to use their reserve units to reinforce their coastal defense troops, or to counterattack in time to be most effective. While this fire was effective in relieving pressure from the coastal areas where the fierce fighting was taking place, it didn't help army morale because the soldiers couldn't see what was benefiting them. They could, however, see the effects of the destroyer fire support because these ships were able to come in very close to the shoreline and rain devastating fire on pillboxes, machine gun emplacements, and entrenched infantry. The accuracy and volume of destroyer firepower surprised not only the German defenders but also our own generals.

There were eight destroyers of the *Bristol* class in DESRON 18 that were engaged in this operation. Each ship mounted four 5-inch 38 caliber dual-purpose guns capable of firing twenty-five to thirty rounds per minute, if necessary, with pinpoint accuracy at the close range of one thousand yards at which they were operating. In addition, they mounted two twin 40mm Bofors and four 20mm guns. I know that some of these ships fired over one thousand 5-inch rounds on D-Day because they had to return to England that evening to replace expended ammunition.

We in flag destroyer *Barton* provided additional fire support for the 116th Infantry Regiment and the 2nd Ranger Battalion operating west of Vierville, while also covering the 5th Ranger Battalion at Pointe du Hoc.

By the evening of D-Day fourteen separate units of the American army had penetrated the defense system of the so-called German "Atlantic Wall," and had established lodgments behind German lines. This put the German defenders in a precarious situation because our troops had cut the Vierville-St. Laurent-Colleville road in several places while also occupying those three towns during the day to rid them of German defenders. We received orders to shell the town of Vierville, and another destroyer was ordered to level Colleville. That was a sad situation because the high command didn't have radio communications with any of the troops that had gained high ground that day, and so sixty-four men of the 2nd Battalion, 16th Regiment who had entered Colleville were killed by friendly fire. I never heard if we had a similar experience shelling Vierville.

By evening St. Laurent was partially secured and Colleville was still under German control. Vierville was totally secured by the 116th Infantry Regiment which had also cut the roads south towards Louvieres and was also pushing west towards the isolated Rangers at Pointe du Hoc.

Later in the evening General Gerow, Commander of V Corps, came ashore to establish his command post above the E-1 draw. At about 2100 he sent his first message to General Bradley that read, *Thank God for the United States Navy.* This was a tribute to the action of the destroyers in providing close fire support to the assault troops. As the evening wore on, we continued firing on German gun positions that attempted to engage us, or harass the men still on the beach.

The soldiers knew that the destroyer *action* against German shore batteries provided the troops with the only artillery support they had during most of D-Day. The positive effect on the morale of the troops on Omaha Beach, by the destroyers' heroic and risky action, was electric.

By day's end 34,000 troops had been put ashore at Omaha while suffering 2,400 army and navy casualties, dead, wounded, and missing. That number of casualties equates to seven percent, which is normally considered very high for one day. In contrast, the German 352 division (which was considered to be made up of crack experienced troops) suffered twenty percent casualties, dead, wounded and missing.

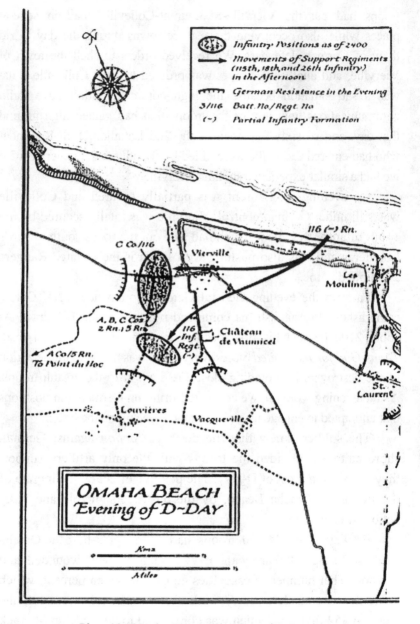

Plate 13: Omaha Beach, Evening of D-Day.

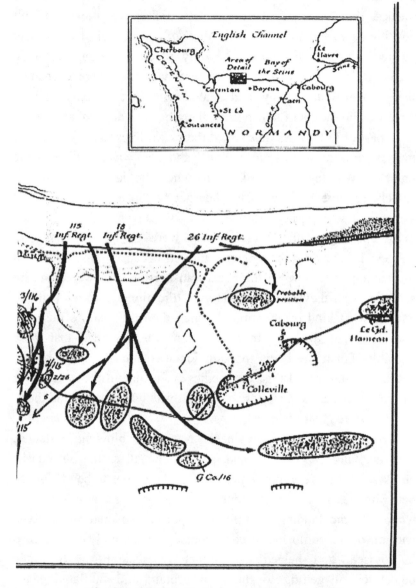

(Source: Stephen E. Ambrose, *D-Day*, p. 464-5.
Map by Anita Karl and James Kemp.)

Before I go further in describing what occurred that fateful day at Omaha Beach, I want to say a few words about the heroics of the medics that attended the wounded under the most difficult conditions imaginable. The shelling of the beach by German gunners was so heavy that the only place affording miniscule protection was the sea wall; therefore, wounded were evacuated there, towards the enemy, and treated with first aid only because there was no means of transporting them back to hospital ships for a large part of D-Day. Medics risked their own lives to drag wounded to these few makeshift aid stations, and many were killed in the process. Walking wounded, men who should have been on stretchers, were helping each other get to the aid stations, while some were attempting to hitch a ride on whatever vehicle happened to be moving in the direction they were going. Doctors were helpless in attending the seriously injured because they had lost all of their equipment when the boats transporting it in were sunk by shell fire—all they could do was give directions as to who should receive what kind of attention. As men died they had to push the bodies out of the way to make room for wounded that were treatable. For many hours the situation was one of bedlam on the beach. In spite of all this, the medics were magnificent and never shirked their duties regardless of all that was going on around them. They deserve great praise!

As the day ended, engineers were still blowing obstacles, covering tank trap ditches, and going about all of the other tasks necessary for more troops, equipment, and supplies to be off-loaded onto the beach. Some of them aided the medics in transporting wounded onto landing craft for transport to hospital ships. Even with all of the confusion of battle, noise, smoke, and shelling, men improvised, and helped each other to accomplish the main objectives of getting to the high ground and outflanking the defenders. With such great confusion the generals were for the most part powerless to command; the junior officers and sergeants made most of the decisions, and it worked.

While the battle for Omaha Beach was in progress on D-Day, and while we did provide fire support for troops in the area, our main objective was to provide fire support for the 5th Ranger Battalion, D, E, and F Companies under the command of Colonel James E. Rudder, at Pointe du Hoc. Companies A, B, and C of the 2nd Ranger Battalion were under the command of Colonel Max Schneider. These especially trained elite assault battalions were attached to the 116th Infantry, 1st Division.

On D-Day the Ranger force was transported to France in two British vessels and one U.S. LCT. When their transport vessels arrived within twelve miles off the French coast the Rangers were transferred to landing craft for their trip in rough seas to their objectives. Heavy seas caused Rudder's first casualties when a supply craft sank with most of its crew and Rudder's supply of reserve ammunition and other vital equipment. The next loss occurred when another British LCA sank with the loss of twenty men plus the commander of D Company.

Companies E, D, and F of the 5th Ranger Battalion were approaching shore when Rudder noticed that they were off course and headed for Pointe et Raz de la Percee. In the darkness the Royal Navy navigator became confused, thinking it was Pointe du Hoc. From the sea the two points look similar, especially in darkness and fog. Rudder noticed the error and ordered the navigator to change course and proceed west to Pointe du Hoc. The error of about two miles proved to be significant.

As the invasion crafts proceeded west along the coast and the fog cleared, Rudder's force became visible to the Germans in the early light, and he began taking fire from their 20mm guns located on the cliffs. When he finally arrived at Pointe du Hoc the Germans were waiting for him and so were we; and he was forty minutes late with no cover of darkness. He had some wounded men from the

20mm fire, and he couldn't execute the original battle plan because heavy shell fire from the battleship *Texas*, and our guns, caused the landing beach to disappear in rocks and mud dislodged from the cliffs. As the invasion boats approached the shore six of the ten boats foundered within 200 to 100 yards from the beach and had to be off-loaded under the most difficult of circumstances. Machine gun, mortar fire, and craters made from our shelling further impeded the ability of the Rangers to unload their climbing gear and other supplies. The original plan had been to split the forces with half of the team ascending east of the point and the other half going up the west side.

As they started their ascent the Germans regrouped and started lobbing grenades down on them from the top of the cliffs. We raked the Germans with 40mm and 20mm fire to drive them from their positions above and near the edge of the cliff where the Rangers were ascending. Our support fire served to disperse the Germans, and each time they attempted to regroup we would hit them again. During this firefight our gunnery officer spotted a company of German infantry reinforcements advancing up the Vierville road from the east. We quickly halted their advance with 5-inch fire.

At 0730 Lt. P. C. Johnson, USNR who commanded the SFCP reached the cliff top and managed to establish communications with us and destroyer *Satterlee* DD 626. He later established communications with destroyers *Harding* DD 625, and *Thompson* DD 627, all three of which were from DESRON 18 and also heavily engaged in this firefight. With their help we were able to control all movements of German units on the roads. When they attempted to bring three tanks up to the battle area we immediately took them out with 5-inch fire.

While all of this was in progress, Companies A and B of the 2nd Ranger Battalion, were waiting well off shore for a signal from Rudder that his men were successful in reaching the top of the cliffs. If the signal "Praise the Lord" was transmitted by 0715, Colonel

Max Schneider was to come ashore with his men as reinforcements. If he didn't receive the signal in time, he was to proceed to the Vierville draw at Omaha Beach, gain the high ground by advancing up the draw, and then proceed west to Pointe du Hoc. By the time that Schneider received the awaited signal it was fifteen minutes past the planned time, and Schneider and his men were on their way to Omaha Beach and the Vierville draw.

Company C of the 2nd Ranger Battalion was also scheduled to land at Omaha and work their way to the top of the cliffs at the Vierville draw. Previous to their arrival, and according to the master plan, Company A of the 116th RCT (Regimental Combat Team) had previously landed at the same spot. Their objective was to clear out the German defenses at the draw in preparation for the troops that would follow them. They never accomplished it—they were almost totally wiped out in the attempt. Company A of the 116th RCT had tried for the east side of the draw, and what few men survived the ordeal were trapped without leadership, radios, and had lost most of their equipment. Their officers were all dead and they were demoralized and suffering from shock.

When Company C of the 2nd Rangers arrived they were faced with the same deadly fire as the men of the 116th who preceded them. The Rangers crossed the beach towards the draw on the west side, and they too suffered heavy casualties. The survivors reached the draw on the west side, only to be fired upon by Germans on top of the cliffs. By this time only thirty-one Rangers were left to fight. In just a matter of a few minutes they had suffered nineteen killed and eighteen wounded.

The Rangers had an advantage over the regular line troops in that they had received training in mountain climbing. While the Germans were lobbing potato mashers (grenades) on them they quickly found a crevice in the cliff, and used their bayonets to carve out hand and foot holds in the side of the vertical cliff, a trick taught to them by their modern day Indian trainers (a thousand-year-old trick of our modern day western Indians handed down to them from their ancestors, the Anasazi). Those who reached the top first secured ropes to mine-field stakes which were placed by the Germans to identify a mine field. The remainder of the men came up the ropes; it was now 0730.

The objective of Ranger Company C was to clear out the section between the Vierville draw and Pointe du Hoc about a half a mile inland and almost two miles long. The plan called for this to be accomplished in about two hours—they were to link up with Companies E, D, and F by noon. As most always happens in battle, it didn't work out that way. Almost immediately upon reaching the top of the cliff they began taking fire from an old Norman stone house. To the Rangers this became known as the "fortified house." It was protected by a maze of trenches, Tobruks, pillboxes, and mines. There was also a radar station in the immediate area.

According to intelligence maps the area contained one 20mm flak gun, three machine guns in Tobruks near the edge of the bluff, one machine gun in a Tobruk at the rear of the compound, and two mortar pits. These defense positions were all zeroed in on Omaha Beach. They had panoramic diagrams of selected target areas of the landing areas and beach, complete with scales giving range and target deflection.

An all-day firefight transpired for control of the area. The Rangers kept killing Germans and the Germans kept getting reinforcements via their communication trenches. Captain Goranson, commanding Ranger Company C, noticed a group of men from the 116th Regiment landing just below the cliff. He sent a Ranger down to guide them to the top, providing C Company with its first reinforcements. By day's end the Rangers and the men of the 116th had finally cleared the Germans out of their fortified positions. It was just one of many engagements they fought on their way to Pointe du Hoc, but it was very important because it reduced some of the fire power that the Germans were using to defend

Omaha Beach. I'm certain that the Rangers and the men of the
116th saved many American lives. Three days later the U.S. Army
Quartermaster burial party buried sixty-nine Germans, but only two
American soldiers.

The Rangers of Company C were not alone in this operation
even though their SFCP never did establish radio communications
with their designated fire support destroyer that day. Lieutenant
Commander Ralph (Rebel) Ramey (as he was known to destroyer
types) commanded destroyer *McCook* DD 496. Early in the morning
he went looking for targets of opportunity and found some in the
vicinity of the area west of the Vierville draw where Ranger
Company C was operating. There were two 88mm gun
emplacements set into the rim of the cliffs that were enfilading the
beaches. Because the guns were pointed down the beaches, and their
gun blasts shielded by concrete aprons on the seaward side, they
were not visible from the sea. The gun boss (chief gunnery officer)
of the *McCook* somehow figured out that they were there, and took
them under 5-inch fire. His shells were bouncing off of the concrete
emplacements and not doing much damage, and being a resourceful
officer he started shooting at the cliff under the emplacement. The
cliff finally gave way and the gun and the emplacement fell off of
the cliff. He then went to work on the second emplacement which
was better protected and not on the cliff edge. The way the gun
emplacement was positioned, the only possibility of destroying the
gun was to put a round through the gun slit, which meant that the
ship just about had to climb up on to the beach to obtain the proper
target angle. In order to position his ship properly for his gunnery
officer, the captain pulled his ship into shallow water with the bow
on the beach and the keel rubbing on the ocean bottom. The gun
boss put a 5-inch round through the gun slit and the gun blew up.
McCook spent the rest of the day firing on targets of opportunity,
from the Vierville draw west to Pointe de la Percee, including the
radar station, which she destroyed.

By 0745 Rudder's Rangers (Companies E, D, And F) had all reached the top of the 136-foot cliffs at Pointe du Hoc. It was about this time that navy Lieutenant Johnson and his SFCP sent us a message requesting a boat and medics to evacuate their wounded. Our captain had the army sergeant report to the bridge, and asked him if he would like to accompany our sailors in the whaleboat to pick up some wounded from Rudder's group. The sergeant agreed to take three of his men and attempt to evacuate the wounded back to our ship. While the whaleboat was being prepared for loading I had the sergeant look through the optics of my torpedo director so that he could see where he was about to go, and what the terrain of the beach looked like. We chatted as we waited for orders. I told the sergeant that he had a grandstand view of the beach and what was happening there, and then I asked him if he was glad he was here on our bridge instead of there on the beach. He said *no, I'd rather be there on the beach.* And so it was—I was trained as a sailor—and he as a soldier.

The whaleboat with its crew of three sailors to run the boat, a corpsman, and four soldiers attempted to approach what was once a good beach landing area, that is, before our early morning bombardment. As the boat approached the landing site it came under fire from two machine guns located somewhere in the cliffs. In the face of this concentrated fire, and two men hit, the coxswain wisely turned about and got out of the area as quickly as possible. Our corpsman and one soldier were both wounded—fortunately not seriously. The boat returned with none of the wounded Rangers, but with twenty-six bullet holes in it, and it was a miracle that more men were not hit.

Our gunnery officer was observing the cliffs for possible enemy action while the whaleboat was approaching the beach, and he observed the machine gun fire on our whaleboat and the location of the guns through the high-powered optics of the main battery director. Firing on our boat was a big mistake because the German gunners gave their positions away. We immediately gave our whaleboat cover fire and destroyed both guns in the process. While our whaleboat was away from the ship the Germans mounted a counterattack on the Rangers. With support fire from us the Rangers repulsed the attack and the Germans left several dead on the field.

There was a concrete command bunker located near the point that directed enfilading fire down on Omaha Beach. About 325 yards west of this bunker was an antiaircraft gun maintaining harassing fire on the Rangers. The Rangers operated in small groups of usually three to a dozen men, and at about 0745 a group of twelve Rangers attempted to destroy this gun; however, heavy mortar and machine gun fire from this defense position succeeded in killing eleven of the Rangers. An additional attack group was sent to neutralize this position, and they too were caught by German artillery and wiped out. Another antiaircraft gun at the eastern end of Rudder's position was also giving the Rangers a lot of trouble. Our SFCP called for help and we killed it.

After their success in repulsing two Ranger attacks on their defense positions, the Germans mounted a second counterattack using a company of what we later learned was the 726 Regiment. The fact that they were committing larger numbers of men to their counterattacks indicated to us that they now realized that we had landed a larger contingent of troops than they had first realized. This regiment attempted an advance up a connecting road, and at the direction of our SFCP we dispersed them with 5-inch fire and stopped the attack. It was now about 0850 hours and some of Rudder's men started clearing out bunkers; the guns that the Rangers were sent to destroy were not there. What were thought to be guns turned out to be wooden telephone poles—the guns had been moved out and relocated on 3 June.

At the time I was wondering why we weren't receiving fire from any of the 155mm German guns known to be in the vicinity. I could clearly see the gun emplacement located on the cliff at

Pointe du Hoc, and I figured that it was knocked out by the heavy shelling of the battleship *Texas* during the pre-bombardment prior to troop landings. It was three years later that I discovered what really happened.

The year was 1947 and I was a student at California State Polytechnic College at San Luis Obispo, California. I noticed a fellow named Les Cline in our class who had a number "1" tattooed on his left arm. I asked him if he had been in the 1st Division. He answered "yes," and when I asked more questions I discovered that he had been a medic attached to Colonel Rudder's Rangers and was one of the men who had requested help from us in evacuating their wounded. When I mentioned the whaleboat that had attempted to beach for the evacuation of their wounded, but was driven off by machine gun fire, he remembered the incident, but of course he didn't know that the whaleboat returned to our ship with twenty-six bullet holes in the hull and two wounded men.

I then asked him if he remembered the destroyer that moved in close to the beach and took out the machine gun nests and other gun positions that had him and his buddies pinned down, he answered,

> *Oh my God yes! We just laid there and cheered as you blew them off of the cliff. We were amazed because German 20mm and machine gun tracers were hitting your ship and you didn't move. You just stayed there and blasted them until you had silenced all of them.*

I had acquired a picture of Pointe du Hoc taken by a navy photographer from our location at sea on D-Day shortly after the main Ranger force had scaled the cliff. I gave a copy to Les in 1980 and it was then that he informed me that there was no gun in the casemate—just a telephone pole.

Les also informed me that the Rangers had advanced to the Grandcamp-Vierville road at Le Guay by about 0830 where they cut the road by setting up defensive positions. As other Rangers attacked German bunkers and heavy gun positions in the vicinity they discovered that there were no guns in these emplacements either. All of the big guns had been removed—so where were they?

Patrols were sent out from the defensive positions at Le Guay with the objective of locating the guns. Ranger Sergeant Len Lommell, with two other men, described in an ITN television interview how they discovered the guns in an apple orchard south of the Grandcamp-Vierville road, well camouflaged. He related the moment of discovery:

> *And there they were, in camouflaged positions pointing towards Utah Beach, with all their shells and everything in readiness to be fired, and their men, about one hundred or so Germans in a field being reorganized by their leaders and listening to their officers. I went down into the emplacement and took my thermite grenades and laid them in the hinges and traversing mechanism, anything that could be melted by a thermite grenade, to make it inoperable.[3]*

Short of grenades, he smashed the gun sights with his rifle butt while his companions stood guard. Lommell and his partner had to return to their defensive position to get more thermite grenades, and then return to the gun location and finish their job of destruction. In a relatively short period of time the guns had been rendered useless and Colonel Rudder had achieved his primary mission.

The success of this operation was extremely important to us destroyer men aboard the *Barton*, and to the other destroyers involved in fire support. We were anchored at "short stay" about 2,500 yards from the shoreline, and somewhat restricted from maneuvering because we were situated in a narrow mine-cleared area in the middle of a mined area. At 2,500 yards we were in easy

---

[3] Kilvert-Jones, *Omaha Beach*, p. 102.

range of these guns, and had they been able to fire on us, we would almost certainly have taken hits which would have resulted in many casualties. We would also have had trouble in returning fire because we wouldn't have been able to determine where the offensive fire was coming from.

It was mid morning when the brass from our guns had accumulated on the decks to the point of obstructing movement of the crew. The officer of the deck broke out seamen to sweep the brass and piles of cordite over the side and clear the decks. Each main battery gun mount produced two brass powder casings and two large wads of cordite each time the mount was fired, ejecting the brass and cordite out of the mount and on to the deck. With the ability of our gun crews to load and fire an excess of twenty rounds per minute, per barrel, brass and cordite could accumulate on the deck fast.

Since the 40mm four-barrel quads, the two-barrel dual mounts, and the 20mm guns could throw off more brass than the main battery because of their rapidity of fire, their brass also built up on the decks at a rapid rate and had to be removed.

By this time it was difficult to see details of the beach because of the fires and smoke created by shelling from both the German and our navy guns. The din of battle combined with the smell of cordite and gas from the guns had the effect of causing my adrenaline to increase to the point where I was no longer tired even though it had been almost seventy-two hours since I had had any sound sleep. I was so busy concentrating on my job that I never thought about the danger we were in, and besides, we hadn't been shot at yet with large caliber guns. Like most men experiencing their first major battle, I still figured I could win the war all by myself—an attitude that would change as the war progressed, and as experience would deflate my ego.

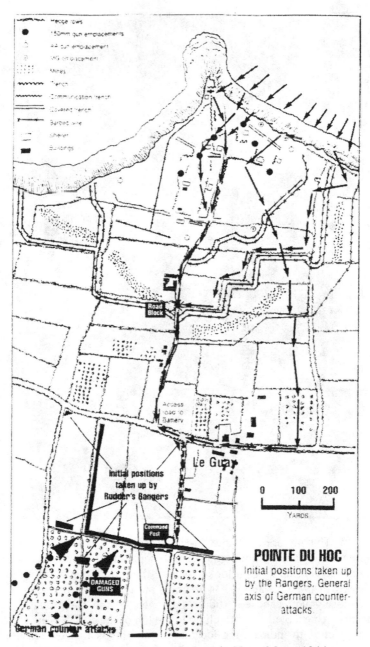

Plate 14: Ranger attack at Pointe du Hoc, 6 June 1944.
(Source: Tim Kilvert-Jones, *Omaha Beach*, p. 103.)

Plate 15: Pointe du Hoc, Normandy, France. (Official Navy photograph. From the private collection of Jerome S. Welna.)

Plate 15: This picture of Pointe-du-Hoc was taken 6 June 1944, some time before noon by a navy photographer who could have taken it from our ship because this is exactly as it looked when I first saw it that morning. It later appeared in the June/July 1944 issue of the *Our Navy Magazine*. If you look closely you can see Rudder's Rangers in the foreground and the ladder which enabled them to climb to the top of the cliff. I drew the arrow on the picture to indicate the location of the pillbox that was assumed to house the 144mm gun, which turned out to be a telephone pole. Note the rubble in the foreground caused by our shelling.

Plate 16: From the cliffs of Pointe du Hoc looking north towards the sea.
(Courtesy of Mrs. James Earl Rudder.)

A view of part of the area overlooking the sea where the battle was fought
on the high ground to drive the Germans out of their defense positions.
Note the bunker in the foreground which survived the incessant shelling of
navy guns. In their effort to take and hold this vital area the Rangers
suffered seventy percent casualties in a battle that lasted two and a half
days from the morning of 6 June to the afternoon of 8 June. Colonel
Rudder was twice wounded in this action but still continued commanding
his troops.

Plate 17. USS *Nevada* in action the morning of 6 June 1944. (Official Navy photograph. From the private collection of Jerome S. Welna.)

Preceding page, Plate 17: The USS *Nevada* was one of the older battleships of the fleet. She was severely damaged by the Japanese attack on the Pearl Harbor fleet the morning of 7 December 1941. She was the only battleship to get underway during the attack, but after constant bombing and heavy damage she was intentionally run aground to prevent her from sinking at the mouth of the harbor and blocking it. She was salvaged, rebuilt, modernized, and returned to the fleet in time for the Normandy invasion. This picture was taken by a navy photographer at 0534 hours as she answered a German heavy battery that had straddled her several times. The flash and hammer concussion from her number four turret of 14-inch 50 caliber rapid fire guns made the picture a little fuzzy in the heavy atmosphere that morning.

Plate 18: Omaha Beach underwater obstacles, June 1944. (Official Navy photograph. From the private collection of Jerome S. Welna.)

This picture of Omaha Beach looking west at low tide, taken by a navy photographer, reveals the extent of the underwater mined obstacles. Wreckage in the foreground resulted from German artillery hits. The LST was hit twice by German artillery and is waiting for a salvage tug to lend assistance. Ships on the horizon are preparing to send in more invasion craft.

Plate 19: Old Norman House at Omaha Beach 6 June 1944. (Official Navy photograph. From the private collection of Jerome S. Welna.)

Preceding page: Plate 19. This is the old Norman House that was used by the Germans to direct heavy fire down on the beach. The morning of 6 June we laid in a short barrage and took out the observation post. Thus the accuracy of our shelling is apparent.

Plate 20: The loss of the *Svenner*. (Photo from the Imperial War Museum.)

The Norwegian destroyer *Svenner* was hit by a German torpedo launched from an E-boat 6 June 1944, at 0537 off Sword Beach in the British sector. The hit occurred amidships with a flash explosion followed by a tremendous second explosion that broke the ship in two. Both halves immediately sank. Few crewmembers survived the attack.

Plate 21: Night air action at Omaha Beach, June 1944.
(Photo by U.S. Coast Guard.)

This photo shows a night air attack over the transport area at Omaha Beach. German aircraft seldom tried to venture into this area unless they were attempting to lay mines. Gun crews aboard the transport vessels were trained to create a cone of fire as evidenced by the tracers in this photo— one out of six shells fired was a tracer. Antiaircraft guns aboard warships were radar controlled and did not use the cone of fire method against attacking aircraft. Note the barely visible transport vessel sinking in the center foreground of the picture, and the two explosions in the background. The three white objects on the right side of the picture may be reflections on the camera lens from star shells that were used to illuminate targets.

Plate 22: Unloading at Omaha Beach D+2, 1944.
(Source: D. Roscoe, *United States Destroyer Operations in WWII.*)

Plate 22: LSTs in the foreground are unloading troops, vehicles, and other equipment. Ships further out at sea are awaiting beach space and orders to proceed in and unload. Note the balloons tethered to some of the ships. Their purpose was to make it difficult and dangerous for low-flying aircraft to make bombing runs on supply ships. German gunners used them as a point of aim, and so they were abandoned by D+3 after several ships were hit by hostile shellfire. They never were used by destroyers or any of the capital warships.

As indicated earlier our captain, seeking targets of opportunity, moved the ship a short distance east so that we could cover Pointe du Hoc, the Vierville draw, and the area in between. We were now about 1,000 yards off shore where we could offer fire support to all locations, which we did throughout the morning.

By noon the noise from our own guns was beginning to get to me when I was suddenly relieved from my battle station so that I could go down to the mess hall for the noon meal. I selected a table in the port wing. The bench for one side of the table was attached to the port hull of the ship. I sat on the bench facing the hull with some of the soldiers who were enjoying navy cuisine. I remember that our meal was a typical hot meal of roast beef, potatoes, gravy, vegetables, bread and butter, milk and dessert. I was thinking of those poor soldiers on the beach with nothing but Spam and hardtack to eat, if they were in any shape to eat; however, the navy had given them the traditional "before battle" breakfast of steak and eggs before they embarked on their landing boats for their long ride to the invasion beaches.

The soldiers were hearing dull thuds against the hull and they asked me what that noise was. I didn't have the effrontery to tell them that dead soldiers were floating by and banging against the hull. I just said that they were floating supply boxes being carried by the current. My explanation seemed to satisfy them when all of a sudden something happened to destroy the peaceful atmosphere of the occasion:

All of the guns of the main battery began firing salvos. There must have been some good targets because they continued firing for several minutes. Each time they fired the whole ship would shake and roll. Paint chips and dust floated down from the steel beams of the overhead and our trays of food jumped around. The sailors shouted, "get 'em Joe"—a reference to our captain, Commander Joe Callahan. And of course there were some other nonprintable remarks concerning our German targets. The soldiers were sitting wide-eyed and wondering what to expect next. When none of the sailors showed any interest in abandoning their food, the soldiers calmed down and also stayed. The noise was especially loud in the mess hall because of the location of the number two gun mount over the mess hall. To us it was all in a day's work. To the soldiers it was "when do I get the hell off of this damn thing?"

When I finished eating I went up on deck to the torpedo shack which was located amidships on the starboard side of the deckhouse under the number one torpedo mount. Several sailors were hanging over the rail talking to someone. I was curious to see what was happening and to my amazement there was a wood fishing boat moored along side loaded with French civilians, mostly women, children, and older men. Since we were port side to the beach, they were hiding behind us for protection from possible German fire, having escaped from one of the French fishing villages at Omaha Beach when the shooting started. They obviously had been able to avoid German mines, probably because they had observed where they had been placed during the construction of invasion defenses. During their travel to our ship, and while they were moored, our main battery continued firing broadsides at German targets—they didn't show any fear about what was happening around them. One of our officers spoke some French and learned that they had left their village during the heavy bombardment that morning. They hadn't eaten and so arrangements were made to lead them out to one of the supply ships and safety where they could be protected and fed. I never heard any more about them, but I am certain that they were properly cared for.

By now it was 1300, 6 June 1944, and I hadn't been in my bunk for over seventy-two hours. I was tired and welcomed the opportunity to wash my face and teeth before hitting the sack until 0400 when I would join my fellow torpedomen in manning the K-guns and torpedo mounts as necessary. As it turned out the Germans were so caught off guard that they were unable to mount a significant attack against us with any units of their navy. Captured German officers said that they didn't think it possible for us to stage an invasion in such foul weather.

Colonel Rudder was hampered by radio communications problems all day long, but he finally did get a message through to V Corps Headquarters via the Navy saying: *Located Pointe du Hoc – mission accomplished – need ammunition and reinforcements – many casualties.*

He later received a relayed message via the destroyer *Satterlee* DD 626. *No reinforcements available.* By late evening, even though he had fire support from us, *Satterlee*, and *Thompson*, his forces were greatly depleted, with one-third of his men killed or wounded. At around 2100 Lieutenant Charles Parker Jr. leading twenty-three men from A Company, 5th Rangers, appeared on the scene with twenty German prisoners. These men would be his first reinforcements. They had made the landings on Omaha Beach and had become separated from their unit during the penetration at the Vierville draw. Lieutenant Parker had led his men inland to the designated assembly area, and when no one else arrived at the rendezvous he carried out his orders and made for Pointe du Hoc. It took him thirteen hours to cover the two miles because he had to fight two engagements on the way.

Our main battery continued firing sporadically all afternoon until dark. At 0400 I manned my ASW (Anti Submarine Warfare) battle station at the port K-Guns along with other members of the torpedo crew. We remained at our battle stations all night long at a "condition two" watch, which meant that half of the crew was to remain awake and alert, while the other half could grab some rest at their battle stations. All was quiet on the beach and we assumed that the troops had bedded down for the night because we were not receiving any requests for support fire from our SFCP. We were using the lull in the battle to relax, sip hot coffee, (which the mess cooks had brought to us), and talk about happier times before the war when all hell broke loose.

It was about 2130 and the Germans had started their third and largest counterattack of the day against Rudder's Rangers, and they were determined to drive the Rangers off the cliff and back into the sea. Our SFCP immediately called for fire support from us and one or two other destroyers in the vicinity. We later learned that we mauled troops of the German 352nd and 716th divisions so badly that they broke off the attack at about 2300. During the battle Rudder and his men were forced to withdraw into a shallow perimeter about 700 feet from the edge of the cliff. When it was finally over, and the dust had settled, Rudder was left with less than a hundred men capable of fighting—he was low on ammunition and food, and needed badly to have his wounded evacuated. At this point I have often wondered if he thought about the British officer who told him, *two old ladies with brooms could knock you off of those cliffs,* when he first proposed the operation at a planning meeting the year before.

The day ended with one lone German observation plane circling over our main formation. He flew low, taking his time, looking over the situation and seemingly daring navy gunners to hit him. He made two or three passes while flying through a wall of flack before leisurely leaving the area unscathed. The gunners of the landing crafts, without the benefit of radar, were trained to throw up a cone of fire that was supposed to prevent an enemy airplane from flying through it. The problem was that it didn't often work.

It was now almost 2400 and D-Day was about to end. We had been at our battle stations for the greater part of the day and had expended a lot of ammunition in support of the invading troops, and had played a vital part in the ability of the troops to effect a breakout from the beach and gain the high ground. The Germans put up a stiff resistance, but our troops not only prevailed, but also dug into positions from which they could not be dislodged by the defenders.

Rommel's worst fears had come to pass. Our troops had broken through the "Atlantic Wall" and they did it on the first day. We now had a fluid front behind the German lines that had no depth—a formidable situation for the German army to overcome—which they never did.

At first light, about 0525, 7 June 1944, I was back at my battle station on the bridge. Shortly after daybreak our SFCP began calling for fire support. The Germans had mounted a counterattack against Rudder's Rangers. Together with destroyer *Thompson* DD 627 we laid down a withering barrage using anti personnel shells and beat back the attack. While the Germans were licking their wounds *Thompson* was relieved by *Harding* DD 625, and we moved closer to the west end of Omaha Beach where we provided fire support for troops fighting on the high ground near Vierville.

It was during this period that I looked over toward the Vierville draw and to my amazement there was an olive drab painted Piper Cub, U.S. Army observation airplane, hovering over the draw. He couldn't have been more than 300 feet in the air, over the high ground, and was apparently spotting for one of the "battlewagons" anchored several miles out to sea. In addition to all the stuff flying around from German rifle and machine gun fire to 150mm heavy shells, the Germans had very effective 20mm AA machine guns (antiaircraft), and they were using them all. They were shooting at this aircraft, but it didn't seem to deter him from his objective. At the same time 5-inch and 40mm shells from the destroyers, and 14-inch shells from the battleship *Texas* were exploding near him. I didn't think a mosquito could fly through all that stuff. I turned to my buddy Jim and remarked that he was going to get himself blown out of the air if he didn't get out of there. I hardly got the words out of my mouth when a heavy shell hit a target under him. The explosion blew his airplane at least 100 feet or more straight up—it then came straight down—and he hit the throttle and took off. I burst out laughing—it reminded me of an old Hollywood comedy I had seen as a kid, but I'll bet he wasn't laughing!

Some years later I learned that the pilot was Captain Oscar Rich who was a spotter for the 5th Field Artillery Battalion. He had arrived at Omaha Beach the afternoon of D-Day aboard an LCT along with his disassembled L-5 airplane (army designation for his Piper Cub). The LCT took a hit in the bow from a mortar as it approached the beach. As it came in close enough to drop the ramp it took another hit in the engine room. The ramp was dropped and two jeeps drove off onto the beach, their drivers forgetting to pull the airplane off. Captain Rich managed to locate a Seabee with a bulldozer who hooked a line to the airplane and dragged it off of the LCT, unhooked it, told Rich he had other work to do, wished him luck, and drove off. Rich was stranded on the beach in the middle of a battle with an airplane, no mechanic, no help, and no transportation.

Stephen Ambrose reiterated a conversation with Rich who explained how he found a beach master who was a navy lieutenant sitting in a captain's chair on the beach, with six or eight telephones and several runners who were also Seabees, calmly and efficiently directing the whole operation of beach management oblivious to the chaos of battle around them. Rich told the beach master that he needed a vehicle to tow his airplane up a draw to the high ground. The beach master pointed to a jeep and told Rich to take it. Rich hooked up his airplane to the jeep and towed it up the E-1 draw that had just been opened by the engineers. It was now about 1300. He miraculously reached the high ground with no problems from the Germans who were preoccupied trying to prevent troops and equipment from gathering on the beach and ultimately working their way up the draws to the high ground.

Once on top Rich located the apple orchard near St. Laurent, where he was supposed to be, and started to assemble his airplane. With no help it was an almost impossible task; however, now and then a startled GI would come by who loved working on machinery, and would give him a hand until an officer or noncom would yell at him to get the hell back to the battle. With such slow going it was dark before he could get his airplane completely ready to fly, and so it was the next day before he could get into the air to do his work.

Sometime during the morning of 7 June three paratroopers from the 101st Airborne Division who had been misdropped wandered into Rudder's position to offer their services. Their pilot had evidently overshot the intended drop zone and dropped them to far east into the area south of the Carentan Estuary the night of 5-6 June. They weren't sure where they were but when they heard the noise of the battle raging at Pointe du Hoc they simply continued in that direction knowing that as the noise got louder they were getting closer to American troops. They were somehow able to escape detection and pass through the German lines while avoiding friendly fire from our warships. I presume they were welcomed with open arms because by now Rudder only had about seventy men left that were capable of fighting. The Germans kept probing Rudder's fortified area and we along with *Thompson* kept firing in an attempt to keep them from breaking further into Rudder's position. About 1300 a boat from the battleship *Texas* showed up with much needed food and ammunition for the Rangers, and then evacuated the wounded and prisoners.

Pressure from the 101st Airborne forces on their left flank, and the 116th RCT and 5th Ranger battalion on their right, finally forced the Germans to give up late in the afternoon and retire to a new defensive position near the River Aure, and just south of road N13. They took up their new position with remnants of the 352nd and 716th divisions which we, with destroyers *Harding, Thompson*, and *Satterlee*, had significantly reduced in numbers since the operation began. At the time I felt that their withdrawal would be an exercise in futility because the River Aure runs east and west in this area, and they were still well within range of navy guns. Time proved me to be right—they couldn't defend the position because, in combination with the air force, we still controlled the roads and they couldn't adequately resupply their position with men and equipment. At that time, however, they hadn't determined that the main objective of the U.S. VII and V Corps was to cut off Cherbourg on the Cotentin peninsula and attempt to trap an entire German army.

We continued firing at the request of our SFCP well into the night. I was at my battle station at the port K-guns from 1600 to 2400. We of the torpedo crew were bored because there was absolutely no activity on the part of the German navy or Luftwaffe. We were on a condition two watch and half of us could alternately get some much needed sleep in our bunks. The German high command still hadn't figured out that they were dealing with the main invasion and not just a diversionary tactic—they still thought the main assault would come at Calais.

Through the morning of 8 June we provided almost constant fire support to the 1st Battalion 116th Regimental Combat Team (RCT) along with the 5th Ranger Battalion which, with a Sherman tank company, blasted its way from Vierville to Pointe du Hoc. This force fought its way west along the D514 road arriving at the point about noon to relieve Rudder and his men who were trapped in their defense perimeter. This culminated the end of one hell of a two-and-a-half-day battle, and both the 116th and the Rangers were magnificent. The successful outcome of this battle was due to the close cooperation between the ground forces and the artillery support of the U.S. Navy destroyers.

At noon, 8 June 1944, the colors were raised at Pointe du Hoc. Rudder's force, in addition to accomplishing its mission, had overrun a fortified German garrison and turned back five German counterattacks while suffering seventy percent casualties. Rudder had twice been wounded during the battle. As a result of the action at Pointe du Hoc Colonel Rudder was awarded the Distinguished Service Cross.

As the afternoon wore on we continued firing at the German positions near the River Aure. The battleship *Texas* and other large warships joined in the shelling and the Germans took a severe beating before finally withdrawing west to the vicinity of St-Lo under cover of darkness. In the meantime men and supplies continued to pour onto Omaha Beach. I don't know how many tanks and artillery pieces had been landed by the evening of 8 June, but I suspect not enough because there was still a great demand for our fire support.

While we were exultant over the success of the Pointe du Hoc battle, we were also very much saddened at the loss of three destroyers during the day. The first destroyer lost this day was USS *Meredith* DD 726 when she struck a mine while on radar picket duty off Cape Barfleur. She was attached to Fire Support Group "U" and had just commenced screening operations in her assigned station when a flight of German "airplane miners" swooped down on the force of U.S. destroyers operating off Utah Beach.

The Germans had developed a method of mining by dropping their mines from low-flying aircraft at night, and this was the first of what would be many nighttime mining forays during Operation Neptune. The mines were of three types, acoustic, magnetic, and pressure—any one of which was capable of sinking a destroyer. The acoustic mines would detonate by the noise of the ship's propellers, while the magnetic mines detonated by the difference in electrical charges between the ship's hull and the mines, and the pressure mines detonated by the increase in pressure when a ship passed over the mine. Of the three types the pressure mine could be the most lethal of them all because it could be set to explode only after one or more ships had passed over it, thus giving ship captains a sense of false security.

The British had discovered the secret of how these mines worked and had developed means of destroying them without losing minesweepers. The problem was that as fast as the minesweepers would clear an area, the German air force would fly in at night and plant more mines. This is thought to be the reason why seven destroyers and several other ships were lost in the invasion area.

The mine explosion had blown a sixty-five-foot hole on the port side of the *Meredith* exposing the after fire room, and forward and after engine rooms to the open sea. The stricken ship immediately went dead in the water without power, lighting, or shipboard communications and began drifting towards Cape Barfleur and the heavy German batteries in the vicinity. The ship started to list badly and the captain ordered all hands to prepare to abandon ship as destroyer *Jeffers* DD 621 came alongside to take on survivors and wounded. *Jeffers* put a volunteer salvage party on board and took *Meredith* in tow to get her out of range of German guns. About 0500 two salvage tugs arrived with one relieving *Jeffers* of the tow, while the second one swept the area ahead for mines so that *Meredith* could be temporarily anchored for salvage about three miles off shore near Grandcamp. Some of the original crew were returned aboard to remove torpedoes, depth charges, and other heavy equipment to lighten the ship, and were relieved late in the evening. Salvage operations were to continue the next day.

For the first two days of the Normandy invasion we saw very few German aircraft; however, all of that was about to change. Early in the morning, under cover of darkness on 9 June, a German bomber force raided the Utah area. We, along with other destroyers fired on them and scored some hits. Several aircraft were shot out of the air, and in the confusion it was impossible to determine which ships scored the hits. More than one ship may have hit the same aircraft. Those German crews that were fortunate enough to survive their attack and return to base probably developed a new respect for the U.S. Navy.

I am not aware that the German bombers hit anything, but they did score a near miss on the anchored *Meredith*. The bomb landed off the port bow and the explosion was first thought to have done no damage; however, the force of the blast (since water doesn't compress) further weakened her structure to the point where she suddenly broke in two amidships and sank immediately with her salvage crew on board. The salvage vessel, *Banncock*, immediately cut her lines and rescued the salvage crew from the water with no losses.

Two officers and thirty-three men were killed, and twenty-six wounded in the original mine blast. *Meredith* was the second ship of that name to be sunk in World War II due to enemy action. The official date of loss on the Navy's roster is 9 June 1944. She was a sister ship to the *Barton*, an identical twin, and we in the torpedo crew really felt her loss.

While salvage operations were in progress with the *Meredith*, the destroyer *Glennon,* DD 620 was also having problems. At about 0803, also on 8 June, she hit a mine in a swept channel off the heavily fortified fishing village of Quineville, about ten miles below Barfluer on the Cotentin peninsula. She was well within the range of a German six-gun 155mm battery which had previously straddled the *Butler* DD 636.

The force of the explosion blew two men, who were on watch on the fantail, forty feet into the air before they landed in the water. Both men were recovered but one was dead and the other severely injured. The force of the blast threw two 270-pound depth charges from the fantail into the air and deposited them on the weather deck near the number two torpedo mount. A 150-pound dan buoy concrete anchor was thrown over 125 feet from the fantail to a 20mm gun mount located near the number one torpedo mount. Sixteen additional men were thrown overboard and had to be rescued. With damage to her engineering spaces she was now dead in the water.

At about 0830 two minesweepers, *Staff* and *Threat* arrived on the scene to take *Glennon* in tow. *Threat* passed a towline to *Glennon* while *Staff* proceeded ahead to sweep a lane to the transport area. While the towline was being rigged destroyer escort *Rich* DE 695, was ordered by Admiral Deyo to aid the *Glennon*. As *Rich* approached *Glennon* she sent a message inquiring if assistance was needed. *Glennon* answered NEGATIVE X CLEAR AREA CAUTIOUSLY DUE MINES. *Rich* slowly passed astern of *Glennon* and headed away when suddenly a Quineville battery opened up with a four gun barrage of 155mm shells which landed about 200 yards astern of *Glennon*. *Glennon* immediately contacted Admiral Deyo over the TBS requesting cover fire from larger ships which was immediately followed by another barrage closer and astern of *Glennon*. The heavy cruisers *Tuscaloosa*, *Quincy*, and *Hawkins* opened fire on the German batteries—they immediately lifted their fire for the time being. The *Rich* had gone less than a mile when, at about 0930, a tremendous explosion occurred. She had detonated a mine that could not be detected by lookouts or other deck personnel. The mine exploded about twenty-five yards off the starboard beam and may have been the pressure type because the *Rich* and minesweeper *Staff* had passed through the same waters a short time before with no contacts. The ship shook from stem to stern and the shock flung depth charges from their K-guns into the water. Fortunately, her torpedomen had their explosive mechanisms set on safe so that they didn't explode in the water. Had they been set for a submarine contact at a predetermined depth they would have exploded and killed all survivors in the water. The shock of the explosion tripped the ship's circuit breakers causing a loss of lights and power which were quickly restored with no further damage.

Rich's crew had barely recovered from the first explosion when a second mine exploded directly under the ship. An explosion under a ship is usually forceful enough to sink the largest of vessels because water doesn't compress. This blast was forceful enough to blow off a fifty-foot section of the ship's stern.

Before the after damage control party could assess the damage and report to the bridge a third explosion occurred, demolishing the bridge and killing every man on the bridge except the captain. Witnesses said that the explosion occurred under the ship about one third back from the bow, probably near the cofferdam of the forward fire room. The ship was now mortally wounded and what chance there may have been for saving her was now gone. There were several torpedo boats and other small craft near the *Rich* that picked up her survivors while the ship went to the bottom in less than fifteen minutes.

Eighty-nine officers and men went down with the ship, and seventy-three were wounded, out of a total complement of 215 officers and men. We of the destroyer force were accustomed to high percentage losses, but these casualties were very high in comparison to that which were more common, and was undoubtedly due to the unusual situation of the ship hitting three mines.

In recognition of his efforts to aid the USS *Glennon*, Lieutenant Commander Edward A. Michel, Jr. was decorated with the Navy Cross. The citation reads:

> *For extraordinary heroism and devotion to duty as commanding officer of the USS* Rich, *while attempting to assist that ship, his own vessel struck and was destroyed by the explosion of two enemy mines. Lieutenant Commander Michel, despite severe injuries, including a broken leg, steadfastly refused to leave his ship and directed and assisted in the removal of all possible survivors until his ship sank beneath him. By his action and example, all able-bodied survivors on board were inspired to remain with the ship and assist in the rescue of the greatest possible number of men.*

While *Rich* was suffering from three mine blasts, *Glennon* was still very much in distress. Minesweeper *Threat* had secured a towline to *Glennon* but couldn't move her. It seems that her severely damaged stern had settled at a thirty-degree angle into the ocean bottom with her starboard propeller securely anchored. Try as she may, *Threat* could not move her, and her captain requested a salvage tug to break her loose.

While waiting for the tug the crew attempted to lighten the stern by shifting weight to the bow and jettisoning depth charges and other heavy gear. Salvage tug *Kiowa* arrived about 1100 after a precarious journey following two minesweepers that cleared a channel through the mine field destroying mines as they progressed. *Kiowa* immediately attempted to take the *Glennon* in tow, but after working for almost four hours gave up and moored to *Glennon* while awaiting instructions from command. At 1630 a message was received from Task Force Commander Moon to abandon all salvage attempts, remove all code books and sensitive material, drop the anchor to prevent the bow from drifting if she broke in two during the night, and transfer all survivors to an LST.

Commander C. A. Johnson, captain of the *Glennon*, was convinced that his ship could be saved and he visited Admiral Moon on the USS *Bayfield* that evening to discuss the situation with the admiral. The admiral agreed to continue the salvage operation the next day, 9 June.

That evening of 8 June, when darkness set in, the soldiers on land settled down for a little sleep and our SFCP ceased calling for support fire. As before, we were ordered to Radar Picket duty, which meant we were to protect vessels of the Western Naval Task Force against attack by enemy surface forces, submarines, and air attack. All destroyers were assigned a section of the Radar Picket Screen invasion area to investigate and identify all unidentified contacts. A continuous all around surface radar guard was maintained. Illumination was by starshell. Ships were to remain in mine swept areas if possible but were to cross unswept areas if our own forces were endangered. All contacts eastward from Pointe Barfleur to the Radar Screen Line were to be considered as enemy.

There were seven German destroyers known to be based at Brest, Cherbourg, and Le Havre, and twenty-seven E-boats based at Cherbourg. We considered the E-boats as the main threat. They served the same purpose as our own PT-boats, being fast, highly maneuverable, hard hitting, and difficult to hit. The E-boat armament consisted of 40mm guns and torpedoes and its main battle strategy was the night attack in combination with bombers, if possible. The E-boat possessed a striking power out of all proportion to its size. With its torpedoes it could seriously damage a battleship, or even sink it.

The German High Command had evidently discovered that there was a real invasion going on and were transferring troops and aircraft from the eastern front—a decision that Rommel called stupid in his notes. His reasoning was that our forces had established a successful lodgment, and with Germany's lack of air cover, and with our superior quality and quantity of equipment, men, and sea power, it was useless to carry on a war that would kill thousands of German soldiers and couldn't be won. Rommel was right!

Even though we believed that the defeat of the Germans was inevitable, they still had a lot of fight left in them. We began seeing more bombers and E-boats coming in to attack our ships.

We learned that four German destroyers were moved up from Royan to Brest the night before.

The British figured that they would try to get to Cherbourg the night of 8-9 June, and that is exactly what happened. In anticipation of this move, the 10th British Destroyer Flotilla was sent to intercept and destroy them.

Contact was made at about 0125 with the four German destroyers and the night action continued until about 0526 when the

Germans finally turned tail and retired. During the engagement destroyers ZH-1 and Z-32 were sunk; Z-24 suffered heavy damage and returned with the fourth destroyer. I have no information concerning possible British losses or casualties.

While the British were engaged with the German destroyers, E-boats were attacking the "Radar Line of Defense." The following is abstracted from the action report of Lieutenant Commander Semmes, Commanding, USS *Frankford* and Comments by the Executive Officer:

> *The Frankford was operating further west from us when at about 0036 she picked up 2 or 3 radar targets at about 13,600 yards. These targets were moving at 20 knots in a southward direction and were near the Cherbourg Peninsula just south of Pt. Barfleur. At 0045 Frankford had closed to a target range of 8000 yards and fired a spread of starshells. She continued closing and at 4560 yards bridge personnel were able to distinguish two E-boats. Frankford commenced firing on the E-boats with full radar control, using AA common shells with fuses set to burst at the target. Her shells must have been hitting too close for comfort because the E-boats immediately turned away while laying down a smoke screen to cover their retirement. Frankford ceased firing, and at 0047 her CIC picked up a third target which was closely trailing the first two. Radar control was transferred to the third target and fire was resumed at about 0050, range 2000 yards. Radarmen indicated that all salvos seemed to be hitting the target, and at 0052 the target disappeared from all radar screens and is believed to have been sunk.*[4]

---

[4] Roscoe, *United States Destroyer Operations in World War II*, p. 359.

The following comments were included by the Executive Officer in the ship's Action Report:

The many hours of haranguing the SG operators not to get too interested in one target finally paid dividends. If the SG operators had not put into effect this training it is quite possible that the E-boat which came in astern of the leading two on the first approach would have torpedoed us after the leading two had turned north.[5]

The battle tactics the Exec. was referring to was standard procedure for the German Navy. E-boats usually attacked in threes with the first two acting as decoys for the third. While the CG radar operators were concentrating on the two decoys, the third E-boat might slip in and torpedo the target. This tactic was also used in combination with bomber aircraft with some success. Even though a separate radar, the SC, was used for incoming aircraft, the main battery director could only direct fire on one target at a time. Would it be the E-boat or the airplane? This was a decision gunnery officers had to make many times during the following days at Normandy.

In a separate action, about 0110, destroyers *Hambleton* DD 455 and *Baldwin* DD 624 made radar contact with two more E-boats, and took them under fire as they cut through the radar screen into unswept waters in hot pursuit at flank speed. It isn't noted in the action reports but there was a third E-boat that attempted to get into range of the anchorage area where the battleships and cruisers were located.

Our SG operators picked up the target at 0120 and we took off at flank speed with all guns of our main battery firing. We raced to the vicinity of the battleship *Texas* and laid down a smoke screen to protect her while maintaining a position between *Texas* and the

---

[5] Roscoe, *United States Destroyer Operations in World War II*, p. 359.

E-boat so as to foil his attempt to launch a torpedo at the *Texas*. I was standing on the weather deck next to the number two torpedo mount with one of the other torpedomen watching the action. We had moved off of the main deck where our K-guns were located because at flank speed and tight turns, water was rushing over the deck waist high, and we didn't want to get washed overboard.

The weather was good with an almost full moon and an overcast sky. Visibility was good and I was watching where our shells were exploding when all of a sudden I saw the telltale wake of a torpedo heading towards us. I immediately notified the bridge; at the same time some other men saw the same thing. I think the bridge had already detected it because while I was on the phone to the bridge, we had already started a sharp turn and the torpedo crossed our wake at about 150 yards astern. We all breathed a sigh of relief at the near miss. I never heard if the E-boat we were firing at survived the action. Was it the one that fired the torpedo?

This was the last engagement in our sector for the day, but it was not the last one in the Omaha area. While we and the other Radar Picket destroyers were fighting off E-boats in our sector, E-boats were raiding the convoy lanes of the central Omaha sector. In the foray they managed to torpedo LST *376* and LST *314*, both of which were part of a five-ship convoy escorted by HMS *Beagle*. LST *314* lost half of her crew in the ensuing engagement.

The morning of 10 June I was back at my battle station on the bridge. The army had now extended their bridgehead far enough inland to have a solid lodgment. Problems with communications between the SFCP and the navy had been solved and our daytime job of providing fire support had become routine. We continued firing throughout the day.

The effectiveness of navy fire devastated whole battalions, regiments, and in one case a division. By now the Germans had committed all of their reserves, and were dependent upon what meager reinforcements could be brought in from other areas at night. Movement of German troops and armor was almost impossible in daylight, and resupply of their forces almost impossible on a significant scale. Until they pulled back away from the coast, they would have no relief as long as their troops were within range of navy guns; however, they would still have to contend with the allied air forces.

In an action report presented by German General Rommel in late June of 1944, he describes in detail the problems the German army faced in dealing with the American forces.

The following is an abstract of his remarks:

Our operations in Normandy are tremendously hampered, and in some places even rendered impossible by the following factors:

a) The immensely powerful, at times overwhelming, superiority of the enemy air force up to 60 miles behind the front. During the day powerful fighter-bomber and bomber formations caused our entire traffic on roads, tracks, and in open country to be pinned down.

b) The effect of the heavy naval guns. The effect is so immense that no operation of any kind is possible in the area commanded by this rapid-fire artillery, either by infantry or tanks. We can expect the enemy warships— unless they are put out of action by our navy and air force—to continue to intervene in the land fighting— above all, on the Cotentin peninsula—with the most lavish expenditure of ammunition.

c) The material equipment of the Americans, with numerous new weapons and war material, is far and away superior to that of our divisions. The enemy armored formations appear to fight their actions at a range of as much as 2,500 yards, using vast quantities of ammunition and with magnificent air support. Also in evidence is their

great superiority in artillery and outstandingly large
supply of ammunition.
d) Parachute and airborne troops are employed in such
numbers and with such flexibility, that the troops they
engage are hard put to it to fight them off. Where they
drop into territory not held by our troops, they dig in
immediately and can no longer be dislodged by infantry
attacking with artillery support. Without air cover our
situation is becoming extremely difficult.[6]

At nightfall I assumed my battle station at the port K-guns as
the ship moved out to sea to take up our position in the Radar Picket
Screen. The sea was calm with very little wind and the seascape was
black as the ace of spades. The sky was overcast and dark with
visibility of about 2,000 yards. It was a good night for a coordinated
E-boat bomber attack. As it happened in so many engagements it
was hours of boredom and seconds of terror. At 2330 it happened
when two E-boats attacked while a Ju-88 (German twin engine
dive-bomber) attacked from a different angle. The E-boats had
approached the formation from an unusual direction where they
were partially out of sight from our SG radar until they were within
striking distance with their torpedoes. The bomber had come in
from shore and was "land locked" until the very last minute before
being detected by our SC radar. The German technique was smart
because they figured we could only bear on one target at a time;
however, our captain wasn't dozing. He reacted immediately
ordering flank speed, a hard left turn which allowed our 5-inch gun
mounts to get off a salvo at the E-boats, and also put us headed
directly towards the bomber. This maneuver created a poor target
for the bomber. Our two forward mounts fired at the Ju-88 and blew
him out of the air. I was looking right at him when a 5-inch shell hit
the nose of the aircraft. The explosion was tremendous as the

---

[6] Liddell-Hart, *The Rommel Papers*, p. 476-478.

aircraft and the bombs he was carrying disappeared in a blinding flash. Pieces of the aircraft fell near us just off our port bow. Our main battery immediately resumed firing on the E-boats which made a hasty retreat in the face of numerous barrages from us and other destroyers in the vicinity. I never heard if the E-boats survived the engagement.

We had an interesting weapon that the Germans may not have known about—Mark-40 5-inch ammunition. (We called it Buck Rogers ammunition after the comic strip of the period.) The Mark-40 shell had a small radio device in the nose that would detect metal and explode without actually having hit the target. A near miss with this shell could sometimes do more damage than a direct hit, especially to an E-boat. E-boats were very lightly armored, and while a 5-inch shell might go through the boat doing light damage, 5-inch shrapnel from a Mark-40 could do a great deal of damage in addition to its effect on morale. This particular evening our gun boss used AA common in the left barrel, and Mark-40 in the right barrel, which was also a devastating combination when used against aircraft.

While we were in action against E-boats and aircraft, the rest of the ships in other sections of the radar screen were busy doing the same thing, as well as protecting the capital ships with smoke. From this night on we were to experience an increasing number of air attacks and mine laying aircraft mining the waters of the channel. The whole invasion area was still a very dangerous place and getting more so all the time.

On 11 June we resumed with support fire to the troops which we continued all day long. In the evening after dark we of the torpedo gang resumed our battle stations at the K-guns ready once again for the night's anticipated action. By now we had learned to expect an enemy attack at about midnight, and this night was no exception. The water was calm, the seascape as black as could be, negligible wind, and visibility 2,000 yards with a dark overcast sky and no moon. Again, it was a perfect night for a combined air and E-boat attack. At 0045, 12 June, our SG radar operators picked up unidentified blips on the radar screen at a distance of 10,000 yards. These were suspected to be E-boats. At about 0100, I was at my battle station when we received a report from the bridge that bogies (unidentified aircraft) were coming in at 350T degrees. They had come from the east and were land locked until the very last instant when they broke out over the formation. We identified them as Ju 88s and began firing immediately as did destroyers *Laffey* DD 724 and *Sumner* DD 692. Some were shot down, but in the confusion who knows which ship (or ships) hit them?

The destroyer *Nelson* DD 623 was anchored about 600 yards off our port quarter on the "Dixie Line" (an imaginary line on the map designating the west radar screen boundary) about 1,600 yards astern of the *Laffey* and 1,600 yards forward of the *Sumner*. Even though it was a dark night, I could see her and an attacking bomber clearly. I saw a terrific explosion on the fantail of the *Nelson* which blew the entire stern off of the ship including the number four gun mount. At the time I figured that the bomber had hit her with a bomb, and maybe it did; however, navy records from the log of the *Nelson* indicate otherwise.

At 0105 CIC (Combat Information Center) reported contact bearing 358T at six thousand yards. Shortly thereafter reported target course 190T, speed twenty. The ship was alerted and FD (radar director controlling 5-inch battery) coached to target by CIC. At 0107 battery was reported on. As required by operation order, signalman challenged, and about fifteen minutes later ship opened fire at four thousand yard range, with entire battery in full radar control. Contact slowed, turned away and separated into three distinct targets. Anchor had been heaved in and chain was up and down. About ten salvos had been fired when at about 0109 ship was hit. There was an explosion aft and ship heeled sharply to port and then resumed an even keel.[7]

The next day she was towed to Portsmouth, England. *Nelson* suffered more damage than the ship's log indicates. In addition to blowing off the stern, the starboard propeller shaft was bent downward with the propeller still attached and dragging at a depth of fifty-two feet. Casualties totaled twenty-four dead and nine wounded, which is about normal for that type of a hit.

Because *Nelson* was required to follow operation orders and challenge unidentified ships using signal lights, the German E-boats may have used the lights as their point of aim. This fact caused her captain to include the following paragraph in *Nelson's* Action Report:

> *It is felt that the ship was hit by an E-boat torpedo. This was fired at the signal light when the challenge was made. Where using a fixed screen around an area, vessels approaching should bear the burden of proving their friendly character. Challenging imposes too great a penalty on the screening vessels. If this ship could have opened fire as soon as control reported on target without challenge, she probably would not have been hit.[8]*

With the hit on the *Nelson* there was now no doubt about the identity of the targets being E-boats. *Laffey* and *Sumner* had also made contact with the targets, and both vessels opened fire with star shells to illuminate the targets, and following with AA common and Mark-40 ammunition. We also switched our fire from antiaircraft, since the bombers had left the scene, to surface targets—E-boats. Since we were not assigned to a fixed position on the screen we were free to give chase to unidentified targets, and it seemed to me that we were chasing E-boats all over the English Channel that

---

[7] Roscoe, *United States Destroyer Operations in World War II*, p. 360.
[8] Ibid.

night, all the while firing star shells, AA common, and Mark-40 ammunition. I don't know what speed we attained but *Laffey* left the screen and reportedly chased the E-boats at flank speed of thirty-two knots (about thirty-six land miles per hour) all the while firing her main battery at them. She pursued them until about 0125 when they intermingled with an Allied convoy and she ceased fire to avoid hitting friendly ships. We quit the chase at about the same time. I don't know how many E-boats made it back to Cherbourg that night, but I do know that our SG radar operators identified six of them at the beginning of the engagement—we certainly had a busy time with them.

The day of 12 June was much the same as previous days, answering requests from our SFCP for support fire. I was noticing that our range requests were getting longer, indicating that the troops were advancing further into enemy territory by the day. In the late afternoon our captain actually pulled the bow of the ship on to the beach, as you would beach a small boat. This was possible because the tide was in and we could float the ship in an area where it would be high for a few hours. We did this in an area of the beach about 100 yards east of the west end of Omaha Beach near the Vierville draw. We could only use our two forward 5-inch mounts for this situation, and we fired one salvo at 15,000 yards, which was followed by a "target demolished" message from our SFCP. As the ship was backed off of the beach I noticed that there were still a few dead soldiers floating in the water. The force of our propellers kicked up sand and debris from the ocean bottom—and soldiers' bodies that had become mired in the mud were forced to the surface.

Ernie Pyle was America's most beloved war correspondent of World War II. He was highly respected by civilians, soldiers and sailors alike. He lived with and wrote about the soldiers who were doing the hard fighting. To my knowledge he never traveled with the navy, but we knew about him and mourned his death when a sniper's bullet ended his life on the island of Ie Shima in the Pacific where we were operating against the Japanese on 18 April 1945.

On 16-17 June 1944, Ernie filed a story about the dead at Omaha Beach and I will quote him here because he described the carnage so much better than I can, and so profoundly:

Here in a jumbled row for mile on mile are soldiers' packs. Here are socks and shoe polish, sewing kits, diaries, Bibles and hand grenades. Here are the latest letters for home.... Here are toothbrushes and razors, and snapshots of families back home staring up at you from the sand.

The strong swirling tides carry soldiers' bodies out to sea and later they return. They cover the corpses with sand, and then in their whims they uncover them.... I walked around what seemed to be a couple of pieces of driftwood sticking out of the sand. But they weren't driftwood. They were a soldier's two feet.

And I wondered about these dead men. Did they have a family back home who hadn't heard from them in a while and were wondering about them? Had a buddy written to the family to tell them how their loved one died? Had they received a notice telling them that their soldier was missing in action? To the families back home their losses were statistics—their loved one went to war and never came back. To us survivors, it was a mangled corpse, a grotesque face staring up at us, a vision, which we will carry until our death. That's the difference.

The cat and mouse game between the destroyers, E-boats, and bombers continued with ever increasing attacks by E-boats and dive-bombers. The German attackers became increasingly brazen in their determination to inhibit our ability to maintain resupply of our invading army's—every night it was the same. We would pick up surface targets on the SG radar at 8,000-10,000 yards. We would attack while firing star shells for illumination (which really bothered E-boat captains), AA common shells with fuses set at target, left barrel, and Mark-40 shells, right barrel. It was like trying to protect a herd of gazelles from a pack of hyenas. E-boats would always attempt to get into the formation of supply ships at anchor, fire their torpedoes, and flee while they were using the supply ships for cover. Even with the difficulty of hunting them down under such circumstances, our destroyers were very effective in preventing ship losses while killing E-boats in the process.

In addition to the destroyers assigned to the Radar Picket Screen, some destroyers were assigned to the reserve group, and we were one of them. This meant that we had no fixed position, but could go anywhere we were needed, for any purpose, especially killing E-boats and protecting capital ships. The day and evening of 13 June was routine. We provided support fire at the request of our SFCP during the day, and patrol duty against E-boat attack at night. The day and night of 14-15 June was more active when we encountered two E-boats attempting to make a torpedo run at the battleship *Nevada* sometime around 0100, 15 June. We circled the *Nevada* with smoke while firing on the E-boats. One of them fired a torpedo at us and missed—we killed him in the engagement. The other one is presumed to have retired back to base.

While the business of fighting off E-boats and bombers continued from 8 June to 18 June, thousands of troops and tons of supplies had to be landed at Omaha Beach. This was first accomplished by running LSTs up on the beach to drop their ramps, run vehicles off, and then unload other supplies. To correct this inefficiency of operation, invasion planners had designed an artificial harbor code-named "Mulberry," after a year of research and planning by British engineers and military leaders.

The harbor was built in sections by British workers in utmost secrecy, and towed across the channel to Omaha Beach where assembly was started on 7 June. A "Mulberry" was also provided for the Utah and English sectors where assembly was started on the following day. Construction of these harbors was completed on 16 June, and this wide open stretch of beach where nothing other than a small fishing boat had ever landed was now a major port of entry. Through 18 June it had received 314,514 troops, 41,000 vehicles, and 116,000 long tons of supplies. Omaha Beach had now become the most active port in France with the greatest capacity. And for the moment it was the most active port of Europe, with the British Beach, Gold, second.

These figures do not include the paratroops of the 82nd and 101st Airborne divisions that totaled some 13,000 men with their attached artillery, engineers, and naval shore fire control parties that were dropped by aircraft and also had to be supplied.

Things were going smoothly with reinforcements, equipment and supplies landing with clock-like precision when the worst storm in forty years hit the area the night of 18-19 June. The wind came up rapidly from the NNE and almost immediately increased to gale force of 90 to 125 miles an hour. Heavy surf began pounding the beaches and tearing at "Mulberry." By noon of 19 June all unloading had to stop. Some ships were dragging their anchors, some were being driven up onto the beach, some collided, and "Mulberry" started to break up. LCTs, LCVPs and other craft were smashed against the piers, which hastened the demise of "Mulberry."

The wind and the heavy seas finally abated on 22 June to reveal devastation more severe than the Germans could ever have hoped to accomplish. Omaha Beach was littered with the remains of small craft of every size and description. Huge sections of "Mulberry" were among the wreckage and debris that littered the beach. The troops ashore had received no supplies for the three days of the storm and therefore had to ration ammunition. Unloading resumed the afternoon of 22 June. The storm gave us some respite from night action—neither E-boats or the Luftwaffe could operate in that kind of weather. Our soldiers weren't very happy; they were all seasick! Some parts of "Mulberry" that could be salvaged were towed to the British sector and incorporated into their "Mulberry-B." The remainder of "Mulberry" was abandoned at Omaha with no attempt to repair it. On 23 June General Eisenhower flew the entire length of the invasion beaches and was astounded at the scope of the damage done by the storm. He states in his diary that he counted over 300 vessels wrecked on the beaches.

The severity of the storm, the unpredictable weather of the English Channel, and the dire need for a dependable port dictated the need to take Cherbourg, the nearest major harbor, as soon as possible. The capture of Cherbourg therefore became the number one objective as of 23 June.

By this time General Collins's VII Corps had sealed off the Cotentin peninsula and had advanced to Cherbourg to meet a German defense perimeter of fortifications on a crescent shaped line extending from eight miles east, four miles south, and seven miles west of Cherbourg. The VII Corps troops were stopped cold and the general requested help from the navy in destroying the coastal guns on the northern and eastern shore of the peninsula, many of which could fire inland as well as seaward. Intelligence had identified twenty casemated batteries of 150mm to 280mm, plus many 88mm and 75mm guns.

The afternoon of 22 June we were ordered back to Portland to replenish our expended ammunition, fuel, and prepare for more action. We transferred our soldiers to a supply ship for return to an army base somewhere in England and reassignment. They were friendly guys and we hated to see them leave, although I think they were glad to get off of the ship and set their feet on dry land once again. I don't know what ever became of them, I assume that they were reassigned to another combat unit. Over the years I have thought about them many times and hoped that they survived the war.

By the evening of 23 June we had finished loading ammunition and taking on stores (food, clothing, dishes and other necessary supplies). The battleship *Texas* had also returned to Portland, England, to load ammunition and the evening of 24 June we moored to her to top off our fuel tanks. It so happened that our starboard amidships 40mm quad gun mount was just across from the 40mm quad gun mount of the *Texas*, and they were both on the same level from the water line. Because we were in a condition red war zone the gun mounts of both ships were manned. The mount on the *Texas* was manned by marines. One of the marines shouted an obscene remark to one of the sailors in our gun mount. Other remarks were exchanged between the marines and our sailors when one of our men had had enough. He picked up a wrench and threw it at the offending marine hitting him on the head. He knocked him out colder than a dead fish. That took the fight out of the marines.

Years later I found myself working with a man who had been an officer aboard the *Texas*. When I mentioned the incident to him he burst out laughing. The marine captain in charge of all marines aboard the *Texas* shared a stateroom with Lieutenant Commander Bill Eidson. Bill told me that the marine captain was so angry that he wanted to sink the whole damn navy, especially our ship. Commander Eidson, who outranked the marine captain, just laughed at him which didn't help improve relations with the marines, as if that mattered to us. At the time it happened I was thinking, "my God, here we are in the middle of a war and these stupid marines want to fight the navy."

That evening we were briefed by our executive officer that we would attack the German defenses of Cherbourg the next day, 25 June 1944, and that our objective was to neutralize the heavy batteries there.

Chapter 8

OPERATION NEPTUNE
THE INVASION OF FRANCE
6 June 1944 to 25 June 1944

BATTLE OF CHERBOURG
25 June 1944

Forward elements of the VII Corps had advanced within a mile of the city of Cherbourg by the evening of 24 June, and hoped to have it completely encircled by the evening of 25 June. The German forces on the capes, east and west of the city, had been pushed into isolated pockets. Best estimates indicate that "Fortress Cherbourg" was garrisoned by over 40,000 men. The German coastal defenses were well constructed with many large Krupp batteries of casemated guns as large as 280mm. German Generalleutnant Karl von Schlieben, the garrison commander, had earlier in the year been ordered by Hitler to make Cherbourg impregnable, as quoted in *The Rommel Papers,* p. 465. Hitler evidently recognized the value of the Cherbourg port to the allies as key to supporting invading troops. Their objective was to destroy the invading forces by denying them resupply.

Following the storm destruction of Mulberry, all incoming supplies had to be diverted through Gooseberry at Sword Beach in the British sector. Supplies then had to be sent overland west for the Omaha beachhead and the Cotentin peninsula to the VII Corps army. Faced with an inefficient supply problem the entire invading forces were stalemated in their present lodgment. VII Corps was dealing with a possible shortage of ammunition. Orders for the VII Corps was to open up the port of Cherbourg with all dispatch and so the army once again requested help from the navy to reduce the heavy fortifications there.

Admiral Deyo was ordered to develop a battle plan for the bombardment of the Cherbourg defenses that incorporated the following restrictions. The battle plan developed by Deyo called for Task Force 129, under his tactical command, to converge on Cherbourg from the seaward side and begin the bombardment at noon, 25 June. It called for a two-pronged attack against the big Krupp guns defending Cherbourg on both the east and west sides of the harbor. Lieutenant Colonel Fred P. Campbell, U.S.A., an artillery liaison officer from the VII Corps, was assigned to assist Deyo aboard the *Tuscaloosa* in selecting targets.

Opposite page, Plate 23: This sketch shows the rapid advance of the U.S. Army in the latter days of June 1944. Note the dotted line extending from just south of Quineville to just west of Carentan, indicating the front line of advancing U.S. forces on 12 June. Next, General "Lightning Joe" Collins's VII Corps cut the Carentan peninsula in half by advancing westward to just south of Barneville, while establishing a secure defense line along the route to prevent enemy reinforcements from breaking through the line before turning north to advance on Cherbourg. By 24 June U.S. troops had broken through the German lines and advanced on Cherbourg forcing German troops into three defensive pockets around Cherbourg. Between 12 and 24 June it became difficult to visualize the U.S. Army in a static position because it was advancing so rapidly. By 25 June this made it a formidable task for the U.S. Navy to execute planned fire support for army troops because of their rapid advancement. During the Cherbourg battle of 25 June, the navy found it necessary to alter the execution of battle plans frequently—sometimes on a minute-by-minute basis in order to avoid the possibility of laying fire on friendly troops. "Lightning Joe" had lived up to his reputation.

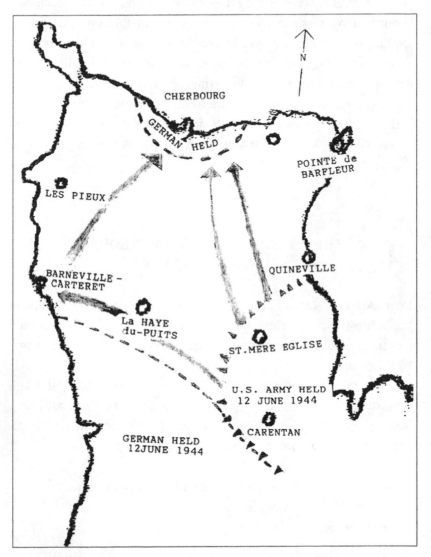

Plate 23: Operations against Cherbourg, 12 to 25 June 1944. (Drawing by Jerome S. Welna. Not to scale.)

At about noon on 24 June, Admiral Kirk conferred with General Bradley concerning the small portion of the peninsula controlled by German forces, and agreed that Deyo's task force would not commence firing before noon, and would fire for only ninety minutes, and that he must take under fire only targets designated and cleared by the army. Both generals, Bradley and Collins, were fearful of naval fire hitting friendly troops. After all, earlier in the drive towards Cherbourg, a called-for air strike caused severe casualties of U.S. troops when the 8th Air Force misplaced their bombs.

THE BOMBARDMENT OF CHERBOURG
Task Force 129

Rear Admiral Deyo's force was composed of three American battleships, two American heavy cruisers, two British cruisers, and eleven American destroyers. The task force was divided into two battle groups.

Group One under tactical command of Rear Admiral Deyo consisted of heavy cruiser *Tuscaloosa* (flagship of Deyo), battleship *Nevada,* heavy cruiser *Quincy*, cruisers HMS *Glasgow* and HMS *Enterprise*, and the following six destroyers:

- *Ellyson* DD 454, flagship of Capt. A. F. Converse, COMDESRON 10.
- *Hambleton* DD 455
- *Rodman* DD 456
- *Emmons* DD 457
- *Murphy* DD 603
- *Gherardi* DD 637

Group Two under command of Rear Admiral C. F. Bryant, consisted of battleship *Texas* (flagship), battleship *Arkansas*, and the following five American destroyers:

- *Barton* DD 722, flagship of Captain W. L. Freseman, COMDESRON 60
- *O'Brien* DD 725
- *Laffey* DD 724
- *Hobson* DD 464
- *Plunkett* DD 431

At 0430, Sunday 25 June, I was at my battle station on the bridge as we were standing out of the harbor at Portland in two groups preceded by United States Mine Squadron 7 and British 9th Mine Sweeping Flotilla. They were to sweep a lane ahead of the gunfire ships directly to Cherbourg. The U.S. Army Air Force provided fighter protection against possible German air attack. Once at open sea we took up our position as Group Two "lead ship" 200 yards off the starboard bow of the *Texas*, and slightly ahead of her.

The sea was calm, weather clear with a slight haze and a light southwest breeze. It was a beautiful lazy day more suitable for yachting, or relaxing at the beach, than going into battle. I was admiring the gracefulness of the ships in our battle group when a junior deck officer, an ensign, came over to me and directed me to follow him over to the port wing of the bridge where the control panel for firing the depth charge K-guns was located. As if I didn't know my job he said, "Whatever you do, don't touch one of these buttons," whereupon he touched one and fired the number one port K-gun, hurling a depth charge right at the *Texas*. Someone on the *Texas* was alert because she immediately made a hard turn to port thus avoiding the charge which landed in the water forward of where she would have been had she not corrected so fast. All of our charges were set on safe and so there was no explosion and no damage to the *Texas*. Had the charge been set to explode at a given depth, even though she had corrected, the *Texas* would have been close enough to the explosion to suffer severe damage, and possibly put out of action before the battle began. If the torpedoman on watch at the port K-guns had been rear the gun when it fired he might have been severely injured or possibly killed.

The minute the K-gun fired the captain came charging out of the pilothouse, looked at me, and yelled, "Who fired that K-gun?" I wanted to say, "That knucklehead ensign," but I knew better. While I was groping for a correct answer the ensign answered in a weak tremulous voice, "I did, Sir." (I think the ensign may have been experiencing a case of pre-battle jitters.) The captain didn't say anything and went back into the pilothouse, and began talking to the officer of the deck. I presume he didn't want to give the ensign hell in front of me, but I'll bet there was hell to pay in the officers' wardroom when the battle was over.

The OOD (Officer of the Deck) secured general quarters and set a condition two watch. (which left half the crew at battle stations, and half off watch) I went down to breakfast to steak and eggs, which was a navy tradition for a ship's company before going into battle. The tradition comes from the old British Navy, as most of our navy traditions do—I have never learned the reason behind it.

A Civil War general once defined all battles as organized confusion. This battle was about to be no exception. At 0900 Admiral Deyo received a request from General Collins to belay all previously planned long-range shoots on coastal batteries lest shell fire fall on friendly troops. Deyo answered by requesting permission to fire on five selected batteries. Collins gave permission for three of them and any others that fired at him, but to leave the rest to the army.

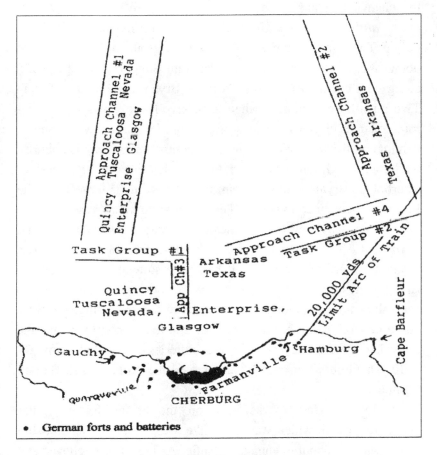

Plate 24: Cherbourg.
Naval Gunfire Support Task Force 129, 25 June 1944.
(Drawing by Jerome S. Welna. Not to scale.)

By 0940 Group One was 30,000 yards from a point about fifteen land miles north of Cherbourg. Our Group Two was several miles eastward. It was at this time that Deyo notified his captains of the change in plans: *"We must not fire before noon unless fired upon, and then only additional batteries designated by SFCP."* Group Two was to join Admiral Deyo's group off Cherbourg at noon. We, as lead destroyer, entered Fire Support Area 2 at 0955 along with our minesweepers. Admiral Bryant commanding Group Two must have been astonished to receive Deyo's message calling for a change in plans because originally *Nevada* was supposed to commence firing on No. 2 (our designation for Battery Hamburg), while we of Group Two were to fire on other batteries east of Cherbourg. Bryant's spotter planes were over their targets and the firing was scheduled to begin when the order to belay was received.

Bryant was now in a predicament because it now meant that *Texas* and *Arkansas* (two antiquated battleships) would have to pass through the arc of fire before it had been softened up by *Nevada*. And, interestingly, by 1034 we were positioned between the battleships and land along with the minesweepers leading, and were not at general quarters. I learned later that the problem was that the army had overrun several of these batteries and killed them. By 1130 our Group Two still hadn't passed the No. 2 target, Battery Hamburg.

After breakfast I was back on the bridge for a regular uneventful watch which was more like a cruise on a vacation ship then a warship about to engage in battle. At 1130 I was relieved and went down to the mess hall for the noon meal. After eating I went back to the after crew compartment and crawled into my bunk for a little rest until general quarters would be sounded for the anticipated battle.

Arkansas' SFCP was positioned on a hill overlooking Battery Hamburg and established radio contact with *Arkansas* and called for fire on the battery. *Arkansas* closed the range to 18,000 yards (nine sea miles) and opened fire. She wasn't doing much damage to Hamburg, and the German naval gunners weren't even answering her fire. They took their time and waited for us to come in easy range and then opened fire on us, and the minesweepers.

I was enjoying a nice Sunday afternoon nap when I heard a crash. It was a noise like I had never heard before and I knew that something was wrong. I called to one of the other men in the compartment who was also napping, "What was that?" He answered, "I don't know." A second later the general alarm sounded all hands to battle stations. The several of us in the compartment all rushed for the ladder leading up and out, and even though I was one of the first up the ladder, the after damage control party was beginning to dog down our hatch and all watertight doors. They were yelling, "Get out of there" as I came through the hatch into the after deck house. I ran out of the starboard door on to the main deck, tore up the ladder to the upper deck by the number two torpedo mount, grabbed my kapok life jacket from the storage box, and saw something out of the corner of my eye—three explosions in our wake. The ship was picking up speed as it was making a hard port turn that caused it to heel to starboard. I raced forward and as I was passing the number one torpedo mount, which was located between the two stacks, I heard the swish of a shell passing overhead, felt the wind from it, and a second later saw it explode just off our starboard side in the water. The shell had passed between the stacks, and had it been a little lower, it might have taken my head off. I continued running forward, up the bridge ladders, on to the flying bridge, and relieved the watch. As I was strapping on my telephone headset I saw three shells exploding just forward of the bow. The German gunners had us bracketed. While shells were falling around us, our main battery was firing as we were heading for the battery that was firing on us.

There was a great deal of activity on the bridge and my job was to stay near the captain so that I could relay information coming over my JU phone circuit, and relay his commands to those on the other end of the circuit in other parts of the ship. As we would change course with hard right and left turns at full speed, the captain would run from one side of the bridge to the other, always on the side of the target with me at his side. Flag officer Captain Freseman, who commanded our destroyer division was on the bridge along with his assistant, Lt. Cdr. Robert B. Montgomery, the then famous movie actor. Lt. Cdr. Montgomery had the misfortune of getting in the way when the captain made one of his famous charges across the bridge as we made a violent course change and he, Montgomery, got knocked down. After that Lt. Cdr. Montgomery hid behind the main battery director base to stay out of the way. Our captain had played football at Annapolis and I think he threw a football block when he encountered Montgomery.

A few moments later I received a call on the JU phone circuit from the after damage control party stating that they had located an unexploded shell in the after port emergency diesel room. The engineering officer in charge also stated that the shell measured over nine inches in diameter, had ricocheted around the diesel room, knocking out bulkheads, including the watertight door separating the diesel room from the crew's compartment where I lived. Both the diesel room and the crew's compartment were partially flooded from water coming in through the hole in the hull created by the shell. The engineering officer advised that they would attempt to jettison the shell through the hole it had created. The shell turned out to be a 240mm (9.4 inch) projectile manufactured at the Skoda Works munitions factory located in the German-occupied city of Pilsen, Czechoslovakia, as indicated by its markings. Had this dud detonated, several of us would have instantly perished from the initial explosion, and possibly followed by a secondary explosion of the port depth charges located just above the shell point of entry. I didn't envy those guys responsible for jettisoning the shell.

Shortly after advising the captain of this appraisal from damage control we learned that the *Laffey* took a hit on her port bow near the anchor. It too turned out to be a 240mm dud fired by the same battery that had hit us. The boys on the forward damage control party aboard the *Laffey* were able to quickly recover the shell and jettison it.

It was at this time that we were steaming west at high speed on a course that was parallel to the land, and the captain was on the port side of the bridge with me to his left a short distance away. Our main battery was engaged in rapid-fire salvos and the captain ordered a hard right turn, which caused the number one and two gun mounts to hit their stops as they were firing. (The stops prevent the gun mount from turning too far and hitting the deck house when it fires.) When the number two gun mount swung further to the left to compensate for the right turn of the ship, it hit the stops, compressed the stops so that it actually traveled a short distance beyond what it safely should have, and fired simultaneously. This brought the left gun barrel so close to the glass wind screen of the flying bridge where I was standing that when it fired it blew the screen out with the blast hitting me full in the face, burning my face and hands. It injured the quartermaster who was standing behind me. I was told that he lost an eye in the accident.

The projectile leaving the gun barrel had actually passed within a foot of my head.

Two corpsmen appeared on the bridge to assist me and the quartermaster. The corpsman suggested that I go down to sick bay for treatment—I declined his very kind offer. I stated that if I were to get killed in this battle it would be at my battle station and not relaxing in sick bay. The corpsman treated me on the spot with a sulfa salve which he applied to my face and hands. The thing that saved me was my steel helmet, heavy clothing, Polaroid glasses, and earphones of my telephone headset. Had it not been for the normal battle dress and gear I was wearing, I most assuredly would have lost my sight and hearing. The glasses were tight-fitting with special adjustable lenses that allowed me to look directly into the sun to spot aircraft, and fit close to the face. I finished the day at my battle station, and other than some discomfort, recovered just fine.

For some strange reason *Texas* was receiving fire from a small battery in the hills estimated to be about 400 yards northeast of Battery Hamburg, and was finally hit by a 240mm dud at about 1234. She also had some shrapnel damage from a near miss. Battery Hamburg was the most important target on the east side of Cherbourg and the one that *Texas* was firing on. Hamburg had two interesting characteristics; its 280mm guns (11.2 inches) had a range of 40,000 yards, twice the range of the *Texas* and even a greater margin over the *Arkansas'* 18,000 range. The second thing about Battery Hamburg was that its arc of fire was limited to a line running thirty-five degrees true north. *Texas* finally got tired of being straddled, moved out of the arc of fire, and shifted her fire from Battery Hamburg to this new offending target. Battery Hamburg with its 280mm guns was now firing on the minesweepers and destroyers. We in turn, along with the other destroyers of our division, were pouring our fire into Hamburg, all the while taking evasive action by executing hard turns and making smoke to protect the minesweepers. Of all the ships in the action, we were closest to the land, and in this engagement we were continually between the land and the *Arkansas, Texas,* and the other destroyers. We were like fire ants biting our prey, drawing their fire, not big enough to do serious damage, but capable of serious harassment. We made ammunition transfers difficult for the German gunners, and they were after us and would loved to have bagged us.

At about 1250, destroyer *O'Brien,* operating off of our starboard quarter, suffered a direct hit from Hamburg. The 280mm shell hit between the port quad 40mm mount and signal bridge, crashed into CIC (combat information center), exploded, and wiped out CIC, the port signal bridge, and the ladder to the bridge. The hit killed thirteen men and wounded nineteen, which included all of the men in CIC, a signalman, and the crew of the 40mm mount. Commander Outerbridge, *O'Brien's* skipper, immediately turned north to exit the firing area while we continued covering fire with protective smoke. Outerbridge soon learned that his radar and communications center was gone and that he had another problem. Without radar, in the intense smoke, he didn't know where the other ships in the formation were, and so he had to exit the area to the comparative safety of the north using dead reckoning and extreme caution to avoid collision.

After three quick hits on his destroyers, and numerous near misses, Admiral Bryant ordered his minesweepers to belay sweeping, and with the destroyers covering the sweepers, retire to the north to open the range. To destroyer types, this maneuver is more commonly referred to as "getting to hell out of there!" As we executed our "well known naval maneuver" we kept firing at Hamburg and laying smoke to cover the minesweepers, all of which escaped without a scratch.

Simultaneously *Arkansas* was busy working over some 150mm (6-inch) guns located in casemates near Fermanville. Guided by her SFCP and air surveillance, *Arkansas* destroyed all four guns. She then went to work on other batteries located in the general area. *Texas* had once again shifted her fire to Hamburg with destroyers *Plunkett* and *Hobson* making smoke for her.

With larger shells and better fire control equipment than *Arkansas, Texas* was better equipped to take on Hamburg.

Under cover from smoke made by destroyers *Plunkett* and *Hobson, Texas* was firing with the aid of her SFCP and making life miserable for the German gunners, when an unexpected shift in the wind blew her smoke cover away and she suddenly became a good target for Hamburg. With no smoke cover the German gunners immediately reacted and put a 280mm shell into her bridge structure, which took out a supporting column of the pilot house, damaged the fire control tower, and exploded. The hit killed the helmsman, wounded eleven men, almost got the gunnery officer, and knocked the captain down. Neither he nor the gunnery officer was seriously hurt. The bridge was wrecked and so the executive officer in the conning tower assumed command of the ship and continued firing on Hamburg under SFCP guidance.

We were immediately ordered to make smoke and cover *Texas*. We weren't firing at that point because the range was too great for our guns. It wasn't long after *Texas* was hit that she repaid the German gunners with a direct hit on one of the four guns in the Hamburg battery. The shell penetrated the steel shield of the turret and the gun blew up. With one gun destroyed the three remaining continued firing.

At the request of Admiral Bryant, Admiral Deyo assigned cruiser *Quincy* to help us out in silencing the three remaining guns of Hamburg. *Quincy* joined the party at about 1330 and contributed fire until 1410 with no direct hits. At that point Deyo decided that with so many ships firing on Hamburg it was impossible for the SFCP, or the plane spotter, to determine which ship was reacting to their target corrections. He therefore pulled *Quincy* back to Group One and ordered her to fire on the battery at Querqueville.

Arkansas now joined *Texas* in dividing fire between Hamburg and a 105mm (4.3 inches) battery that seemed to have a charmed life. This troublemaker had been fired on by almost every ship in Group One, had been silenced more than once, but always came back to life. The two battleships stayed about 18,000 to 20,000 yards off shore, outside Hamburg's arc of fire, firing on their two targets for most of the afternoon; however, at about 1447 both *Texas* and *Arkansas* with *Plunkett* and *Hobson* accidentally moved within the arc of fire to be met by a furious volley of fire from Hamburg and the 105 battery. The two covering destroyers made smoke and the four ships escaped with no damage.

In the meantime we continued harassing a 105mm battery nestled in the hills east of Hamburg. We were firing without benefit of SFCP guidance but under the orders of engagement we could fire on this battery because they were firing on us. As long as we kept them busy trying to hit us, they couldn't train their guns on the advancing army. Without benefit of CFCP fire control, I don't know just how much damage we did because this battery was so well camouflaged.

While we of Group Two were dueling with the German batteries east of Cherbourg, Group One was working over the guns west of the city. Group One had made landfall at 0940 and was forced to sail in circles because of the army's request not to fire before noon, unless fired upon. Nothing happened until 1206 when a Querqueville battery, (designated target 308) three miles west of Cherbourg, opened up on HMS *Sidmouth*, the leading minesweeper for Bombardment Group One. Four 150mm shells whistled over the ship and were quickly followed by another salvo that exploded between two of the other minesweepers in the group. Minesweepers are good targets for shore batteries because they can only make five knots with sweeping gear streamed.

Four destroyers immediately began laying a smoke screen as Admiral Deyo ordered *Glasgow* to engage the offending batteries with direct fire. At 1214 she opened fire and HMS *Enterprise* joined in a moment later. A Spitfire spotting for the two ships couldn't identify where the shells were falling because they were kicking up so much dust. By 1230 the Querqueville battery had straddled every minesweeper and Deyo ordered them to retire beyond the main force and lay-to where they would be out of harm's way and out of the way of the gunfire ships which were steering elliptical courses in Fire Support Area No. 3. The destroyers laid smoke to protect the heavy ships and closed the range to use their main batteries more effectively.

The German guns concentrated on *Glasgow* and *Enterprise* for the next half hour when at 1251 *Glasgow* took a hit in her port hangar, followed by a hit in her aft superstructure. She immediately checked fire, turned away, and surveyed the damage. Having ascertained that her propulsion was not affected, she requested and obtained permission to rejoin. Later *Enterprise* learned from her spotter plane that two guns of the Querqueville battery were out of action. By 1440 the other two guns were out of action, but only temporarily. It had taken 318 rounds of 6-inch to neutralize one battery.

Simultaneously, Deyo's group was answering requests from SFCP for help to VII Corps. *Nevada* opened fire at 1212 on a target about two and a half miles southwest of Querqueville. Her 14-inch shells almost immediately began digging in, and after about twenty-five minutes of fire the battery showed a white panel, but *Nevada* was advised to keep firing, which she did. The army had learned not to pay any attention to white flags displayed by the German Army. *Nevada*, with the help of *Quincy*, silenced two more batteries during the day, expending 112 rounds of 14-inch and 985 rounds of 5-inch.

Meanwhile *Tuscaloosa* was distributing her fire among several targets. Her SFCP requested fire on a target one mile west of Querqueville. At 1315 she made direct hits with her 8-inch guns on the battery which exploded with such force that it damaged two spotter planes flying overhead, forcing them to retire from the scene.

At 1207 destroyer *Ellyson* reported gun flashes from target "346" (a battery of four 150mm guns) located near the village of Gruchy. *Glasgow* sent her spotter plane over, and at 1311 commenced firing. She apparently silenced the guns before retiring.

Destroyer *Emmons* began receiving fire from Fort de l'Est, located at the end of one of the harbor breakwaters. She fired sixty-four rounds at this small fort from a range of 15,000 yards, silencing it, when she started receiving increasingly accurate fire from a battery she could not locate. At this point her captain decided it was best to retire while he was ahead.

As the ninety-minute firing period established by command expired, Admiral Deyo signaled VII Corps inquiring, *Do you wish more gun fire?* Several enemy batteries still active. General Collins replied at 1405, *Thanks very much—we should be grateful if you would continue to 1500.* Deyo immediately turned *Tuscaloosa* inshore to once again bombard the Querqueville battery which had come to life opening fire on destroyer *Murphy*. *Murphy* had finally made contact with her SFCP at 1327 when the Querqueville battery found her range and straddled her four times in twenty minutes. As she ducked behind a smoke screen, *Tuscaloosa* came to her aid at 1342 with 8-inch salvos on Querqueville. She fired seventeen rounds before scoring a direct hit on the target, resulting in a burst of flame and an explosion. The German guns continued firing, though more slowly; so destroyers *Ellyson* and *Gherardi* joined in with 110 rounds of 5-inch. *Quincy* then entered the fray, firing for half an hour when *Nevada's* SFCP called for 14-inch fire. Her fourth salvo fell squarely on what appeared to be the one active German gun. SFCP reported—*I do not see any need for further firing.* But target "308" had a charmed life. After the combined efforts of a battleship, four cruisers and several destroyers, it came to life as our task force retired, and defiantly tossed a few more shells in our direction.

The endurance of this battery was truly amazing—the equally amazing thing about it was the inaccuracy of its gunners. Considering the number of shells this battery fired, it is truly remarkable that it scored so many near misses and so very few hits. The same can be said for the batteries we encountered in Fire Support Area Two. My personal opinion at the time was that the German gunners couldn't hit a bull in the fanny with a banjo—fortunately for us!

While the navy was attempting to destroy as many German batteries for the army as possible, the army was continuing its advance on Cherbourg, and was more concerned with the defense fortifications near the city. Fort des Flamand, located at the eastern end of the breakwater, had a battery of eight dual-purpose 88mm guns that were holding up a whole regiment of the 4th Division. At 1432 an SFCP called for fire on the battery and destroyer *Hambleton* answered with 5-inch fire at 14,250 yards; but after only eight salvos, 240mm shells from Battery Hamburg began to drop around her. She retired and left cruiser *Quincy* to take over with her 6-inch guns—she knocked the battery out and the army once again was able to advance.

Target "346" near Gruchy came to life again, and at the request of an SFCP, HMS *Glasgow* fired fifty-seven rounds of 6-inch, and destroyer *Rodman* thirty-six rounds of 5-inch; but when "346" seemed to be getting the range of *Rodman,* she retired out of range to let *Glasgow* handle the situation.

The new deadline for firing set by General Collins was 1500, and Admiral Deyo reluctantly ordered his group to cease fire. He then ordered Admiral Bryant to have our Group Two to follow him out of the bombardment area. Deyo was so reluctant to leave that when a request from an SFCP came in requesting fire on target "322" (75mm field gun casemates, on the dock at the entrance to the naval arsenal) he allowed *Tuscaloosa*, already on her way out, to answer the call. She commenced firing at 1515 at a range of 25,400 yards (12.7 sea miles) and continued until 1540 when the range had opened another mile and a half. She scored a direct hit on one casemate with an 8-inch shell and damaged another with a near explosion.

Nevada did not cease firing until 1525, and for four minutes the batteries on the west side of Cherbourg continued to fire on her, as they had been doing since 1206. During the battle she was straddled by large caliber shells over twenty times, with one shell passing right over her superstructure and exploding on her disengaged side. She had no casualties and received only superficial damage from fragments of shells exploding close by. She had a charmed life!

In a conversation with Comdr. Bill Eidson I learned that *Texas* had experienced a direct hit of a 280mm shell. It too was a dud which was discovered in the bunk of a crewmember when the battle was over. During the heat of the battle no one noticed that they had been hit because there was no explosion and no personnel in the compartment at GQ.

For us in Group Two the battle lasted for three hours and forty-five minutes. This time will vary for each ship because many ships, including ours, were still firing beyond the 1500 cease-fire deadline due to the aggressiveness of the German casemated batteries still in operation. The German batteries finally went silent as our Task Group Two withdrew northeastward, having been ordered back to Portland, England, by Admiral Deyo.

With some German batteries still firing, were we successful in this operation? Commenting on the bombardment and fire support action of Task Force 129, General Collins made the following observations in a letter to Admiral Deyo and the personnel of the entire task force on 29 June. *I witnessed your naval bombardment of the coastal batteries, and the covering strong points around Cherbourg. The results were excellent, and did much to engage the enemy's fire while our troops stormed into Cherbourg from the rear.*[1]

Lieutenant Colonel Campbell, the liaison officer, who returned to VII Corps, wrote to Admiral Deyo on 20 August that all Army officers he had talked with agreed that the bombardment broke the back of the German defense of the city. I took a look for myself, and

---

[1] All communications were posted at the quarterdeck for the crew to view. General Collins added: *Fortunately we did not ask the navy to shell Fort du Roule—fortunate in that it contained among other things a well-stocked wine cellar.*

am convinced that you did tremendous damage to those batteries. Some were never active after the bombardment, and still pointed out to sea when the city fell, even though they could have been turned;[2] and, the supreme commander, General Eisenhower wrote: the final assault was materially assisted by heavy and accurate naval gunfire.[3] German General von Schlieben, reporting to Field Marshall Rommel on 26 June, referred to the heavy fire from the sea as one of the factors that made resistance useless; and Admiral Krancke in his war diary, after the fight had ended, referred to *naval bombardment of a hitherto unequalled fierceness* as one of the contributing causes to the loss of Cherbourg.[4]

As our two bombardment groups entered Portland Harbor Sunday night, Captain Clarke of HMS *Glasgow* called Admiral Deyo on the TBS radio and said he hoped to have the honor of holding the captains' conference on his ship. All of the captains went aboard the HMS *Glasgow* at about 2100 for an after battle meeting and a splice of the main brace in the captain's cabin, which was well ventilated by shell fragments.

Admiral Ramsay visited Portland the next day and personally thanked both flag officers and each CO of a bombardment ship. This operation, he wrote in his Dispatch on OVERLORD,

> *was carried out with skill and determination by Rear Admiral Deyo, but it is considered unfortunate that it was not found possible to adhere to the original plan, which provided for the initial neutralization of the enemy long-range batteries, as, had better fortune attended the enemy gunners, they might well have inflicted heavy damage to*

---

[2] These communications were posted for the crew to view.
[3] Ibid.
[4] Ibid.

our ships at the relatively close range at which they were firing.[5]

Admiral Deyo considered the Cherbourg operation successful. Following the battle he wrote in his report:

Much regret is felt at the damage and casualties suffered by this force. It is believed, however, that under the circumstances we got off very lightly indeed and that the results attained were such that the army was probably saved a good deal of damage which would otherwise have been received.[6]

Admiral Bryant, Commander of Task Group Two, had some definite observations concerning the operation:

A major caliber, heavily casemated or turreted, and well dispersed coast defense battery cannot be silenced without excess expenditures of ammunition and great risk to the bombarding force unless the firing can be carried out from a blind bearing or from a greater range than that of the shore battery. Such a mission should not be undertaken unless its successful accomplishment is of sufficient importance to justify unrestricted expenditures of ammunition and the risk of serious damage to the bombarding force.[7]

Looking back on the operation after we were safely back in Plymouth, we of the torpedo crew all agreed that Task Force 129 was extremely fortunate indeed. Casualties were light for an operation of this size and length with only fourteen sailors killed and thirty-five wounded. Damage to ships of the task force was also light. Even though more than half of the ships had been hit or

---

[5] These communications were posted for the crew to view.
[6] Roscoe, *Destroyer Operations in World War II,* p. 362.
[7] Ibid., p. 363.

sprinkled with shell fragments, only the *Texas,* HMS *Glasgow,* and destroyer *O'Brien* were severely damaged—destroyers *Barton* and *Laffey* had lesser damage.

The Cherbourg bombardment concluded Operation Neptune for the DESLANT Force. Even though the destroyers of the DESLANT Force were at the forefront of the attack on the beaches, and had suffered the loss of four great warships, *Corry, Meredith, Glennon,* and *Rich,* the contributions and successes of DESLANT were proportionately greater than their losses. There is no question but that the destroyers provided the punch needed to prevent a disaster on the beaches, plus the necessary support to the troops in getting up to the high ground. In the face of heavy German fire on the beaches, they provided the only artillery support the troops had on D-Day, and most of what they had for several days to follow. The unorthodox improvised methods of the captains and their crews will serve as an example in training future naval officers for years to come.

Years later I was telling the story of the dud, which hit our ship during the bombardment of Cherbourg, to a friend who happens to be a Czech naturalized citizen of the U.S. Born in Pilsen, Czechoslovakia, Charles Kucera lived in Pilsen during World War II under the occupation of the Nazis. The duds which hit the *Texas,* *Laffey,* and *Barton,* all bore the markings of the giant Skoda Munitions Factory at Pilsen, Czechoslovakia. Chuck talks of his relatives who were forced to work in the munitions factory as slave laborers, and since they were all Czechs who hated their German masters, it became routine to sabotage shells when ever possible—at the risk of death. I owe my life to one of these fearless Czech workers who risked death to sabotage the shell that hit us, 25 June 1944, and I am truly grateful! I speak for all of the sailors in the task force when I say that I would love to express my gratitude personally to all of those brave workers who sabotaged shells, for God only knows how many sailors owe their lives to them.

THE LIBERATION OF CHERBOURG

While Task Force 129 was pounding the German batteries at Querqueville and Fermanville on 25 June, the U.S. Army captured Fort du Roule from the rear, which guarded Cherbourg. On 26 June the 9th and 79th Divisions advanced into Cherbourg forcing German General von Schlieben and the naval commander, Konteradmiral Hennecke to surrender. These officers had been ordered by Hitler to defend the city and port to the last man. By 1 July most radical Nazis had been captured or killed by American forces, and the mopping-up operation of isolated German units was for the most part complete. On 16 July the first freight was unloaded from Liberty ships. By the end of July estimated tonnage of cargo unloading had been reached, and Cherbourg quickly became the second largest port in France by September. This accomplishment allowed the U.S. First Army to resume the offensive on July 25, seven weeks after D-Day. It also silenced the armchair generals, admirals, visiting congressmen, and the press back in Britain and the United States who had been carping at Eisenhower for what they perceived to be a futile stalemate. These same people, all of whom had little knowledge of what they were talking about, had also been critical of Overlord—prophesizing disaster. They didn't understand that the battle for position and building up of supplies and reserves had been slowed by the loss of "Mulberry" and "Gooseberry." These people could not know the facts. They couldn't understand that if everything in war were common knowledge there would be no opportunity to surprise an alert enemy. They didn't understand the detrimental effect their carping had on morale. Of morale, Eisenhower wrote:

> *In temporary stalemates, however there always exists the problem of maintaining morale among fighting men, while they are suffering losses and are meanwhile hearing their commanders criticized. The effect of carping becomes more serious when soldiers find it in letters from relatives at home who have been led to expect the impossible.*[8]

I was told by a flag officer that German Konteradmiral Hennecke was awarded a high decoration for his Battery Hamburg supposedly sinking two American heavy cruisers. The same officer told me that the Germans accused our navy of putting numbers on cruisers. The confusion probably arose from the fact that the *Barton, Laffey,* and *O'Brien* were *Sumner* class destroyers of the latest design, with heavy armament not common to destroyers of any other navy, and were therefore mistaken for cruisers. In addition to being named, all destroyers of our navy have a hull number which appears on both sides of the bow. Of course the Germans didn't sink any of our ships that day, so was it a case of CYA on the part of the German admiral? Or was it Hitler's propaganda machine trying to minimize the loss of Cherbourg to the German people?

---

[8] Eisenhower, *Crusade in Europe*, 265.

Chapter 9

BELFAST AND HOME

The next day, 26 June 1944, we refueled, took on more stores, and loaded ammunition. At this time I was informed that I had passed my examination for second class torpedoman; however, I could not be rated at this time because the navy had enough second class torpedomen. The navy had trained enough torpedomen of all classes to sufficiently man all existing surface ships and submarines.

The Western Task Force was disbanded because troops had advanced in France beyond the range of navy guns. Because the battleship *Texas* had suffered battle damage she was sent somewhere in the British Isles for repairs. Some of the damaged destroyers were immediately sent back to the United States for repairs. The remainder of the Western Task Force was given a new designation and ordered to Belfast, Northern Ireland. We were ordered to screen the Belfast force and we all set sail a day or two later. As we sailed into the anchorage at Belfast and anchored in the harbor I was amazed to see the place all lit up as if there was no war going on. While Northern Ireland was at war with Germany, Southern Ireland was not. Evidently Northern Ireland was out of range of German bombers.

The next day a third of the crew was given overnight liberty starting at 1200 and ending at 0800 the following day. Jim Dudly and I were in this first group. We were anchored so far out into the harbor that land was hardly visible from the ship, and it took quite a while for our whaleboat to get to the dock where we were deposited on land for the first time in over a month. There was a very broad street leading from the dock up a gentle incline, and what we saw was a sea of white hats—a thousand sailors from our task force had landed minutes before us and were invading Belfast. I stopped short and surveyed the situation. I told Jim, this would never do, let's go left on a side street into the residential section where there are no sailors. The side street was lined with "row houses" built against each other with no room between. Some had the front door open so that we could see inside as we walked along. What we observed was deprivation beyond anything I had ever seen in the poor neighborhoods of Chicago. It was very sad and I experienced despondence for these poor people and their obvious state of despair. Our poor people in the many large cities I had visited were rich in comparison. Even the poor people in the provinces of Montreal and Quebec, Canada, where poverty prevailed to a much greater degree than in any place I had been in my travels over the United States, were better off by far.

We soon came to a neighborhood pub that looked interesting and we decided to go in and visit with the local people. The place was small, quaint, and rather dingy with the short bar on the inside wall opposite the windows. The windows were hinged so that they opened out and their sills were about three feet from the floor. There were no drapes over the windows, and no decorations in the place—only a few tables and chairs, but no bar stools. The bartender greeted us in a friendly fashion. When we asked what he had available to drink he offered Guinness's Extra Stout. It was warm but very good. We concluded it was better than what we had in the states. We chatted for a while and were just finishing our beers when I took particular notice of three young men sitting with their backs to the windows. I noticed that they weren't drinking—they were just watching and listening to us with keen interest. I looked them over carefully and concluded that they looked at least ten to twenty years older than we were. They were shabbily dressed and it was obvious that they were from the neighborhood of row houses. We ordered another round and told the bartender to set these men up with a drink. That broke the ice and brought them into the conversation. I can't remember exactly what we talked about, but it wasn't about the war. I do remember thinking that we were probably the first American sailors these men had ever seen. When we finished our second round we ordered another for the house. One of the men told the bartender to get out the cognac. The bartender reached under the bar and came up with French imported cognac. It was excellent—these men may have been poor but they knew good booze. They weren't dumb either—after all, we were buying! Anyway, I think we were good ambassadors and made some poor Irishmen feel good about Americans. After several rounds of drinks we were ready to move on and the bartender gave us directions to downtown Belfast where the restaurants and department stores were.

We boarded a double-decker bus, which was a bit of an experience for me. I have never considered myself a big man, but at just under six feet and 180 pounds, I felt like a giant on that bus. I had to stay all hunched over so as not to crack my head open on the low ceiling. I remember the women ogling me, and the men intently surveying me—they couldn't seem to take their eyes off me. I don't know what they were thinking, but I was thinking that I shouldn't sit in one of those double seats because there just wasn't room for me and another passenger. Jim had already gone up to the upper deck and I decided to join him there. There was a vacant seat behind him and I piled into it to enjoy the ride. I noticed that he occupied about two thirds of his seat, and he wasn't quite as big as I was. Now that I think back on the situation we were not wearing navy issue uniforms, but tailor made dress blues, as did most petty officers. In contrast, British and French sailors wore government-issue uniforms which were not of the same quality as ours. No wonder they resented us.

We wandered around downtown Belfast and found a decent restaurant on the second floor of a department store. We were able to buy a basic meal of meat, potatoes, and vegetables. I think we had tea to drink. I was surprised that the meal was as good as it was because the submarine blockade, by now rather ineffective, was still on. However, I later learned that the U.S. Army had a huge number of troops stationed there waiting to go into France. I think that the U.S. government probably supplied the civilian population with much needed food supplies. While I was contemplating all of this, the other patrons were looking us over carefully—we were the only American sailors in the place, and they seemed to be wondering where these two characters were from, and whether we were part of the invasion force.

When we left the restaurant it was getting dark and we located a cocktail lounge on the second floor of what appeared to be a commercial building of some sort. We went up the carpeted stairs into a nicely decorated room to land in the middle of a brawl. There were some sailors from the *Tuscaloosa,* and some from another ship and they were tearing the place up. We beat a hasty retreat down the stairs to meet the shore patrol coming up. They didn't pay any attention to us, but kept on climbing the stairs to straighten things out.

We found the dance hall the Irishmen had told us about and were standing outside looking things over. It was located in a town square where all the streets came together like the spokes in a wagon wheel. In the center was a statue of some kind, a fountain, benches, and some U.S. sailors. Some American soldiers approached us and one of them said, "Are we glad to see you guys." I asked, "Why?" He replied that "there were too many British sailors, and each time they tried to get in the dance hall the 'Limeys' in the place would throw them out." I said, "Let's go in!" When the

British sailors saw us coming they didn't offer any resistance for some reason. There weren't that many of us, perhaps we looked too mean. I headed for a table where two British sailors were sitting with two girls in British Army uniforms. I picked out a good looking redhead and asked her for a dance. She accepted and when she stood up one of the British sailors stood up to knock me down; however, he had a problem. He was almost a head shorter than I was, and when I told him to sit down and behave himself he did. While he grumbled, I danced with the girl who turned out to be very friendly, personable, and a good conversationalist. I don't think she was too enamored with the British sailor; she seemed happy to get rid of him. I spent the entire evening with her and ended up seeing her home, which was not too far from the dance hall. It seems that the army had her billeted in a private home.

Jim and I found our way to a sort of barracks for the navy. It may have been a U.S.O. facility because it didn't cost us anything to stay there. The next morning the lights went on at 0600 and we washed up, were provided with a toothbrush, got dressed, and were given breakfast. We grabbed a cab which took us to the dock where we met our whaleboat to be taken back to our ship.

The cab driver was a kindly old gentleman who seemed pleased to have us in his cab. I don't remember him asking any questions about our ship or us, but he was pleased to discuss his cab, which was interesting—it ran on coal gas. It had a big bag on the roof, which had a suitable pipe that connected it to the vehicle's carburetor. As I remember it, that was the only source of fuel for running the vehicle. It looked funny, but it worked. All privately owned vehicles had these gas bags on their roofs because of the gasoline shortage. The coal gas didn't provide the power of gasoline, but it got the cab down to the dock with four sailors squeezed into it.

Our whaleboat appeared at the appointed time and so did some of the other guys from our ship. We piled into the whaleboat for the trip back to our ship and arrived in plenty of time to check in with the OOD. When we came aboard he asked if we wanted to go back for another day of liberty. No one turned down that offer, and so after chow we gathered at the quarterdeck ready to depart in our whaleboat for another day of liberty in Belfast.

That evening Jim and I went back to the dance hall on the square. By now the entire fleet had discovered the place. The square was a sea of white hats with a few soldiers milling around. We went in and had no trouble meeting a couple of girls. After a couple of hours things began getting rough on the dance floor so we took the girls up into the balcony where we could get a seat and watch the crowd below. There were as many as four fights going on at one time on the dance floor—it was all American sailors fighting each other. I don't remember seeing any American soldiers involved. During one fight there were sailors and their girls surrounding two sailors battling when a female spectator, who was having trouble seeing the slugfest, made a run for the group and took a dive over the cheering crowd, landing on the heads of a couple of sailors. There was no shore patrol in the hall, management didn't interfere, and the disagreements simply ended with the better man winning. It's no wonder American sailors have a questionable reputation, especially when they get a couple of drinks under their belts. If they have no enemy to fight, they'll fight among themselves!

We finally decided to go for a ride in a horse-drawn cab. The girls thought they had latched on to a couple of crazy millionaires, especially when we tried to buy the horse and cab. If we had made a deal I don't know what we would have done with it, but we ended up having a fun night.

The next day when we reported back to our ship we were advised that we would be leaving in the morning and that all further liberty was cancelled. The next morning we weighed anchor at daybreak, all hands were called to GQ and we got under way in company with our sister ship *O'Brien*. We stood out of the harbor and remained at GQ until the sun was up well in the sky.

It was sometime after 0800 when a condition three watch was set and I took over the watch at the port K-guns as we were headed out across the North Atlantic which had seen so much bloody action from 1940 to 1944.

The U-boat war, also known as the Battle of the Atlantic, had by now simmered down in stark comparison to what it previously had been. We had no idea of the numbers of ships lost to German actions of all kinds, but we did know that while we were in danger of torpedo attack by German submarines, our chances of making contact with one were much less now than they had been a year before. Allied losses in tonnage had decreased dramatically by the end of 1943 due to the introduction of long-range aircraft such as the RAF's Sunderland flying boats, and the U.S. B23 Liberator bombers which were equipped with centimetric radar. These four-engine bombers could penetrate deep into the mid-Atlantic ocean where the wolf packs operated, saving many a beleaguered convoy. They could join the Jeep carrier hunter-killer groups for the attack. Also, unknown to us was the fact that the capture of *U-505* on 4 June 1944 had provided Naval Intelligence with all of the code books and hardware needed to know exactly where all German submarines were operating, and where they were to be on any given day in the future.

By the end of the war aircraft were scoring many more kills on U-boats than surface escorts.

It was 4 July 1944 and we were sailing in the North Atlantic in the company of the *O'Brien*. I had just come from a Fourth of July celebration in the mess hall and a great meal of pork chops with all the trimmings. It was a beautiful sunny day without a cloud in the sky and I was feeling relaxed and a little lazy. I assumed the 1200 to 1600 watch at the port K-guns and crawled up onto the weather deck by the number two torpedo mount to relax on a stowage locker. There was nothing coming over my telephone headset except an occasional check from the bridge. I was watching the *O'Brien* as she would dive into a ground swell with her bow disappearing clear back beyond the number one gun mount to the deckhouse. There was no crewmember foolhardy enough to be on her forecastle in this kind of a sea. After being submerged for a short spell her bow would start up out of the water to climb another ground swell exposing her red bottom all the way back to the sound gear on her keel. Great amounts of water would spill from her bow deck as she hung there momentarily before crashing down and digging into another ground swell. Each time the bow would dig into a ground swell the stern would come out of the water exposing her screws and rudders. I watched this episode for a while, and then it dawned on me—since we were an identical ship we had to be doing the same thing!

We were headed for our homeport of Boston, Chelsea Navy Yard. A few days later I was standing my watch on the bridge instead of the K-guns. As we neared the harbor at Boston it was decided to inflate the barrage balloon for display as we entered the congested harbor. The special sea detail, some deck apes, (seamen) and the OOD tried for almost four hours to inflate it with no luck. I smiled and thought how happy I was that we didn't need it during the heat of battle. I never did find out why they couldn't get it inflated.

Upon entering the harbor we sailed parallel to a ferryboat going in our direction at our same speed on our starboard quarter. Her passengers immediately all went over to her port side for a better view of us, causing a slight list of the boat. They got one of the closest and best views of a warship possible. Many of the passengers were waving and calling to us. Word of our arrival had somehow preceded us. Finally we entered the navy yard and headed for our usual dry dock, which was empty and awaiting our arrival. A tug turned us around and pushed us in stern first. About an hour later the water had been pumped out and we were sitting high and dry in the drydock—the time was about 1600.

The rumor aboard ship was that survivor leaves were to be granted; however, instead of an announcement concerning liberty or leave, the OOD announced that two service .45's were missing and until these sidearms were found no one would leave the ship! About two hours later they turned up and all was forgiven, except for the guys who had them. Two seamen were taken away in irons and liberty was announced.

Somehow we of the torpedo gang had come into possession of an army cot, some army blankets, navy blankets, and some other odds and ends that were left over from when we had the soldiers aboard. We had the army cot set up on the fantail near the starboard depth charge rack.

We had landed all of our depth charges the first morning in drydock. Quite a few of our seamen had been transferred and replaced with boots fresh out of boot camp. They were typical of most kids fresh out of boot camp, not yet familiar with protocol aboard ship. We had the army cot sitting on the fantail near the starboard depth charge rack and I was sitting on one end of it writing a letter. One of the new boots sat down on the other end with a bucket of water and started washing his clothes. Ordinarily I wouldn't have said anything; however, his action was causing the cot to jiggle up and down, and that made it impossible for me to continue writing. I turned around and yelled at him to "knock it off, I'm trying to write." He kept on bouncing up and down so I called once more with no response—at that moment I laid my pen and tablet down, went back to him, grabbed him by the shirt and slammed him against the number three gun mount. I ordered him off of the fantail and that was the end of that. The next time I went through the chow line he was there serving as a mess cook. He addressed me as Mr. Welna and asked if he had put enough food on my tray. I guess someone had clued him in about messing with that mean torpedoman.

While in the yard we were directed to do complete maintenance on our depth charge racks including painting. There were two deck plates adjacent to both the starboard and port depth charge racks that had been removed for access to both of the rudders. I was working on the port rack, when without thinking, I stepped back. The problem was that there was no deck there and I fell eight feet into the after seaman's compartment and continued down several feet lower into the after steerage compartment, landing on the ring which the rudder pin normally passed through. I landed on the ring in a sitting position with my legs and feet dangling out of the ship's bottom. If I had passed through the ring I would have landed in the drydock twenty feet below. During the fall I had scraped against ragged metal resulting in all kinds of lacerations and bruises from head to foot. I managed to get myself to sick bay unaided where the corpsman patched me up. That evening, with bandages visible on head, arms and hands, I went ashore by myself on liberty to my favorite bar. People were staring at me and wondering what in hell had happened to me—I was in no mood for conversation! I kept thinking, what an irony, I survive twenty days of battle without getting killed, and in thirty seconds I almost kill myself in drydock.

During the first ten days in the yard I was assigned to gangway watches with an occasional fire watch. Men who had been trained in firefighting school stood these watches on a twenty-four hour basis because of the amount of activity by welders and other yard workers who were busy tearing our bridge structure out. Fire hazard was a great consideration. Naval architects had redesigned the entire bridge structure to eliminate the open flying bridge. That suited me fine because in rough weather water would come over the bow and soak us on the open bridge. We had no protection from the weather on the flying bridge and the men in the pilot house were crowded.

The entire crew was granted a ten-day leave that was divided into three sections. I requested section two and went home to Chicago on leave. I arrived home as my folks were preparing to leave for California. Dad was ill with chronic bronchitis, which was thought by the doctors to be caused by the dampness of Lake Michigan—we lived, and he worked, near the lake. We now know his problem was caused by cigarettes. After spending some time in Arizona they finally settled in San Diego.

When I returned from leave I found a big change in our ship. The hole in our hull from the hit at Cherbourg, the interior damage of the after diesel room, and our crew compartment had all been repaired. Our bridge was half rebuilt; the entire ship was dusty, dirty, and with power lines, welding lines, and other service lines all over the place. It was a dangerous place to be. The entire crew was unhappy with the conditions caused by the repair work.

Fortunately for me I didn't have to spend much time on a fire watch in all of that dust and dirt. Most of my duty was on shore patrol. Many Boston policemen had been drafted into the navy and given the rate of chief petty officer. They were known as the roving shore patrol. The destroyers in port supplied two men with right arm rates for stationary shore patrol duty, mostly in the bars. The roving SP was available for emergency, and to check on the stationary SP. Most of my watches were SP duty. I was always stationed in some den of iniquity (along with a torpedoman from another destroyer) to keep peace in the place.

One evening I was standing watch in a bar (which I can't remember the name of) that was located in downtown Boston. For lack of a name I will call it the "Corner Bar." The "Corner Bar" had one large room, well lit with many tables and chairs. Since this establishment was located on the corner, it had two entrances with the bar located near the side entrance. I was standing at the end of the bar and yawning from boredom. The place was loaded with U.S. sailors, many with their girlfriends. In the center of the room I noticed one table with two sailors and their girlfriends. The two sailors left the table and went downstairs to the men's room. While they were gone two French sailors came in and went directly to the table where the girls were sitting. When the two U.S. sailors returned they welcomed the Frenchmen and offered to buy them a drink; the French refused and attempted to push the Americans off. A fight immediately started—a crowd formed around them, my buddy grabbed one of the Frenchmen and I jumped into the fray and grabbed the other one. I threw my Frenchman out the side door and my buddy threw his out the front door. The crowd settled down, and when they tried to get back in we barred them from entering.

The bartender mixed me a drink, in thanks for services rendered, and all was well until they returned with our roving SP in about an hour. I told the chief what had transpired and that I wasn't about to let them in again. They went away again and came back in about another hour, this time with one of our officers and a French officer. I told our officer what I had told the chief, and when they tried to get by me because their officer was present, I stood in the doorway and blocked their entry. There was much jabbering in French from their officer—our SP officer got rid of them for us. I thought we were through with them for good, but they kept coming back by themselves, sometime to the front door, and sometime to my side door, and we kept blocking their entry. Just before closing I advised our two sailors to take their girls and go somewhere else to avoid getting jumped by these two crackpots. Our two sailors hadn't been gone very long when these two idiots came back again, I was hoping that one of them would lay a hand on me so that I could arrest him and send him off to our brig. It astounded me that these two creeps wasted a whole evening of liberty trying to get into our bar, when there were so many other ones nearby. This was my first experience with the French Navy.

A couple of nights later Jim Dudly and I had just left the yard when a sailor came at me cursing me because of my campaign ribbons. I told him off and as we were walking away he hit me from behind and broke my nose. Blood was spurting all over the place turning my white uniform red. I had to return to the yard gate and the guards—I couldn't fight in that shape. I was taken to the Chelsea Naval Hospital and admitted. The next day a navy doctor reset my nose—he and the nurses never quit kidding me about how it all happened. He then transferred me to a recovery unit where I relaxed for a couple of weeks. One day our corpsman showed up and informed me that our ship was to leave in two days. I immediately went to my doctor and requested to be released so that I could stay with my ship. He signed my release with a note to our ship's doctor concerning my recovery—and I reported to my ship for duty. We did leave for a few days but then returned to the yard for more work on the ship.

I later learned that there were dissidents employed in the yard who were threatening to strike and tie up the yard so that repairs on warships would be delayed or halted. The navy threatened them with reprisals if they did strike. They challenged the navy and did strike; the navy responded by having them drafted into the navy—they were then put back to work on the same job they had been doing before as civilians. These former civilians then took out their anger on the sailors, and not knowing the situation, I had stumbled into one of them ending up with a broken nose.

While work was being done on the ship all of the silver in the officers' wardroom disappeared. It was determined that a yard worker had stolen the silver—and a notice was then posted at the quarterdeck stating that yard workers were not to be allowed on the ship after 1700 hours (5 o'clock P.M.). Personnel standing gangway watches were to take whatever steps necessary to enforce the order. This order further enraged some of the yard workers. I think the yard worker dissidents attempted to test the order, and just happened to choose a time when I was standing a gangway watch. One man attempted to board the ship after 1700. As he started up the gangway I ordered him to stop. He continued until he was halfway up the gangway when I took out my service .45, pulled back the slide to put a round in the chamber, and threatened to shoot him if he attempted to come aboard. He stopped, started cursing at me, turned around and left. I really didn't want to shoot anyone, but I also didn't want to be charged with dereliction of duty. That was the only incident of that kind that I know of as long as we were in the yard.

There was a huge park in down town Boston called the Commons. The Commons had a band shell in the center where a symphony orchestra performed every evening until dark. Having been educated in classical music, I spent many evenings in the park enjoying the concerts, which were free for all of the people. One evening I met a very attractive brunette girl who also liked classical music. We began dating and hit it off. It turned out that she lived not too far from the navy yard with her parents in a nice respectable neighborhood. Mary was an only child, which may be why her parents took a shine to me and had me over to their home on several occasions for family gatherings and parties. I quickly learned that her father was a foreman of one of the crews that worked on the refit of the *Barton*. He was very knowledgeable and he taught me much about the design of the ship. One evening Mary announced that we would not be seeing each other again because "your ship is due to leave in the morning," and so we did—that was the last time I ever saw her. We corresponded for a while, but with numerous actions in the Pacific, and censoring, I couldn't write very much to anyone—I just wrote mostly to my parents to let them know that I was still alive.

By now it was early September and we were operating in the Atlantic looking for German submarines. The weather turned violent and we were suddenly in the midst of a hurricane. To add to our problem we were ordered to make contact with the USS *Warrington* DD 383. She had sent out a distress signal and then went silent. We were later informed that she had capsized and we were ordered to look for her survivors. With mountainous seas and almost zero visibility to contend with, that was a very large order almost impossible for us to comply with. Our ship was heaving and rolling in excess of forty-five degrees, and it was extremely dangerous to be on the main deck with the risk of getting washed overboard from the huge waves coming over the side. Fortunately, we had an interior companionway that did allow passage from the stern deckhouse forward to the outside ladder leading to the upper deck, forward deck, and bridge.

We approached the location where the *Warrington* was thought to have gone down and had extra lookouts on the bridge scanning the sea, hoping to spot survivors. Our captain covered the area as best he could considering weather conditions. He had a real problem trying to make turns without getting the ship parallel in a trough that might cause us to also capsize. After two days of searching the area he gave up and we started for Norfolk. The official navy records give the date of loss of the *Warrington* as 13 September 1944. Most of the crew went down with the ship; however, there were a few survivors that were picked up by a passing ship after the storm subsided. While we were in the area we picked up a submarine contact which may have prompted our captain to leave when he did. He may not have wished to risk his ship and crew when the submarine had all of the advantages.

When we arrived in Norfolk we remained there just long enough to refuel and take on stores before departing for Panama. At Panama we went directly to the canal entry lock and proceeded through the canal that same evening. As we sailed through the waterway our boatswain took advantage of the situation and had our seamen wash the entire ship off with the fresh water. At intervals there were small contingents of U.S. Army outposts. The jungle looked wild to me and I wondered if it was really necessary for them to be there. I later learned that there was a real threat from spies in Panama, and so the troops had to maintain their lonely vigil. The tropical climate of the area was hot and muggy and I was happy to get out of there.

We didn't stop at Panama City on the Pacific side but continued south through the Gulf of Panama before turning west and then north west to proceed up the coast to San Diego, California. We entered one of the finest natural harbors in the world at about 1500 hours, took on a harbor pilot, and went directly to the destroyer base where we tied up. That same evening I was given liberty because my parents had recently moved to San Diego. Dad was now working at the navy base at North Island and was informed when our ship sailed around the island to dock at the destroyer base, so my arrival was not a complete surprise.

After several days in port eating good old home-cooked food, meeting my parents' newest friends, and seeing my relatives again, it was time to shove off, this time for Pearl Harbor. The ride to Pearl Harbor was a smooth one—much smoother than the Atlantic—it felt more like a pleasure cruise. We arrived in Pearl Harbor about the middle of October. There was lots of liberty during the day but we had to be back aboard ship by 1700. Jim Dudly and I spent lots of time just sight-seeing around the island of Oahu. We hitchhiked north up to the vicinity of Kaena Point on the west side of the island where we could overlook the ocean. That was my first observation of the variety of colors of the shore water of the Pacific. The colors ranged from emerald green along the shore to a beautiful blue in the deeper water. We sat there in the soft breeze for a while marveling at the gentle white surf, the only sound adding to the peacefulness of the area.

We soon discovered a plantation that had been acquired by the navy for enlisted personnel. It consisted of a large mansion complete with badminton courts and other recreational facilities. The main house had a library, rooms for listening to records, and an ice cream parlor. Jim and I played some good badminton sets. I enjoyed going there because it was a very pleasant restful atmosphere. No one ever bothered me to have a piece of cake, soft drink, or to move furniture as they sometimes did in a U.S.O.

We spent time wandering around Honolulu, the palace, and whatever historical places we could find. The Royal Hawaiian Hotel had been taken over by the navy as a rest area for submarine crews in port. We were able to use their facilities to change clothes and rent swimming trunks for a swim at Waikiki Beach. The water was warm, and the surf high enough for body surfing—I felt like I was in heaven. I remembered listening to radio broadcast from the Royal Hawaiian in pre-war days and I never imagined at the time that I would ever visit the place.

We had been in port for a few days when I suddenly got jerked back to reality. I was walking along a pier when I suddenly came across the battleship *Arizona*. There was no sign identifying it and it took a few minutes for me to figure out what I was looking at. The ship had no superstructure, her main battery guns had been removed leaving large round holes in her deck where the turrets had been. Her main deck was awash, oil was seeping from her bunkers—she was just a hull serving as a resting place for 1,000 members of her crew. It was, and will always be, a sobering reminder of 7 December 1941 when the Japs attacked Pearl Harbor.

We were now spending many a night and day at gunnery practice firing at sleeves and sleds. A sleeve was a target towed by an airplane, and a sled was a target built on a water sled and towed by a ship. It was obvious that we were preparing to join the battle fleet in the South Pacific. One day an officer approached me and stated that the USS *Sterett* DD 407 was in need of an experienced torpedoman. He asked if I was interested in transferring. I checked with our chief who knew the history of many of the destroyers; and when he filled me in on the history of the *Sterett,* plus the fact that she was being ordered to Australia, I decided to transfer. I always wanted to see Australia. On 29 October I packed my gear, picked up my orders, and carrying everything I owned on my back, walked a quarter of a mile to where the *Sterett* was moored. I reported to the OOD and was now a member of the crew of the *Sterett*.

Chapter 10

USS *Sterett* DD 407

T he *Sterett* was one of the ten older destroyers of the *Benham* class, all built in 1938-39 under the London Naval Treaty of 1936, and commissioned in 1939-40. These ships were therefore a little smaller than our naval architects, or the Navy, would have desired. She displaced 1,637 tons (standard); 2,250 tons to 2,286 tons (full load). She was 340 feet, nine inches long with a beam of thirty-five feet, eight inches. She developed 50,000 horsepower at 38.5 knots. Bunkerage was 484 tons giving her a range of 6,500 nautical miles at twelve knots.

In 1942 at the time of her refit following the Battle of Guadalcanal (Third Savo) she received radar and four single 20mm guns as replacement for her six .5 machine guns which were landed. She also received two twin 40mm mounts along with two Mark 51 directors on the after deck house.

She did not have the sleek appearance of the newer *Fletcher* or *Sumner* class destroyers, but by the time I transferred aboard she had been updated with the latest SC, SG, and Mark 20 radar systems. Her main battery consisted of four 5-inch 38 caliber dual-purpose guns. Because of the addition of the new radar systems and the additional personnel to man them, and the space required for the new CIC, there had to be compensation for the added weight; therefore, the gun houses for the number three and four 5-inch guns had to be removed, creating open mounts. She mounted two quad torpedo mounts of eight torpedoes total and the usual complement of depth charges for A/S (antisubmarine) work.

The *Sterett* was a destroyer with one of the most envied and famous battle records of the destroyer fleet—indeed, the entire navy. Her illustrious career began in the winter of 1940 when she was ordered to do patrol work along the upper eastern seaboard and into the North Atlantic as part of the Neutrality Patrol. At that point in time there was growing friction between the United States and Germany concerning freedom of the seas. Our navy was active in maintaining that freedom for the United States by challenging German submarines and the *Sterett* was active in that mission.

January of 1942 the *Sterett* attacked and depth charged a German submarine that had torpedoed a U.S. Coast Guard cutter just south of Reykjavik, Iceland. The *Sterett* was in the company of the *Lang, Stack*, and *Wilson*, which comprised the four destroyers of the 15th Destroyer Division. As usual, the North Atlantic was very rough and the submarine escaped. The following March of 1942 a task force comprised of the battleship *Washington*, cruisers *Wichita* and *Tuscaloosa*, destroyers *Wainwright, Plunkett, Madison, Lang, Wilson* and *Sterett* were transferred to Scapa Flow to join with the British Navy in North Sea operations. Scapa Flow was the main base of operations for the British Home Fleet. It is a cold and dismal anchorage in the north of Scotland that has nothing to offer the sailor for liberty.

In a conversation with Captain Ray Calhoun, U.S. Navy Retired, he reiterated how happily the British received our navy personnel. He told of how the British assigned ten of their signalmen to become temporary crew members of the *Sterett* for the purpose of instructing *Sterett* personnel in how to communicate with the Royal Navy. All of the British signalmen had ten to twelve years experience. They were trained to read and translate tactical signals, and to understand the tactical maneuvers required to execute the commands received. Our signalmen of that period were not trained

Plate 25: USS *Sterett* DD 407 after refit at Mare Island, February 1943. (Official Navy photograph. From the private collection of Jerome S. Welna.)

Plate 26: USS *Sterett* DD 407 showing planview, quarterdeck, aft. Circles indicate alterations. (Official Navy photograph, February, 1943. From the private collection of Jerome S. Welna.)

to execute a signal command. Now, with this training, our signalmen could advise the officer of the deck on specific tactical responses, and our navy could more fully utilize the capabilities of our enlisted men.

To hide the fact from the Germans that the U.S. Navy was involved in a combined operation with the Royal Navy, the British gave the code name of HMS *Steadfast* to the *Sterett*. The other U.S. Navy ships of the task force were also given special code names for communication purposes. After a couple of months of training in gunnery, A/S warfare, and communications with the British, the USS *Wasp* (an aircraft carrier) showed up at Greenock, Scotland, with her flight deck loaded with Spitfires (British fighter aircraft). The next morning the *Sterett*, in company with the *Wasp*, HMS *Eagle*, (a British aircraft carrier), *Lang*, and British destroyers HMS *Echo* and *Intrepid*, departed for the island of Malta in the Mediterranean. The task force never went directly to Malta but close enough to launch their aircraft. This was quite an accomplishment because the pilots had no previous experience taking off from carriers, and their aircraft were not designed for carrier takeoffs; nevertheless, it went off with only one accident. The Spitfires that flew to Malta to reinforce the air defenses there arrived in the middle of an air raid and shot a bunch of Germans down. Somewhere in the operation the *Sterett* splashed one German aircraft—I have no record of where or when it happened, but I do know that the ship was officially accredited with one hit.

May 27 found the *Sterett* in the Portsmouth Navy Yard, Virginia, where she was fitted with her first radar systems—air-search and fire control. By 18 June she was in San Diego, having made the trip with the *Wasp*, battleship *North Carolina*, cruisers *Quincy* and *San Juan*, and the destroyers *Lang, Stack, Wilson, Farenholt*, and *Buchanan*. This task force arrived in San Diego 18 June and added one amphibious cargo ship and three large ocean liners loaded with marines to the task force—destination Tongatabu in the South Pacific. This task force, in the company of other task forces, was destined to conduct the first U.S. offensive operation of the war by seizing and occupying Guadalcanal, in the Solomons.

These islands were long recognized as one of the best natural fleet base sites in the world. This knowledge was not lost on the Japs who had taken possession of Tulagi, Rabaul, New Britain, the north coast of New Guinea, and all of the Solomons. They were confidently building an airstrip on Guadalcanal which would give them a stepping stone to Australia.

The *Sterett* was in action 7-9 August 1942 for the Guadalcanal-Tulagi landings, the capture and defense of Guadalcanal 10 August to 13 November 1942, and the Battle of Guadalcanal (Third Savo) 12-15 November 1942. The Japs were running heavily escorted night convoys (known as The Tokyo Express by our navy) down the New Georgia Sound (The Slot) past Savo Island to reinforce their troops fighting on Guadalcanal. The battle of "Third Savo" was a night action in which the *Sterett,* as part of a U.S. task force, assisted in sinking a Jap battleship and cruiser with torpedoes, and unassisted sank a Jap destroyer with gunfire. In that fight she suffered heavy battle damage from eleven major projectile hits resulting in fifty-five casualties—twenty-eight dead, four missing, thirteen critically wounded, and ten with minor wounds. In this action one torpedo mount, the after deck house, and the number three and four 5-inch guns were blown away.

In April of 1943 the *Sterett* was operating off of the southeastern tip of Guadalcanal screening transport ships during the consolidation phase of the Solomon Islands when she came under air attack. Her executive officer, Lt. C. Raymond Calhoun, was wounded in this action and required evacuation to the hospital in Espiritu Santo. After surgery he was transferred to the navy hospital in Oakland, California, for additional surgery and physical therapy.

The *Sterett* continued in almost constant operations including the New Georgia-Rendova-Vangunu occupation 20 June to 31 August 1943.

Rear Admiral Kelly Turner handed Commander Frederick Moosbrugger, commander of Destroyer Division 12, a tough job—stop the Tokyo Express in the Vella Gulf. The night of 6-7 August 1943 the 12th Division of six destroyers did just that with the *Sterett* sinking one Jap destroyer, assisted in sinking a cruiser and a second Jap destroyer, and finally sinking a giant barge loaded with supplies and Japanese troops. The last surviving Jap destroyer turned tail and took off at thirty knots for Bougainville. Once contact was made the battle took less than fifteen minutes to stop the Tokyo Express. The U.S. Task Force had no losses.

The *Sterett* continued on to participate in the Treasury Bougainville operation, code named "Cherry Blossom," a small task group comprised of the carriers *Saratoga, Enterprise*, and six destroyers. Two strikes were made, one on 5 November 1943, and one on 11 November 1943. Beginning 1 November the *Sterett* escorted the carrier *Saratoga* to her position where on 5 November she could launch planes together with those of the *Enterprise* for a raid on the Japanese fleet at Bougainville. Their planes not only stopped the Japs from making a counterattack on our beachhead at Bougainville which would have been catastrophic to our troops there, but sank or damaged six Jap cruisers and four destroyers, while shooting down twenty-five intercepting aircraft. On 11 November, the *Sterett* was screening the carriers *Essex* and *Bunker Hill*. While their planes were making another strike on Rabaul and Bougainville, the task unit was attacked by at least fifteen torpedo bombers and dive-bombers. The *Sterett* shot down one Jap unassisted and splashed one other Jap with the assistance of another destroyer in the screen. These two strikes were critical and two of the most important of the Pacific war.

Next came the Marshall Islands Operation 26 November 1943 to 2 March 1944. The *Sterett* operated with Task Force 58 screening fast carriers *Bunker Hill* and *Monterey*. She was in action when the carriers struck Roi and Namur islands in Kwajalein Atoll. She participated in the attack of the heavily defended Japanese base at Truk 12 February 1944. She was in the action during the strikes on Tinian and Saipan in the Marianas five days later. During these actions the *Sterett* had to take on fuel and stores at sea every three or four days while under way. It was a grueling pace involving huge air battles with U.S. planes defending against Jap air attacks on the carriers and other surface ships. *Sterett's* gunners were also firing on Jap aircraft as both U.S. and Jap planes were falling from the sky.

The following summer the *Sterett* was once again in action, this time in the Marianas Operation of 10 June to 27 August 1944. On 15 June the *Sterett* gave fire support to marines who stormed ashore at the heavily fortified island of Saipan. By late afternoon 20,000 marines and their artillery were ashore, but still on the beach—deep penetration was impossible because of heavy artillery fire from the Jap defenders. The next morning a banzai attack made up of thirty-six light tanks and 1,000 Jap soldiers charged down from the hills to drive the marines into the sea. The *Sterett*, along with two other destroyers delivered accurate shellfire to repulse the attack—more than three-fourths of the Jap force was destroyed and the marines were not dislodged!

On 16 June picket submarines operating in the Philippine Sea reported a large Jap fleet forming east of the Philippines for an attack on our fleet in the Mariana Islands. By the morning of June 19 the carrier planes of the U.S. Fifth Fleet and the planes of the Japanese combined fleet were close enough to each other to clash in a severe air battle. U.S. Navy Hellcat fighters (which had replaced the Wildcats) were superior to the Jap Zeros, and after a year of training these combat experienced airmen were superior to the Japanese pilots. The results were dramatic—the Japs lost half of their aircraft in their first strike, and of the few that did get through to the formation, only twenty-eight escaped the deadly antiaircraft fire of the surface ships. One Jap did manage to score a rather insignificant bomb hit on the *South Dakota*. This was the start of the Battle of the Philippine Sea which would result in so many Jap planes being shot down before the day was over that it became known to American pilots as "The Great Marianas Turkey Shoot."

At around 0900 a second strike of 130 aircraft was launched from the Jap carrier *Taiho* just before a torpedo from the USS *Albacore* struck her—she had run into the Task Force 58 submarine picket line. Since the carrier could still make twenty-six knots, a third strike of 130 planes was launched. The second strike which preceded them ran into a bigger "turkey shoot" than the first with only thirty-one of its fighters, torpedo attack planes, and bombers escaping. The third strike didn't fare any better than the first two—it couldn't even find the Fifth Fleet. American fighters were vectored onto it by radar and added another ten to their increasing score. At about 1130 hours a fourth Japanese strike force of eighty-two aircraft was sent out to locate a nonexistent American force south of Guam. This group was directed to land on Guam to refuel, but as they were landing they fell victim to another American strike force. By this time Japanese Admiral Ozawa had lost over half of his aircraft and hadn't scored one hit on an American carrier.

At 1222 hours the submarine USS *Cavella* put a spread of four torpedoes into the Japanese carrier *Shokaku*—by 1500 hours, flames from the torpedo hits reached magazines and she blew up and sank. It was a fitting end for one of the Jap carriers that had hit Pearl Harbor December 7, 1941. At 1520 the Japanese carrier *Taiho*, flagship of Admiral Ozawa, was burning fiercely with spreading fires following the earlier torpedo hit. The fire was so hot that rescue destroyers had difficulty getting close enough to the wreck to get Admiral Ozawa off of the ship. Finally, a gigantic explosion from a buildup of hydrocarbon vapors tore the ship apart and sent her to the bottom along with 1,650 crew members—the result of using Borneo crude oil for fuel. Admiral Ozawa was having a bad day.

By 1540, 20 June 1944, Admiral Spruance had come within extreme range of the Japanese fleet that was conducting refueling operations. Even though his fliers would have to attack at near sunset, and then make night landing on their carriers, he decided to attack. Within a few minutes he had 216 aircraft in the air and on their way to meet the Japanese. With insufficient time to coordinate their attack, the American aircraft sank a light carrier, three tankers, severely damaged two light cruisers, two heavy cruisers, and of the eighty Jap aircraft that managed to take off, sixty-five were shot down.

The Battle of the Philippine Sea was a great victory for the U.S. Navy, but a disaster for the Imperial Navy. The Japanese navy lost a third of its remaining carrier force, and all but thirty-six of its surviving aircraft. Highly trained carrier pilots necessary for them to combat the skilled carrier pilots of the U.S. Navy were impossible for them to replace.

When the battle for Saipan finally ended on 9 July 1944 the *Sterett* was still there lending fire support to the Marines. The capture of Saipan allowed the building of an air base for B-29 bombers that brought Tokyo within their range. From early July to 15 August the *Sterett* was alternating screening of the carriers with shore bombardments of Guam, Tinian, Palau, Yap, and Ulithi.

By mid August 1944 the *Sterett* was back in the United States again at the Puget Sound Navy Yard for eight weeks. During that time minor repairs and updating was done to the ship's radar, CIC, and AA armament. By mid October she was back at the Hawaiian Islands for a concentrated period of training, and on 29 October I transferred aboard as a permanent member of the ship's company.

The *Sterett* was still undergoing intense gunnery practice and one of the first things we did after I came aboard was to fire a practice torpedo. The firing of a torpedo involves the use of a black powder cartridge to propel the torpedo from the tube by creating suitable pressure. After the firing the tube must be cleaned out thoroughly and can only be done by a man crawling into and through the 22-inch tube and washing it out with diesel oil. It is one of the most distasteful jobs imaginable. Because I was new to the crew the guys decided that I was the man for the job. Because I was a rated petty officer, and in addition had passed my second class examination, I could have refused. In reality, it should have been done by a striker, but since I wanted to dispel the notion that I was above and better than any one else because I had transferred from a newer, larger destroyer, was a former college student, and a graduate of two navy service schools, I decided to prove that I was a good sport who was not afraid to get his hands dirty—I did it in good humor without protest. I dressed in the oldest dungarees I had and tied a rag around my head leaving only my face exposed which I greased with torpedo lubricant to protect me against powder burns. One of the guys would pass diesel oil and new rags to me as necessary. When I had everything cleaned up I took off all my clothes, threw them overboard, and stepped into the shower. When I showed up at the torpedo shack I was now one of the guys—with a little more ribbing they accepted me into the gang.

About a week later our captain, Lt. Comdr. Joe Blouin, ordered the entire crew to report to the fantail. He advised us that we would be leaving for the Pacific war zone within a day or two, that we would begin loading ammunition and fuel oil, and if we had any room left, stores (food). No one grumbled, the attitude was "what's new?" A day later yard workers showed up on the ship and welded eye cleats onto the deck of the quarterdeck between the torpedo mounts and the K-guns on both sides of the ship. Next, additional cans of 40mm ammunition appeared and the yard workers strapped them to the eye cleats with special tools so that the cans would not shift in heavy weather. Our captain wasn't kidding! By now I had figured out that we had a well trained ship's company with a core of veterans of many engagements, with some officers and men who were plank owners. I felt comfortable and proud to be associated with this crew.

The next morning we put to sea headed for Guadalcanal to join a battle group there. We were in the company of our sister ship the USS *Wilson* DD 408 and we immediately began more training in target identification, radar controlled gunnery, and torpedo firing. I was immediately ordered to stand my condition three watches in CIC for additional indoctrination. I spent several days in my new training environment working with target plotting, and torpedo fire control by radar.

About four days out from Pearl Harbor all of us polliwogs were ordered to the forecastle to be served a "subpoena and Summons Extraordinary" commanding that we appear before the Royal High Court of the Raging Main. This was the start of the ancient initiation of polliwogs—persons who have never crossed the equator and been duly initiated into the Solemn Mysteries of the Ancient Order of the Deep. Each of us polliwogs were read the charges against us, and briefed concerning initiation protocol—from that moment on the initiation was in progress. During the initiation, which was to last three full days, the ship was actually in control of the shellbacks, the sailors who had actually been duly initiated at a previous crossing. During this period officer polliwogs were actually taking orders from enlisted shellbacks. I remember our engineering officer working in the crew's mess engineering dirty dishes around at the orders of the boatswain. Before leaving Pearl Harbor we took several officer passengers aboard—they were all bound to join Admiral Halsey's staff. One of these men was a young warrant officer who happened to have steel blue eyes; therefore, someone dubbed him "Baby Blue Eyes." I had an 0800 to noon watch on the bridge and there was "Baby Blue Eyes" dressed in an asbestos firefighting suit looking through a fire hose nozzle searching for the equator.

Finally we were about to cross the equator. All of us polliwogs were gathered up to face the final initiation at 0900 in the morning. We were lined up on the starboard side of the ship at the break in the main deck and went up the ladder (stairs) to the forecastle deck where the Royal Judge was presiding over the ceremonies. He had a fiery red beard and high black silk hat. He wore a stiff starched color, no shirt or tie, and sported a black cutaway coat, all of which was suitable for the occasion. His dungarees were cut off just below the knee and he wore marine boots. He stood at a wood podium and was read the charges brought against each polliwog by an aid as they stood before him, hat in hand, to which he replied "guilty in the first degree" as he banged his rawhide maul down on the podium. The next stop for the polliwog was the royal barber who unceremoniously cut all his hair off. The polliwog was then blindfolded in preparation for his visit to the Royal Doctor/Dentist who did an oral examination of the mouth in which he jammed some stuff that tasted like cold beef fat. I think it had some Novocain in it because I couldn't taste food for a couple of meals afterward. Finally we had to walk the plank blindfolded—instead of landing in the ocean we landed in a tank of water and garbage. I remember being hit in the butt with a cattle probe—I flew out of the tank onto the deck like a launched torpedo, and was released back to the crew as a shellback. No one got hurt, we all had a good time, and we were all duly initiated. When it was all over we all laughed about it and looked forward to the day when we could do the same to future polliwogs.

A couple of nights later we made contact with a Jap submarine at about 2100 hours. We were only about 125 miles northeast of Manus in the Admiralty Islands, well in the range of Jap operational warships. Our sister ship, the *Wilson*, covered us while we made our attack on the sub. The crew was called to GQ and I took over the port K-guns to fire depth charges. Our captain maneuvered the ship so as to cross over the sub in a figure-eight strategy while we dropped three patterns firing charges from the K-guns while simultaneously rolling charges off of the fantail racks. After the third pattern we lost contact and I don't know if we got him or not.

The next morning we put in at the advanced navy anchorage in Manus to refuel and replace our expended depth charges. We took on more stores and the following day left for Guadalcanal arriving in early November late in the afternoon. My first recollection of Guadalcanal was the colors as we entered the anchorage at about five knots—the flag hung like a wet dishrag from the mainmast. There wasn't a breath of air moving as we moored to a destroyer tender. I was sweating profusely and experiencing dizziness from the intense heat and humidity. When I told the chief that I was overcome by the heat and humidity he told me to go below and rest. I went below to my bunk, but it was so hot in the compartment that I went back topside, lay down under a 40mm twin gun and passed out. That evening after dark I hauled my mattress up to the starboard torpedo mount and tried to sleep, but it was still too hot, so I kept experimenting with places to sleep topside. The next day I was sent over to the tender to have a routine examination of my teeth. The dental spaces were all air-conditioned and I didn't want to leave the facility and go back out to the heat and humidity. The dentist found a cavity in a molar that he filled with silver. That was OK with me because I could stay longer where it was cool. He did a good job because it lasted for almost twenty years. I invented every way possible to get off of the ship to a place where it was cool. I encouraged the supply officer to send me over to a supply ship with a work party to get fruit for the crew because I knew it would be cool in the hold of the ship. I managed to get myself sent over to the tender with the ship's binoculars to have them checked because I knew that their facility had to be air cooled also. I swore I would rather fight the Germans in the cold of the North Atlantic than the Japs in the heat of the stinking islands of the South Pacific.

A short time later we put to sea to patrol among the Solomon Islands, the Bismarck Archipelago, and New Guinea. Due to the strategy of island hoping (bypassing certain areas of Jap occupation), there was still a possibility of Japanese counterattacks in these areas. We didn't make any contacts with Jap naval units of any description, and I took the opportunity to locate a place to sleep on the deck—it was too hot with foul air in the crew's compartments. My first try was the deck on the starboard side of the number two 5-inch gun. That location worked out fairly well for me, but the guys who had to wake me up at night for watch in a rain squall didn't like it because they would get all wet doing it. I never got wet because I had perfected a way of using my fire-and-waterproof mattress cover to protect me from the elements. I would put the mattress cover down, then the army blanket, and then my foul-weather jacket for a pillow. The waterproof mattress cover would deflect rain and two or three inches of water going around me on the deck. If it was raining hard, with careful manipulation I could get my stuff up and still use it for cover to get to a protected area without getting wet. After a few complaints I decided to try a 20mm ammunition box by the forward 20mm AA gun under the port wing of the bridge. The box was just wide enough for me and about seven feet long—it worked perfectly and I had no complaints about the location because there was overhead shelter from most rain squalls. I spent a lot of my time in the tropics sleeping on this box during night hours. I also discovered a storage box on the deck house near the starboard twin 40mm AA gun that worked fairly well during condition two watches when I had to be in that vicinity at night.

The Japs were laying low, there was no action, and the captain decided to give the crew a little relaxation. We were in the Russell Islands and the captain decided to anchor and allow the crew a chance to go for a recreational swim. The boatswain rigged a line from the yardarm of the foremast so that we could use it to swing from the bridge (about thirty feet from the water line). The way the line was rigged we could swing out in an arc parallel and away from the ship, let go of the line at the end of the arc, and go sailing through the air to dive into the water. It was really fun and a great thrill. The gunnery officer and I were having a big time seeing who could swing out the farthest when the captain saw us and put a stop to it. He said he didn't want to lose a gunnery officer and a torpedoman. Since I could no longer swing out on the line I did a thirty-foot swan dive from the bridge. When the captain saw that he closed the bridge to all swimmers!

During this quiet period of patrolling in the Solomons I decided to make a knife. I had plenty of off duty time and our torpedo workshop was well equipped with all of the tools I would need for the job. I had developed a close buddy in Dave Vestal, a very talented torpedoman—he had just started making a knife and he helped me to get started on mine. I would see what he was doing and how he solved certain problems and that helped me with my project. We worked together in testing different steel alloys and other materials that might be suitable for our projects. One alloy we tested could not be drilled and would burn out our drill bits, but it could be easily cut with a hacksaw. Another alloy could be easily drilled but was impossible to cut with a saw.

We finally located enough suitable steel alloys and miscellaneous junk to make our knives. For the handle I gathered scrap pieces of stainless steel from bulkheads, Monnel (a form of hardened alloy steel used for gun mount bearings), Bakelite, from old electronic switches, and Plexiglas pieces from the main battery director. I located a worn-out, hardened-steel machine hacksaw blade that I ground down for the knife blade. Discarded gun covers with leather reinforcement yielded the heavy leather needed for the scabbard. The final result was a knife that would not rust or pit from the salt air, was strong, sharp, and lightweight, would retain its edge, and would never need polishing. My knife measures ten inches overall including a six-inch blade. It weighs eight ounces without the scabbard—and over the years has been used for everything from prying open ammunition boxes to shaving. Several officers on the *Sterett* tried to buy it from me from time to time but I never considered selling it. I have displayed my knife at several lectures I have given and it always attracts a great deal of attention.

We refueled and took on stores at Rabaul, New Guinea, then proceeded some 1,250 miles north to Ulithi Atoll which lies approximately five hundred miles southwest of Guam at latitude north 10 degrees and longitude west 140 degrees of Greenwich. We then proceeded west—our mission was to locate any Japanese naval units prowling in this area of the Pacific between Ulithi and the Philippines, a thousand miles west to where the invasion of Leyte was taking place, and where the battle of Leyte Gulf had occurred. We didn't encounter any Japanese naval units of any kind.

By the time we returned to Rabaul we had been living on something called *Chicken-ala-King and rice*. The *Chicken-ala-King* was lavishly laced with cockroaches and the *rice* had an ample supply of worms. The officers, who paid forty dollars a month for their food, had the same fare. One day I was standing my watch on the bridge near the captain who was sitting in his chair. An officer's steward appeared on the bridge with the captain's noon meal on a tray that clamped on to the arms of his chair. The tray had a white linen napkin spread out with another napkin in a silver napkin holder, a dish of his food with a silver cover, a silver coffee pot, knife, fork, and spoon of silver and fine china. It was an impressive spread. The captain lifted the silver cover from his food to reveal the same thing we were eating. He didn't say anything, but he got a look of disdain on his face. The ship fitter happened to be on the bridge repairing something and as he passed behind the captain to leave the bridge he said "Forty dollars a month." I almost choked trying to keep from laughing. The captain gave me a dirty look and drank his coffee—I made a hasty exodus to the wing of the bridge and I never knew if he ate anything.

When we returned to Rabaul the supply officer immediately commandeered a Higgins boat from somewhere, and along with some seamen located fresh fruit and other decent food. When he returned with the goodies they tossed crates of fruit onto the deck. Officers and men alike broke into the crates to get at the fruit. I bit into an apple and blood ran out of both sides of my mouth because my gums had deteriorated from lack of proper diet. I could actually wiggle my teeth in my gums. When we ate the oranges we ate the skin and all. It didn't take long before the crew responded to the proper foods. We spent a few days in the anchorage at Rabaul resting.

Every evening the electricians would set up the movie projector and screen on the fantail and we could watch a Hollywood movie. Some of them were good and some were boring, especially the war movies—some were so far from reality as to be pathetic. Most of the crew would wander off, and those who stayed would jeer the film.

Plate 27: USS *Sterett* DD 407 in the South China Sea, January, 1945. (Official Navy photograph taken from USS *Marcus Island* CVE-77. From the private collection of Jerome S. Welna.) We were coming alongside while under way to receive a transfer of mail.

Chapter 11

LIBERATION OF THE PHILIPPINES, PART I

Supply and Protection of Leyte
Resupply of Mindoro
7 December 1944 to February 1945

About 1 December 1944 we entered Leyte Gulf in the Philippines and anchored for a short stay. While there some natives in a dugout canoe showed up and tied up to the rudder guard on our fantail. They had a parrot, monkey, and some sake that they wanted to trade for clothing. One of the seamen traded some skivvies for the sake. One other sailor traded some clothing for the parrot, and Harry Howard, our acting chief torpedomen, traded for the monkey.

The monkey, which the chief named Pancho, turned out to be a disgustingly filthy animal and we all hated him—more about the monkey later. The sake was akin to real firewater. Nobody would drink it and so it went overboard. The parrot—I don't remember its name—lived in the forward seaman's compartment for a while and then died. We also had a little dog named Gismo that looked like a cross between a sausage hound and a Heinz 57 Variety. He also lived in the forward seaman's compartment. He was a cute little guy and didn't bother anyone. He was a real sailor who had been aboard for many months—he never got excited when we were engaged and firing our guns.

273

While at Leyte Gulf one of our seamen went AWOL and ended up on the beach at Leyte. He was apprehended by the army who wanted a sack of potatoes as a reward for his capture and return. Our captain offered two sacks of potatoes if they would keep him an extra day. Since we couldn't see land in any direction I don't know how he ever got to the beach, unless he bribed a native visitor to transport him in a dugout canoe.

The Japanese were landing a steady flow of troop reinforcements and supplies on the western coast of Leyte. Destroyers were routinely sent into Ormoc Bay to stop this movement of Japanese shipping. The evening of 2 December three destroyers were ordered to conduct the fourth Ormoc Bay sweep of enemy shipping—they were the *Allen M. Sumner* DD 692, *Moale* DD 693, and *Cooper* DD 605.

As they entered Ormoc Bay under cover of darkness the *Cooper* detected a surface target by radar which she engaged at about 12,000 yards. After pumping 5-inch shells into the target for several minutes it exploded in a ball of flame—it turned out to be the Jap destroyer *Kuwa*, which was transporting infantrymen to the Jap defenders. The next day over 250 dead Jap soldiers washed up on the beach for burial. *Cooper* then shifted her fire to another target that she sank before being struck by an enemy torpedo. She immediately exploded, broke in two, and sank along with ten officers and 181 men. About 168 of her crew were later saved.

On 7 December U.S. troops of the 77th Division were put ashore near Ormoc on the west coast of Leyte. The objective was to drive a wedge between the Japanese troops in the rear positions. This landing of assault forces occurred just prior to a Japanese attempt to land reinforcement troops near the same area. The Japanese transports and escorting naval units were forced to retire when they experienced heavy losses from attacks by our destroyers, and covering marine fighters and bombers.

At this time we were operating in Leyte Gulf, Surigao Strait, and the Mindanao Sea, doing radar picket duty (detection, identification, and engagement with enemy surface and submarine contacts). We came under attack by kamikazes on two separate occasions, but I can't remember if we shot them down, or our CAP (Combat Air Patrol) splashed them. Two of our destroyers were hit by kamikazes in this action, but suffered only minor damage.

The capture of Mindoro was essential to MacArthur's planned invasion of Luzon because of the island's geographic location and strategic airfields. Those airfields were needed so that army air could cover the Lingayen landings on Luzon. On 15 December a special U.S. Army assault force was landed on Mindoro and had it secured in five days. Their greatest problem was the kamikaze attacks on their convoy during the three-day run from Leyte Gulf to Mindoro when one of the escorting carriers took a hit that required it to retire to Ulithi for repairs.

We returned to San Pedro Bay at Leyte Gulf to take on ammunition, fuel, and stores. The captain assembled the entire crew on the fantail and announced that we would leave for Mindoro as part of the screen of the Third Echelon Supply Group the next day, 27 December. He further stated that we would come under ever-increasing kamikaze attack, and that our radar would be landlocked at times (which meant that Jap planes could fly low over the islands below radar detection, and pounce on us in just a couple of minutes). To improve enemy aircraft detection additional telephone circuits were added to allow special lookouts to communicate directly with CIC, in addition to the bridge. He then gave us the encouraging news that fifty-percent casualties were expected on this run. He also said that he couldn't give us suitable advice if we were captured—he just concluded with: "if you are captured, God bless you." In conclusion to his briefing it became crystal clear that if we were to survive this and future battles, it would require the complete cooperation of every man and officer in the crew. I, personally, was not worried because I had complete confidence in my shipmates. We were all ready and eager to do battle with the Japs.

Once an invasion has commenced, troops are landed, and advancing, it is essential that resupply of these troops takes place according to plan. To keep them provided with all that is needed for them to accomplish their objective is often more difficult than the original landing. To accomplish this objective convoys are used to deliver supplies to the new beachhead, and the enemy will do their best to interrupt or prevent needed supplies from arriving. Vicious battles often erupt in these situations, and this one was no different. The Japanese were concentrating on these convoys with ever-increasing ferocity, as we were about to experience.

The next morning we joined the convoy and took our assigned position as the lead destroyer on the starboard side of the formation. The echelon was a large one and consisted of one hundred ships of all classes from APAs (attack transport) to PT boats including nine destroyers of the screen. The 21st RCT (Regimental Combat Team) of the 24th Division was transported in the landing craft. The entire convoy was under the command of Captain J.B. McLean, and had the code name of "Uncle plus 15."[1]

The convoy proceeded through Leyte Gulf on 27 December with no incidents. Everyone on our ship was expecting trouble as we approached the Surigao Strait, and our concerns were well founded. At 0330, 28 December all hell broke loose and continued for the next three days with a call to general quarters every hour or two for the next seventy-two hours. We were called to general quarters fifty times during those three days. As our captain and radarmen had warned, the kamikazes would pop up over the hills through low cloud cover on our starboard side, and jump us almost immediately because of their short run. There were as many as

---

[1] Uncle plus was a synonym for D-Day, and this convoy was due at the beachhead fifteen days later from receipt of orders.

twenty-five Japs in each attack. We assisted in shooting one of them down that morning.

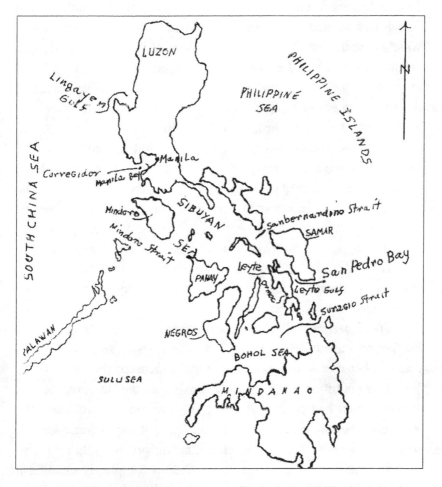

Plate 28: Where the great battles were fought in the Philippine Islands.
(Drawing by Jerome S. Welna.)

It was about 1000 in the morning and I was standing at my battle station on the quarter-deck when three landlocked bogies dropped out of the cloud cover on our starboard side. One of our destroyers shot the first one out of the sky. The second one hit the forecastle deck of the Liberty ship *John Burke* (an ammunition ship) which was located about 500 yards astern of us in the formation. I watched with disbelief as the Jap exploded on contact. A split second later the *John Burke* disappeared in the most violent explosion I have ever seen. The whole ship seemed to vaporize and the smoke from the explosion rose up through the cloud cover over a thousand feet and mushroomed out like the detonation of an atomic bomb. The concussion hammer came at us like a gray wall with such force that some of the crew thought we had been hit. I ducked when I saw it coming, and it tore the colors off of the mainmast. Pieces of the ship kept raining down for what seemed like a long time; and, as the convoy continued moving, pieces fell on other ships. The explosion was so great that it damaged the LST that was in the column 300 yards on the port side of the *John Burke*. When pieces finally stopped falling from the sky it was as if the *John Burke* had never existed.

The Liberty ship *William Sharon* was hit by the third Jap, and her entire superstructure was aflame. Our sister ship the *Wilson* came to her rescue to fight the fire and evacuated the entire crew. When ammunition in her ready boxes started to explode the *Wilson's* men had to cease fighting the fire, be removed, and she was forced to clear until the ammunition quit exploding. When it was safe to return the *Wilson* closed again, put firefighting crews back on board again, and was finally able to completely extinguish the fires. The *William Sharon* was left anchored in the Mindanao Sea until a salvage tug towed her back to Leyte. The guys on Mindoro had to wait for their gasoline, ammunition, trucks, rations, and beer (the most important part of the entire cargo).

Our CAP retired at about 1515 leaving us completely unprotected. During the rest of the day we fired on many targets along with other ships, and I don't know how many planes we assisted in knocking down. I do know however, that we were credited with two more assists during the day, one at about 1706, and another one about 1717. At 1925 we shot one down unassisted using full radar control. That evening at about 1830, twenty-five or thirty Japs jumped us as we passed the southern point of Negros Island. We expended a lot of ammunition that night and I don't know how many more Japs were shot down by us, either assisted, or unassisted in the attack which lasted almost two hours. By the time the attack was over at about 2015, LST *750* had been hit and mortally wounded. The escort commander, Captain McLean, ordered destroyer *Edwards* to sink her, after making certain that all her crew and wounded had been removed.

Even though the attacks were over for the day, we had bogies in the area all night long.

Sylvester Williams was a chief mess attendant for the officers' wardroom. He was more commonly known as "Big Willie" among both officers and crew. Big Willie was a giant of a black man, the nicest guy you ever wanted to meet. He had a jovial disposition and was well respected by officers and men who came in contact with him. Willie used to come back to our torpedo workshop to drink coffee with us because we had a coffeepot that was always hot. Once in a while he would repay the favor with some delicacy from the officers' mess. One day Willie and I were fooling around when Willie got my arm caught in his and carefully applied enough pressure to cause me to yell "knock it off." With his great strength he could have crushed my arm.

In a private conversation Ray Calhoun, recounted an incident concerning Big Willie and a subordinate mess attendant:

Our ship's doctor, Lt. Lea (MC), was in charge of the officers' mess. The navy was all segregated in those days and Doc Lea noticed that one of the black attendants was habitually belligerent, surly, uncooperative, and abusive in language as well as manner. Doc's solution was to speak to Big Willie about the situation. He told Big Willie that his subordinate was a trouble-maker and that his reputation as a leader was hurt by his apparent inability to discipline him effectively. The next day Doc had a new problem—Big Willie had broken the "undisciplined" mess attendant's jaw. Doc had to take him to a dental surgeon aboard the battleship Massachusetts *to have him patched up. Apparently the culprit made the mistake of reacting to Willie's reprimand with his fists. From that day forward the troublemaker's attitude improved markedly.*[2]

Big Willie was well known for the many times he went over the side into the water with a harness and line to swim to a downed pilot. He would bring him back to the ship and because of his great strength lift him aboard. Many a downed carrier pilot owes his life to Big Willie.

Big Willie's reputation was legendary as the first loader of the number two 5-inch gun mount which was his battle station. As first loader he would remove the 5-inch shell (which weighed fifty-four pounds) from the projectile hoist and place it in the tray (slide). If the gun was being fired under full automatic control from the main battery director, the fuse would have been set automatically as the shell came up the hoist from the ammunition handling room located beneath the gun. The powder can would come up the powder hoist from the handling room below the gun. The powder man would receive his powder can from the powder hoist, remove the safety

---

[2] Raymond Calhoun, Captain, USN Ret. was Executive Officer of the *USS Sterett* at that time.

from the rear end of the powder can, and place it in the tray (slide) behind the projectile. The gun would then automatically ram, fire, and the hot powder can would automatically be ejected. While this seemed like a slow process, well-trained gun crews could put twenty-three rounds a minute through a 5-inch gun. Big Willie and his powder man Tex could go as high as thirty-two rounds per minute.

During one attack in the afternoon of 29 December I went up to the number two 5-inch gun mount (for a reason I can't remember) that was firing on a kamikaze approaching our formation. Both doors of the gun mount were open, and as I approached the mount it suddenly quit firing. I thought this was strange because the other three mounts were still firing. I stuck my head in the door and Big Willie had his projectile in the tray, but there was no powder can behind it; therefore, the gun couldn't be fired. Tex, the powder man, had a powder can between his legs and was struggling to release the safety from it. Big Willie looked around and yelled at him *throw it away, get anoder one, dere's a million moe in dat hole!* A ship fitter, a buddy of mine, also witnessed the event. We both busted out laughing, and I made my way back to the quarterdeck, laughing all the way. To this day I still laugh when I think about it.

Captain McLean felt that the situation was serious enough that if we didn't receive more air cover, there was a definite possibility that the Japs would wipe out the entire convoy. During the evening of 28 December Captain McLean pleaded with MacArthur's headquarters and the Mindoro command for continuous dawn to dusk air cover. Aircraft based on Leyte couldn't fly because they were socked in by bad weather. We had no escort carriers in the area, and I don't know why. The next day, 29 December, Mindoro replied with everything they could put into the air including witches' brooms. During the day we had constant cover from P-61s before dawn, to be later relieved by F4Us flown by USMC Pilots, and P-38s, and P-47s from A.A.F. (United States Army Air

Force)—they were all excellent pilots. The Japs were having a bad day on the 29th because every time they attempted to attack our formation our air cover, with the help of our radar direction, would knock them down. We would shoot down any Jap that got by the CAP; however, they were forced to retire at dusk, leaving us vulnerable again. And sure enough, the Japs came out at about 1730 with twenty-five or thirty planes to do their dirty work. Two P-61s came to our aid, and with the help of our radar direction and ships' gunfire, killed several Japs and kept the rest away in spite of the full moon.

The next morning at dawn, we again came under kamikaze attack and the formation shot down several more Japs. It was mid morning, 30 December, when we finally reached our destination and put into Mangarin Bay, Mindoro. By early afternoon our supply ships were busy unloading their cargoes. The Japs had a reception committee awaiting our arrival and they made their appearance at about 1540. Five Vals (Aichi 99, single engine Navy dive-bomber) broke through the air cover and made suicide attacks on both the destroyers *Gansevoort* and *Pringle,* tender *Orestes*, and avgas *Porcupine. Orestes* (a converted LST) was hit by a Jap in flames, probably dead at the controls—he hit the water in flames and then bounced into the starboard side of the ship. He was armed with a bomb that deflected upwards and exploded inside the ship. The *Orestes* burst into flames losing all power. She was unable to fight the fire and two LCIs came to her rescue—they extinguished the fire and towed her into shore near Caminawit Point where she was beached. She was later towed into Leyte for repairs. Fifty-nine men were killed in the attack—106 were wounded including her captain and members of the Diversionary Attack Group staff.

A second Jap crashed into the destroyer *Pringle* DD 477 within a minute of the crash into *Orestes*. The Jap hit the after deck house but didn't do serious damage. *Pringle* was still able to contribute her share of fire support against the suiciders.

At about the same time as the attacks on *Orestes* and *Pringle* were occurring, *Porcupine* also came under attack. The Jap hit her with a bomb and then followed the bomb in to blow a huge hole in the main deck. The plane's engine passed through the ship tearing a large hole in the hull below the water line. The explosion that followed put the *Porcupine* out of commission, killing seven men and wounding eight.

The fourth Jap of the attack group hit the destroyer *Gansevoort* DD 608 in the after engine room killing fourteen men and wounding thirty others. We were immediately ordered to close on her port side and render assistance fighting fire. I was given instructions to remove the detonators from our starboard depth charges in preparation for our assistance to her. A seaman torpedo striker by the name of Jim Agneu was assigned to help me.[3] Agneu was a recent transfer aboard from boot camp and had never seen a depth charge detonator, and had no idea of where it was located in the depth charge, or how to remove it. I proceeded to give him some on-the-job training while we were under attack by more bogies. I took a detonator out and explained that he had to be extra careful not to bump it against anything or drop it. I watched him as he attempted to remove his first detonator. He was scared to death, shaking, and nervous as a whore in church. I warned him, "Whatever you do don't drop it." I hardly had the words out of my mouth when he dropped it. Lucky for him, he was so scared that he had the heel of his right foot on the deck with the toes of his foot pointing up. This created a cradle for the detonator as it landed flat in it. Had it landed any other way it might have blown his foot off. I sent him back to the torpedo shack to the chief. When the chief came back to see what had happened I told him to keep Jim somewhere else so that he couldn't blow the ship up, and I would remove all of the detonators

---

[3] A striker was a seaman who wished to advance to petty officer by study, learning on the job, and then passing the appropriate examination.

myself.[4] I removed all of the detonators with one eye on attacking bogies, and the other eye on what I was doing. I had just completed the job when the chief came back with an order from the bridge to put them all back in. We weren't going to the aid of the *Gansevoort* after all. The destroyer *Philip* DD 498 was to assist our sister ship the *Wilson* DD 408 in aiding the *Gansevoort*. Her fire was brought under control and she was towed to the beach and given the job of knocking the stern off of the *Porcupine* with a torpedo. The *Porcupine* was on fire and the object was to prevent the fire from spreading to the forward holds of the ship and igniting the avgas stored there. Because of the shallow water the torpedo hit was not very effective and the fire did finally spread to the avgas igniting it. Burning gasoline spread across the sea causing the *Gansevoort* to be towed to another location, while *Porcupine* burned to the water line. While all of this was happening the Liberty ship *Hobart Baker* was hit by a Jap bomber and sunk off Mindoro beachhead. A Betty tried to skip bomb us but the bomb hit a wave and jumped over the forecastle without doing any damage. When the Jap flew over us we clearly saw the meatball painted on his fuselage. Our ship was made of Texas horseshoes.

Jap mortar batteries on a ridge began shelling the transports unloading on the beach. We were ordered to take them out, and our captain skillfully ran the ship so close to the beach that we were almost aground. We took them under fire with deadly accuracy. When the last battery was destroyed and we ceased firing, our guns were red hot from firing so fast and for so long. Captain McLean declared that he had just witnessed some real fancy gunnery.

---

[4] The depth charge detonator was about five inches long and slightly bigger around than a ballpoint pen. It was filled with an explosive material that was quite stable; yet, would not take a lot of rough handling. One end was especially touchy because it was part of the exploder device designed to receive a firing pin that would initiate its detonation, and set off the main charge of high explosives.

Captain McLean formed a convoy of twenty-one empty LSTs, a couple of merchantmen, and the remaining seven destroyers for the return to Leyte Gulf—the other supply vessels remained at Mindoro to be unloaded. We assumed our position in the convoy screen and departed for Leyte Gulf that evening. I read somewhere that "our return trip to Leyte Gulf was uneventful." Whoever made that statement was evidently not there, and had no idea of what he was talking about. We beat off kamikaze attacks for the entire trip starting at dusk 30 December. The next day we beat off several attacks with the help of our CAP. When our CAP retired at dusk we came under attack again at nightfall. We had Jap planes flying low on the water between our LSTs raising all kinds of havoc. Their technique was designed to induce our gunners from all of the ships to fire on them, and in so doing, hit our own ships and personnel. To some degree they were successful because LST gunners were trained to set up a defensive cone of fire. The night sky around the convoy was lit up with tracers from 40s and 20s going in all directions, and ricocheting off of LSTs in the formation. I ducked for cover to keep from being hit by friendly fire. There were Jap planes on fire falling from the sky to explode in the water, while others were attempting to bomb our ships. Some were attempting to crash into the ships but were missing their target to crash in the water and explode creating a fireball that would light up several ships in the vicinity. I remember saying that this was the damnedest display of New Year's Eve fireworks I had ever seen. I can't remember how long this fight lasted, but at the time it seemed like hours. When the fight ended and the action report finally completed, we were amazed to learn that we hadn't lost any ships, casualties were light, and damage to ships was minimal.

The next day, New Year's Day, we were attacked again during the day but beat them off with the help of our CAP. That night, however, we again came under attack when the CAP was forced to retire at dusk. This attack was not as heavy as the one of the previous night, and we fired on several aircraft, but I don't remember if we scored any hits. In the confusion of battle with two or more ships firing at the same target, it was sometimes impossible to determine who actually downed the bogie. I know that we assisted in downing more enemy aircraft than we had credit for.

We finally entered Leyte Gulf at 2330 while condition red was in effect. Since we were practically out of ammunition, and since no enemy aircraft were attacking us, we didn't fire. We were conserving what ammunition we had left for our defense in case of a direct attack. Officers and men had hours ago passed the stage of extreme fatigue—we were absolutely exhausted! At dawn the next morning a Jap Betty flew over our force, dropped a bomb, and flew off unmolested by the gunners of our formation. I remember Lt. (jg) Neale Fugate, our torpedo officer, standing next to me as the Betty flew over our ship, dropped a bomb on the *Wilson*, (which missed) and flew off as if he owned the territory. We just stood there like dummies and said "oh, an airplane." Not one of the ships sounded general quarters, and not one ship fired one round at him. I've often wondered what the Jap thought of the stupid situation. The extreme fatigue of the navy crews was not lost on the high command, and was dealt with in detail in their action reports concerning 3rd Echelon Resupply.

The losses of ships carrying critical supplies to the army at Mindoro created a difficult problem for both the army engineers and the navy. Army engineers were delayed in preparing the airfields for S-Day (the invasion of Lingayen) the following week. They needed their expected supplies of bitumen, timber, instillation materials and other supplies. Construction of airfields was delayed until these supplies could be delivered. During the first week of January several merchantmen waiting unloading were damaged so severely that their cargoes were lost. One of these happened to be an ammunition ship that blew up from a bomb hit. It did a tremendous amount of damage to other ships in the anchorage. Never had the navy experienced so much resistance in supporting an amphibious operation following the initial landing. The situation at Mindoro had a definite effect on how the navy changed their plans for the Lingayen operation.

The kamikaze proved to be a very formidable weapon, and strict censorship was imposed on the news media so that the Japanese command would not be informed of just how effective it was. The run to Mindoro and back, which was supposed to be tantamount to a tourist cruise, turned out to be one of the most exhausting tasks of the war. The cost in ships and cargo exceeded by far the best estimates of the planners; and, navy casualties were more than one thousand sailors—officers and enlisted men who could not be easily replaced.

In his comments to all ships of the task force concerning the new tactics developed as a result of the Mindoro action, Admiral McCain wrote in part:

> As never before, the offensive air strength of the fast carriers has had to be spread to cover the enemy in his large island systems and land mass dispersions. At the same time the force has found it necessary to concentrate its defense to a degree never before considered necessary. Before the innovation of suicide attacks by the enemy, destruction of 80 or 90 percent of his attackers was considered an eminent success. Now 100 per cent destruction of the attackers is necessary to preserve the safety of the task force.

There was a huge anchorage in Leyte Gulf a couple of days after our entry and I spotted the *Barton* standing into the area. As soon as I saw her anchored I hitched a ride on our whaleboat to the *Barton* to visit my old shipmates. The first news I learned was the death of Moose. (I can't remember his real name) He was killed when a line snapped while lowering the whaleboat. I felt really bad about his passing because he was a real nice kid and a conscientious torpedo striker. He was ceremoniously buried at sea. I also learned of Admiral Halsey's Task Force 38 and his bad luck in encountering heavy weather 15 December in the eastern half of the Philippine Sea at a rendezvous point for refueling his destroyers. These ships were dangerously low on fuel following their three days' strikes on Luzon. They had to refuel at sea from oilers or capitol ships and it immediately became a dangerous business with a rapidly increasing thirty-knot wind with heavy seas.

Refueling at sea under way required the ship receiving fuel to sail on a parallel course at the identical speed with the ship supplying the fuel. Even though I was a qualified helmsman I never trusted myself to handle the ship in this very touchy situation. In a heavy sea the destroyer had a tendency to bounce up and down while moving away or into the supply ship, requiring the helmsman to make tricky adjustments with the wheel to avoid a collision.

When both ships were in their correct positions to each other a line was shot from the supplier to the receiver. When it was recovered by the receiver it was hauled in along with the fuel hose, which was then deposited in the receiving fuel trunk. When the fuel hose was made secure the oil was pumped from the supplier to the receiving ship. If the sea was rough the fuel hose would sometimes break and oil would spill and spray over the receiving ship creating a big mess.

We once broke five fuel hoses while refueling from the battleship *West Virginia* in very rough weather. During one of those breaks the hose snapped, whipped around, and sprayed oil into the officers' wardroom.

As the ship would use up its fuel, seawater would be pumped into the empty fuel tanks to maintain proper ballast. Receiving ships would be notified hours in advance of time and location for refueling. This would give them lead-time for pumping water out of their fuel bunkers. It was a tricky business in heavy weather because without normal bunkerage and ballast, ships were buoyant, subject to excessive rolls, capsizing, and just hard to handle. It therefore depended on the ability of the aerology officer to predict weather forecasts. In those days meteorology hadn't progressed to the science that it is today, and weather reports from weather stations and aircraft were at least twelve hours old when received by task force commanders—lack of recent suitable information resulted in many serious mishaps.

Most of the ships low on fuel were destroyers and escort carriers. Halsey had orders from Nimitz to strike Luzon again on 19 December and it was imperative that refueling operations be completed by then if he were to carry out his orders. His one big problem was the nasty weather which seemed to indicate no change for the next few days. It had already become impossible to refuel certain needy ships depending on where the ships were in the formation. Because of lack of reliable information on the storm's path, he was not able to get out of the way and find smoother water. What actually happened was that the whole task force sailed right into the teeth of the storm as it developed into a full blown typhoon with counterclockwise winds of over 100 knots and ever worsening seas by noon of 18 December, depending on the position of the ship referenced. The weather had already caused the task force to break up and it became every ship for itself with ships scattered over 2,500 square miles of ocean; however, by 0800 18 December most ships of the task force were steering southerly courses which would eventually lead them out of the path of the typhoon. By mid morning of 18 December Halsey had lost three destroyers and he didn't know it due to the ferocity of the typhoon. Some COs of destroyers reported visibility as low as three to four feet and rolls as much as seventy-two degrees in mountainous seas. How they recovered without capsizing is beyond me. And yet I have experienced rolls almost that bad in an Atlantic hurricane and a

Pacific typhoon, and if that doesn't scare the hell out of you, nothing will!

The three destroyers lost were the *Spence* DD 512, *Monaghan* DD 354, and *Hull* DD 350. I have no specific figures for actual personnel losses, but I do know the normal complement of these ships, and based on the number of men rescued, close to 1,000 officers and men went down with these three ships. The men of the *Barton* told me that the ship had actually started to crack in two. Her captain must have taken skillful action to save his ship. At the Court of Inquiry Admiral Halsey did receive some blame, but I'm not certain that he was treated fairly because he was judged on the bases that there were weather warnings of an impending typhoon—in fact, he did not receive weather reports indicating there was something more than a normal tropical disturbance. In 1946 I saw the *Barton* again in San Diego. Long steel bars had been welded to her hull at the quarterdeck area, main deck level, to shore up the weakness where the stress had occurred to threaten her breakup. Luckily for us we had been operating far to the southwest of where Halsey's force was and had no contact with bad weather.

Due to the persistent slow travel course of the typhoon, Task Force 38 could not carry out the strike schedule on enemy airfields on Luzon 19-21 December. After refueling, the task force returned to Ulithi for rest, repairs, and reconditioning. On 30 December Task Force 38 sortied to strike Japanese air bases on Luzon once again.

Chapter 12

LIBERATION OF THE PHILIPPINES, PART II

Luzon Operation
Lingayen Gulf Landing
12 December 1944 to 18 January 1945

Once back in Leyte Gulf we replenished our ammunition and fuel oil. While we were enjoying a little rest our acting chief torpedoman proceeded to service our smoke tanks. He put on heavy rubber gloves and other clothing which was designed to prevent the caustic F.S. mixture (a chemical mixture used to create smoke) from coming in contact with skin during the recharging procedure. These tanks had to be maintained and operated by torpedomen who generated smoke during surface engagements when it was necessary to screen larger ships from enemy shellfire.

When the smoke tanks were recharged and ready for service the chief decided to give Pancho (his monkey) a bath since he (the chief), was all suited up and ready for the occasion. The only problem was that Pancho wasn't crazy about the idea. He wasn't about to have a bath and he fought the chief tooth and nail, turning him every way but inside out. Since we all hated Pancho, none of us were about to enter the fray. The chief finally won out and Pancho had his bath—sort of! When released, Pancho took off and ended up sitting on the SC radar atop of the foremast. The chief, after licking his wounds, disappeared for a rest after his long ordeal—he was not in a jovial mood! We were hopeful that Pancho would drop something on the bridge, or better yet, the captain. That would be a sure way of getting rid of him.

While resting in the gulf, our ship fitters built two mesh steel cages for the collection of spent brass from the two 40mm antiaircraft guns which were located atop the after deckhouse. This was an improvement because it kept the brass casings from accumulating on the deck during air attacks. Pancho discovered these cages and took a liking to them—he would crawl down into them and hide—until hot brass would fall in on him during an air attack.

I think it was actually 2 January when we were served a turkey dinner to celebrate the New Year. I remember it well because the mess cook dumped a turkey leg on my tray. I thought I had it made until I tried to bite into it. No matter what I did I couldn't get a bite out of the thing. It had been in storage so long that it had atrophied. I felt like hitting the mess cook over the head with that leg.

We got under way at 0600 and I relieved the watch on the bridge at 0800. We were attached to Task Force 78 as part of the Seventh Fleet. I had entered the bridge on the port side where there was nothing but ocean to view. I strapped my telephone headset on and walked over to the starboard wing of the bridge. I looked out in a southerly direction and to my amazement saw ships on the horizon strung out from east to west as far as the eye could see. The invasion force was under the command of Vice Admiral Oldendorf and numbered over 1,000 ships of all classifications. There were eight battleships, six heavy cruisers, twelve escort carriers, many destroyers and destroyer escorts, destroyer transports, destroyer minesweepers, attack transports, tugs, and all kinds of support vessels. All of the task groups required for the Lingayen operation had made rendezvous at Leyte Gulf during the past couple of days, and the battle fleet was now formed up for passage through the

Surigao Strait and on to Lingayen Gulf. What I was looking at was the entire invasion fleet under way for the battle that we were to be a part of. We were sailing in the opposite direction of the main fleet and it took most of the day to get to our assigned position in the formation, which was the San Fabian attack force, one of the two groups that made up the entire invasion force under Admiral Kinkaid—we were to screen the light carrier *Manila Bay*, one of twelve light carriers in the invasion force.

Richard Rodgers told a magnificent story with music in *"Victory At Sea."* I have never seen this historic film, and yet there is a certain passage in his music that recreates a picture in my mind of the assembly of warships forming for the battle of Lingayen Gulf. There is another passage which recreates my feelings of patiently waiting to go into action, when men are quiet, each with their own thoughts—and then there is the score of the raging battle and its aftermath. Whenever I listen to his music I once again experience the scenes and emotions of all the experiences I ever had in the South Pacific during World War II.

Because of their slow speed, the Minesweeping and Hydrographic Groups had already left two days before with salvage and LCI groups. They came under attack by bombers that dropped bombs the afternoon of 3 January, but caused no damage. That evening, however, the first suicide attack occurred when a Val hit the deck of the oiler *Cowanesque* killing two men but doing little damage to the ship. This was just the beginning of what would turn out to be a worse battle than the Mindoro operation.

Our formation passed through the Surigao Strait and once in the Sulu Sea formed two groups around a screen of escort carriers. Our carriers provided air cover of forty planes around the clock and was supplemented by additional army fighters which increased the total to about seventy. Navy fighter direction was from the carriers *Makin Island* in the vanguard, and *Natoma Bay* in the rear. During the next two days about twenty kamikazes were able to penetrate the air cover and execute their suicide dives on the formation sinking one escort carrier, the *Ommaney Bay* on 4 January.

On 5 January we were steaming about 150 miles from the Japanese airfields on Luzon. Bad weather on Mindoro had the army air grounded and so we had to depend on our own CAP for air cover. Kamikaze attacks began at about 0800 and continued throughout the day with the CAP shooting most of them down and turning the remainder back. It was about 1700 and we were about a hundred miles off Corregidor when twenty-one bogies came in on our formation.

It was hard for the Jap pilots to miss our invasion armada because our ships were strung out for over forty miles. Even with our air cover it was possible for just a few to get through and crash a target ship, which in many circumstances caused the loss of the vessel. Even though we bagged another bogie, and our CAP knocked most of them down, enough got through to do a lot of damage.

The heavy cruiser *Louisville*, the flagship of Rear Admiral Chandler, was hit on her number two turret by a Judy (an Aichi, Navy dive-bomber), killing one man and wounding fifty-nine with her captain being badly burned. The resulting fire was quickly brought under control and the ship continued as a fighting ship. At the same time another Judy crashed HMAS *Australia* with a bomb that killed twenty-five men and wounded thirty; however, it did not do a lot of damage to the ship. HMAS *Arunta* suffered a near miss that killed two men but did no damage to the ship. The escort carrier *Savo Island* escaped when the attacking kamikaze was defeated by the ship's searchlight which blinded the pilot causing him to clip the ship's radar antenna and splash without doing any other damage to the ship.

While we were covering the escort carrier *Manila Bay* two bogies came in low on the water at high speed. Our radar was not useful at that low altitude so we had to use local control which wasn't as effective because they had approached low over the land at high speed making it difficult for our gunners to quickly get locked in on them. At about a half-mile distance they pulled up to about a thousand feet, rolled out and made their dive for the carrier's deck. The first one hit the base of the ship's island superstructure, penetrated into the hangar deck and exploded setting some airplanes on fire, killing twenty-two men and wounding fifty-six. Even though the damage to the superstructure was serious, damage control got things under control and she continued firing. The second one missed the ship and splashed harmlessly in the ocean.

The USS *Safford*, a destroyer escort, was badly damaged by a hit that created a sixteen-foot hole in her starboard side, flooding her number two fire and number one engine rooms killing two men and wounding twelve. A bogie went after the destroyer *Helm* DD 388. He hit her mainmast, wrecked her searchlight, and crashed into the sea. Six men were lightly wounded.

At about 1700 the minesweepers that were working in the gulf closer to shore came under attack by four bogies. Three of the sweepers were able to deflect the bogies that crashed in the water close to them causing no damage or casualties. The fourth hit *LCI(G)-70* (LCI gun boat) killing two men, wounding six, and knocking eight men overboard. That ended a busy day, but the next day, 6 January, was to be worse. I don't remember how many times we went to battle stations, but I do remember that we spent most of the day at general quarters firing at bogies. I think we received credit for two kills that day, but I am certain that we bagged more than that.

Early in the morning of 6 January we were sailing just west of Cape Bolanio which resembles the thumb of a mitten, west of Luzon to form the Lingayen Gulf. The main formation then broke up into small battle groups to execute the main plan. We headed for San Fernando Point to prepare for our scheduled bombardment. Our escort carriers moved further northwest of the gulf where they could provide protection for the invasion force with less fear of kamikaze attack. My old buddies of the 60th destroyer division (Flagship *Barton, Walke, Sumner, Radford,* and *Leutze*) went ahead to provide fire support protection against shore batteries that might attempt to knock out the slow moving minesweepers. By sunrise four groups were on battle stations at Lingayen Gulf, many banged up but all of us eager to kill Japs.

The preliminary bombardment had just commenced when about ten enemy planes swooped down on our formation. Our CAP shot down five of them with a loss of one of ours and no ships were damaged. Between 1130 and 1145 they began to attack in large numbers.

One bogie tried for destroyer *Richard P. Leary* but only grazed the number two gun mount before harmlessly crashing in the water.

The battleship *New Mexico* was the flagship of our San Fabian Fire Support force. She was bombarding the area at San Fernando with important passengers on board. A Jap bogie in flames hit the port wing of her navigation bridge where Lieutenant General Herbert Lumsden (Winston Churchill's personal liaison officer at General MacArthur's headquarters), Captain R.W. Fleming the ship's commanding officer, his communications officer, an aid to General Lumsden, and *Time Magazine* correspondent William Chickering were all killed instantly. Twenty-five crewmen were also killed and eighty-seven were wounded. Even though the damage to the bridge was extensive she continued firing.

Destroyer *Walke* was attacked by four kamikazes around noon and splashed the first two; the third one hit the port side of her bridge in flames fatally wounding her captain who died shortly after of severe burns. A kamikaze hit the destroyer *Sumner* in her after deckhouse and number two torpedo mount shearing off several torpedo warheads that were not armed and therefore didn't detonate. Her after 5-inch magazine flooded and was not cleared for three days. Fourteen men died and twenty-nine were wounded in the attack.

A few minutes past noon two Zekes (Jap Navy Mitsubishi Zero fighters) came in low on the water to attack the minesweeping vessels. One headed for destroyer minesweeper *Long*, hitting her port side abaft the forecastle at the water line and setting her on fire. The sea going tug *Apache* extinguished the fires but before a salvage party could board her another bogie hit her and the explosion broke her in two—she sank the next day. Her crew was rescued by *Hovey* (destroyer minesweeper)—thirty-five men had burn wounds and one died. Moments later destroyer transport *Brooks* was hit losing three killed and 11 wounded in the crash. HMAS *Warrammunga* came to her aid, extinguished her fires, and towed her free of the gulf.

Later in the evening at about 1800 several kamikazes dropped out of the clouds over the gulf and attacked the fire support force. Two attacked the destroyer *Newcomb* but one Jap pilot changed his mind and peeled off to crash the battleship *California*. *Newcomb* shot the Jap out of the air but the one that hit the *California* did considerable damage. Shells from a nearby destroyer also contributed to the forty-five men killed and 151 wounded on *California*. *Newcomb* also received a shower of both 40mm and 5-inch shells from a friendly source that may have contributed to two of her crew killed and fifteen wounded. This, along with a couple of other incidents, caused me to be more concerned with our own trigger-happy guys than the Japs.

These friendly fire incidents caused Admiral Oldendorf to issue a stern warning to all ships of the task force.

A day which was characterized by brilliant performance on the part of many ships was seriously marred by indiscriminate, promiscuous, and uncontrolled shooting. Ammunition was wasted, death and injury to shipmates inflicted, and material damage caused to our ships. All hands are enjoined to make certain that their guns are fired at the enemy and not at their shipmates.

Light cruiser *Columbia* was also attacked by two kamikazes, the first of which splashed close aboard after passing between her masts without doing much damage. The second Jap hit her on her port side doing extensive damage. Her damage control parties did a tremendous job of saving the ship. An hour later power was restored and her gunners shot the tail off of a Jap trying to crash the HMAS *Australia*; *Columbia* suffered thirteen killed and forty-four wounded.

The ordeal for HMAS *Australia* was not over—she received a second crash from a kamikaze that added another fourteen killed and twenty-six wounded to her losses of the previous day. She lost a gun mount, but like the ships of the U.S. Navy she kept on fighting. I personally met some of these Australian sailors at Ulithi after this operation and I found them to be a great bunch of sailors.

The cruiser *Louisville,* having been hit the day before, now took a second one more serious than the first. One kamikaze tore out a large section of her bridge and a 40mm mount on the starboard side. Rear Admiral Theodore E. Chandler was severely burned by flaming gasoline; nevertheless, he helped handle a fire hose and took his turn with the enlisted men for first aid, but because his lungs were seared from the flames he died the next day. Thirty-one men were killed (in addition to the admiral) and fifty-six were wounded in the attack. The damage to the *Louisville* was so severe that it put her out of action. Since she could not continue her battle assignment, Admiral Oldendorf's flagship *California* took over her bombardment and fire support duties, and she left the battle area with a returning convoy.

I have always said that I had a guardian angel on one shoulder, and lady luck on the other, because both destroyers I served on survived many situations that could have been deadly. The *Barton* was a very lucky ship, and I wonder, did I leave lady luck with it when I transferred to the *Sterett*? The *Barton* was the only ship of the 60th Destroyer Division that survived the entire Philippine and Okinawa campaigns unscathed. It was mid afternoon when *Barton* and *O'Brien* were covering minesweepers in the gulf. It happened that *Barton* and *O'Brien* were passing each other close in on opposite courses. Two Zekes dropped out of the clouds at high speed diving on both ships. The first one missed both ships hitting the water only about ten feet ahead of *Barton*. The second one hit *O'Brien* on the fantail ripping off the deck plates, three 20mm guns, flooding two compartments including the magazine for the 5-inch gun mount effectively putting it out of commission. I have no record of fatalities from this hit. *Barton* then relieved *O'Brien* of her duties and escorted the minesweepers into the gulf.

At about dusk destroyer minesweeper *Southard* was hit by a kamikaze on her port side of the number two fire room at main deck level. Steam lines were cut, fire ensued, and she was dead in the water. She was towed outside of the gulf to safety where her damage control crew worked on her all night repairing the propulsion damage. At mid day she was back at work minesweeping. Luckily, only six men were wounded, and none were killed. She was the last ship to be hit on 6 January—this brought the total ships hit or sunk from 3 to 6 January (inclusive) up to twenty-seven. Two ships were sunk during the period, and six ships sustained more than one attack. Counting the three that sustained two hits the total attacks numbered thirty. During this short period 314 officers and men were killed and 763 were wounded, for a total of 1,077. Most of the losses had occurred on 6 January with a loss of sixteen ships hit or sunk, 165 killed, and 502 wounded for a total of 667 for the day.

When Admiral Kinkaid totaled up the score for ships and personnel lost for the day of 6 January he, as well as every high-ranking officer, was very much alarmed. With a fifty percent increase in loss of ships, and thirty-one percent increase in personnel loss just three days before the scheduled troop landings, something had to be done to prevent embarking troops from being slaughtered. He had therefore contacted Halsey and requested help from his carrier cover of Task Force 38, which was located about 120 miles southeast of Cape Engano. Halsey sent his bombers in to attack the Jap airfields, but bad weather over Luzon prevented satisfactory results and only a minuscule fourteen planes were destroyed in the air, and eighteen on the ground. Recon photos indicated 237 planes ready to fly in camouflaged locations, mostly near Clark Field. Had it not been for the fact that Task Force 38 did provide as much cover as weather permitted, our losses would have been even higher.

We were very lucky this day. While we expended a lot of ammunition against the suicide planes, we were not attacked. I don't know if we had any accredited kills or assists, but I suspect that we did bag at least one or two with long-range radar control. It may be that because we were operating further away from the beaches of the gulf, the Japs may have figured that their chances of success were better if they concentrated on slow moving minesweepers and the screening ships whose radars were land-locked because of the close proximity of the mountains to the shore. It was an exhaustive day, or as one fleet officer put it "one helluva day."

The night of 6 January was a bright moonlit night with no activity until past midnight. At around 0430 in the morning of the seventh, two bogies came over the hills and attacked destroyer minesweepers *Chandler* and *Hovey*. *Chandler* hit one bogie just as it dropped a torpedo that hit *Hovey* sinking her in just a few minutes. I don't know if the second kamikaze splashed harmlessly or was shot down—*Hovey* lost forty-six officers and men.

Our naval bombardment by both the San Fabian and Lingayen groups commenced 7 January at 1030 in the morning. The morning was beautiful, the air crisp, visibility clear and temperature in the low seventies. Resistance to our bombardment was very light. We only detected two or three Jap shore batteries exchanging fire with our group. We killed one Jap mortar battery with counter battery fire. The few enemy aircraft that appeared were quickly shot down by our screening ships; however, in the evening about 1830 a Jap bomber popped over the hills and dropped his bombs on minesweeper *Palmer*. He made a direct hit and *Palmer* sank within a few minutes losing twenty-eight killed, and thirty-eight wounded.

If 7 January was considered an easier day for the navy, 8 January would be anything but. Seven ships would be hit throughout the day—two would sustain extensive damage. The other five damaged ships would be classified as minor. One ship, the HMAS *Australia*, would be hit once early in the morning and experience only minor damage; twenty minutes later it would be hit again and suffer extensive damage. It is my understanding that Admiral Oldendorf offered to allow HMAS *Australia* to retire after being hit the fourth time, but the Aussies refused and wanted to continue the fight, even with a fourteen-foot hole in the side of their ship at the water line. These guys were our kind of sailors and we were proud to have them on our side.

In the evening around 2230 we were called upon to bombard a sector of the beach where the San Fabian assault force would land the next day. We began firing one broadside every twenty seconds port side too. Pancho, the monkey, showed up and took up a position on the port rail just forward of the port K-guns. He could easily sit on the rail because the top of the rail was bent over in a semicircle, which gave the monkey a place to sit, walk, and grab onto for security. He sat down as the guns fired their first salvo. He went "eep" and immediately scampered forward on the rail about forty feet when the guns fired their second salvo. He went "eep" turned around and scampered back to his starting place, which he reached as the guns fired their third salvo. This went on for about twenty minutes with him reversing direction and going "eep" every twenty seconds as the salvos were fired. During that time I felt sorry for him because he was on the firing side of the ship and getting the gun blasts which had to be hurting his ears. I tried to get him off of the rail to the other side of the ship, but he wouldn't leave. He must have been completely confused and couldn't understand that he should get out of there and that I was trying to help him. When we finally ceased firing he left the rail for other parts of the ship.

During the early morning of 9 January the San Fabian attack force moved into position to disembark troops in the eastern sector. We took up a position 4,000 yards from the beach and started our assigned bombardment at 1030. We were on the eastern edge of the formation dueling with some batteries hidden in caves and behind rocky formations on the side of the mountains. The area was lightly defended in comparison to previous beaches, but more heavily defended than the area where the Lingayen Task Force went in at the western sector. A few well-hidden batteries did manage to take pot shots at our destroyers and landing ships, doing some damage and causing some casualties. Our counter battery fire was not very effective because we couldn't see where they were hidden. The army sent some hunter-killer patrols into the hills to locate them— with army and navy cooperation the destroyers helped to kill them all, but it took four days. The main Japanese defending force was dug in on a ridge well out of range of naval guns. The Japs had learned their lesson not to try outgunning the United States Navy during an amphibious operation. A few kamikazes got by the CAP and harassed us, but even though most were shot down, some managed to get through and hit four ships. Our biggest problem was friendly fire. The battleship *Colorado* was hit in a critical fire control area of her bridge by a friendly 5-inch 38 caliber shell that knocked out a sensitive fire control station of her bridge killing eighteen and wounding fifty-one men—she now had no air defenses and seriously reduced combat efficiency.

HMAS *Australia* received a fifth hit from a kamikaze that caused more structural damage but no casualties. She had been beaten up enough by this time to be ordered back to a repair facility. Light cruiser *Columbia* was hit again for the third time and suffered another twenty-four killed and sixty-eight wounded. The additional damage and loss of personnel did reduce her effectiveness, but she still had more fight left in her, as she stood by to provide more fire support. The battleship *Mississippi* took a hit that did minor damage, but resulted in twenty-three killed and sixty-three wounded. The fourth ship hit was the destroyer escort *Hodges*. She suffered minor damage and no casualties.

In the evening when the CAP retired, smoke ships (specially modified and equipped LCIs and LCVPs—Landing Craft Vehicles and Personnel) commenced generating smoke. They were stationed to windward and seaward of the transports that were either unloading, or waiting to approach the beach to unload. The blanket of smoke generated made it very difficult for the kamikazes to select targets and attack the larger warships and transport vessels. We hoped to get some respite from the evening air attacks, but relief was not to be. Destroyers and other escort vessels were not under the smoke blanket and we caught hell because we were the best targets around, and had no protection.

Not only did we have to put up with the kamikazes, but the Japs came up with a new surprise for us—suicide boats. These little gems were wooden boats about twenty feet long. They reportedly carried two 260-pound depth charges, a light machine gun, some hand grenades, and a crew of two or three men. They were designed to infiltrate our Lingayen invasion fleet and attack any ship available by approaching the ship as close as possible so that the target ships guns could not be brought to bear on the suicide boat. They would then roll a shallow set depth charge over the side, which if close enough would blow a hole in the hull of the target ship. Over eighty of these little devils reportedly took part in the attack that damaged several supply ships. While they were a very effective weapon, the Japs never had a chance to use them again the following night because our destroyers shot up or damaged most of them. I don't know how many bogies or suicide boats we fired on, or how many we may have hit, but between the suicide boats and kamikazes we had a very busy night

January 10 was a quiet day for us. A few kamikazes came in at dawn to attack mostly the ships unloading cargo. Most were shot down, but one did hit the destroyer escort *LeRay Wilson* causing extensive damage and killing six men and wounding seven. We went to general quarters before dusk in anticipation of bogies attacking after our CAP retired. One bogie came in and hit an APA, (Attack Transport) killing thirty-two men and wounding 157. We were dive-bombed and strafed; the bomb missed, we had some minor damage from the strafing, but no casualties. He had come in over the hills so fast that our gunners didn't have enough time to really get a good shot at him and so he escaped.

Late that night we were picking our way through a mine field that hadn't been cleared. Visibility was 175 yards maximum due to the smoke blanket, the water was smooth as glass, and there was no wind. We were crawling at less than five knots and there was an eerie quiet about the whole scene, with no one talking, except those men using the ship's communication phones and the officers giving orders on the bridge. Special lookouts were posted to hopefully detect floating mines before we ran into one. A special lookout was posted on the bow with a phone line connected directly to the bridge. The special lookout was a petty officer who spent only twenty minutes intensely scanning for mines before being relieved. Men who were known to have good night vision were assigned to this special duty. I had the dubious honor of taking my turn. Needless to say we didn't run into any mines. I don't remember what our mission was, but whatever it was, every man on the ship was happy to get out of there.

We were reassigned to the outer protective screen of destroyers covering the convoys arriving at the gulf and those departing after unloading their cargo. There was also an inner screen of destroyers that contributed to a tight defense against large submarines, suicide and midget submarines, and all kinds of surface vessels. One dark night about 2400 we were patrolling in the company of our sister ship the *Wilson*. We picked up a radar contact that indicated two unidentified Jap destroyers sneaking north through the little islands just north of Bolina at the north entrance of Lingayen Gulf. They were evidently trying to get into the South China Sea and escape to Formosa where the Japs had a large naval base. We were north and west of them and the *Wilson* was south and east of them when we both opened fire. We had them at the apex of the target triangle, with a little island between the *Wilson* and us. When they ducked behind one of the larger islands we shifted our fire from armor piercing to star shells. This illumination gave the *Wilson* the ability to see them and increase her accuracy. I think they thought they had the whole U.S. Navy after them because they hightailed it around another island and went north at flank speed. I think they were hit more than once but it didn't affect their propulsion machinery. We were ordered not to chase them because there was the possibility that they were decoys attempting to draw us away from the screen so that a suicide submarine(s) could get through to the transport vessels unloading. Our picket submarines were alerted to be on the lookout for them and to sink them if possible. If they failed to make contact, the CAP would hunt them down in the morning.

On 12 January we had nine ships hit by kamikazes. Included in that number were two destroyer escorts, one destroyer transport, four submarines, and two LSTs. Casualty figures for the day totaled 179 killed and ninety-two wounded for a total of 271. Six of the ships hit suffered extensive damage and had to be retired to a repair base for temporary repairs, and then to Pearl Harbor or a West Coast repair facility. Three more ships were hit on 13 January—one escort carrier, one destroyer transport, and one LST. Casualties for the three ships totaled twenty-five killed and 122 wounded.

By 13 January we had undergone twelve days of kamikaze attacks, shore bombardments, and surface engagements. During that period I was able to record the most important incidents at wars end including the number of ships hit each day; however, the names of the many ships hit, and their stories, became one huge muddle over the years. Information on casualties was not usually available until commanding officers filed their battle reports—by then we were involved in other actions and had already put it out of our minds. It was one big problem trying to chronologically reconstruct all of the events accurately that occurred during that period.[1]

I might also add that we weren't interested in preserving our exploits for the annals of history. That was Captain Samuel E. Morison's assignment, and he did an excellent job of it. We were all tired and our main interest at that time was in doing our assigned task as well as possible, and then getting the hell out of there in one piece.

The next evening we were patrolling among the islands of the gulf and things seemed really quiet. I had a 2000 to 2400 watch on the bridge and had just been relieved. I went down to my bunk, grabbed my gear that I used to make a bed topside, and discovered a radar jockey sacked out on my favorite 20mm ammunition box under the port wing of the bridge. I thought, "the audacity of him crapped out on my ammunition box." Since I outranked him I contemplated jerking him off of "my box." I then had a second thought—his battle station was in CIC, which was just around the corner of the deck house, and if we had a bogie contact he would be needed in CIC in a hurry. I decided, "to hell with it," he can stay there.

---

[1] For a more complete list of ships sunk, damaged, and casualties, please see Morison, *The Liberation of the Philippines,* Vol. XIII, pages 103–156, and pages 325–326.

I went looking for a place to spread my gear and decided on the amidships port 20mm gun location. I carefully made my bed on the deck under the gun so that my feet were towards the starboard and my head was to port. I was on my back and noticed that the SC search radar on the top of the foremast was not turning 360 degrees as it normally would be doing. It was searching an area of target angle about forty-five degrees. That was an indication that there may be a bogie out there. I watched it for a little while and then drifted off to sleep.

I don't know how long I had been asleep when I was rudely awakened by an explosion. When I first opened my eyes I saw the black silhouette of a Jap Betty roaring overhead in the black sky. The general alarm immediately sounded and we all rushed to our battle stations. By the time we were battle ready in a little over two minutes he was long gone. My main reaction was that he ruined my sleep. By the time we secured from GQ it was time to go down to the mess hall for breakfast. At breakfast I learned what really happened. He had dropped a bomb on us that hit close enough to the ship to poke a hole in our hull at the forward fire room, just below where I was sleeping. His bomb almost landed on me. When it exploded, shrapnel from the bomb hit the under side of the port wing of the bridge and ricocheted off to hit the 20mm ammunition box. The radarman was not there. He had been called into CIC, but had left his mattress on the box, which was all torn to hell from the shrapnel hit. Had I kicked him off the box I would have been there and would have been killed. I was happy that he also escaped being killed. This was the second time that my guardian angel had saved me from certain death.

By 18 January our part of the Lingayen operation was over. As near as I can determine it took the lives of 738 sailors, with 1,377 wounded for a total of 2,115 casualties from 2 January to 17 January. During that period fifty-four ships were hit, some more than once, four were sunk, and all survivors were damaged enough to require various degrees of repair before being returned to their squadrons. The closer we came to Japan the more fierce the Japanese resistance and the higher our casualties and losses. These statistics were not lost on the navy high command.

A couple of days later we were ordered to Guadalcanal for rest and minor repairs. On the way to Guadalcanal we put into Leyte Gulf to refuel and load ammunition. As we were standing in to the anchorage I saw the *Barton*. She was moving at our same speed on a parallel course. I was admiring the grace of the ship as she cut through the water, and there near her number two torpedo mount stood my old buddy, Jim Dudly. Jim spotted me at about the same time that I saw him and we waved at each other. He began signaling me that they had just sunk a Jap submarine. I acknowledged his signal, they increased speed and turned away. That was the last time I ever saw Jim. Two years ago I called him at his home in Kansas and we spoke for an hour. He gave me more details concerning the sinking of the Jap submarine.

We spent a few days in Leyte Gulf resting up and collecting our mail. One day I came up to the torpedo shack (our name for the torpedo work shop), and found my buddy Bob Burns asleep on his back on the work bench. At the same time I spotted the monkey sitting on the overhead pipes of the shack. We didn't want him in there because we kept our battle helmets attached upside down by there straps on those pipes, and God knows what he might do, as filthy as he was. I grabbed a wrench and threw it at him as I let out a roar. When it hit him he went "eep," took a giant leap landing on Bob's bare chest, went "eep" again and in one large leap was out the door headed for the fantail. Bob woke up and ran out the door yelling "where are they?" as he was scanning the sky. He thought we were under air attack! There were several guys relaxing near the torpedo shack and every one had a good laugh at Bob's confusion. I personally laughed until my side hurt. I think that one reason Bob reacted like he did was that he was a gunner on the forward starboard 20mm antiaircraft gun, and being half asleep he expected the general alarm to sound, and when it didn't he became confused for a couple of minutes.

Chapter 13

OPERATION ICEBERG
Okinawa Gunte, Nansei Shoto Operation
17 March to 11 June 1945
1 April Landing 1945

W hile in Leyte Gulf we came under air attack when a Jap Betty came over a hill at low altitude and dropped a 500-pound bomb on our sister ship the *Wilson*. The bomb hit the after deckhouse and penetrated into the crew's compartment below deck where it finally came to rest. In the confusion of the attack no one realized they had been hit. The bomb didn't detonate and was discovered by one of their guys from the after damage control party doing his routine compartment inspection. We stood by to give assistance should they need it while they removed the bomb and jettisoned it.

We arrived in Guadalcanal late in January for replenishment and minor repairs. We were only in port a short time when we were ordered to Rabaul. We entered the harbor at Rabaul and dropped the hook at about 1800. Most of the crew was lounging and relaxing topside when a DUKW[1] showed up with army personnel (both soldiers and nurses) aboard. They greeted us with welcoming cheers and many complimentary shouts as they came in close while

---

[1] The DUKW was an amphibious diesel powered vehicle that could carry twenty-five troops or 2½ tons of cargo, function as a boat or land vehicle because of its wheels, and only required one driver. It could haul supplies to an inland land dump without requiring handling at the water's edge.

311

circling the ship. They were apparently impressed with the number of Jap flags, indicating our battle score, that were painted on the wing of our bridge. I think we were the first warship they had ever been close to.

At 1830 a Jap snooper (reconnaissance airplane) showed up to leisurely fly over the whole anchorage. The electricians started to set up the movie screen and projector at about the same time. Someone dubbed the snooper "Sewing Machine Charlie." Each evening at precisely 1830, Sewing Machine Charlie would show up and fly over the anchorage. You could set your watch by him. While we were gathering for the movie we would wait for Sewing Machine Charlie to make his appearance, which he did for several days in a row. One day the admiral ordered him shot down and that ended the entertainment—we later learned why. It was announced on 16 March that Iwo Jima had just been captured by U.S. Marines; however, it wasn't until 26 March that all pockets of resistance had been mopped up in heavy fighting. Iwo Jima in the Bonin Islands was seized to provide emergency airfields for B-29s and to base P-51 fighters for escort of the B-29s in raids on Tokyo. Rabaul was an important base of operations and our command didn't want the Japs to be knowledgeable about our ship movements. We didn't know it then, but we now know that intelligence knew that the Japs figured we would be pushing towards Japan, but they didn't know which islands would be our next objective.

The Japs didn't have long to wait. The next objective was Okinawa, an island of the Ryukyus in the East China Sea about five hundred miles south of Kyushu, the southernmost main island of Japan. About fifteen miles west of Naha (the largest town in southern Okinawa) is a group of ten islands called the Kerama Retto, all part of the Ryukyus. Between the larger and smaller islands of the Kerama Retto (meaning string of islands) are several large roadsteads (passageways of water open on both ends) capable of accommodating many large ships. One of the roadsteads was suitable for sheltered anchorage of seaplanes, their tenders, and a water takeoff and landing area. These roadsteads were twenty fathoms (120-210 ft.) deep and so situated as to accommodate antisubmarine nets. Admiral Turner chose the Kerama Retto as an anchorage for ammunition replenishment, refueling, and repair of the Okinawa invasion fleet. The Kerama Retto, which was lightly defended, was taken on 26 March in preparation for the Okinawa invasion. By 31 March the objectives of the Kerama operation were almost 100% complete and prepared for any Japanese attack. Ships were already being replenished with fuel oil, ammunition, food, and other necessary supplies, and radar installations were operational to detect Jap air and surface activity. The stage was now set for the invasion of the island of Okinawa.

Immediately following the announcement of the capture of Iwo Jima we departed Rabaul for an island where the 1st Marine Division was to conduct an amphibious rehearsal for the invasion of Okinawa. We sailed northwest along the Bismarck Archipelago. It was there that we saw a sight that few of us will ever forget. The setting sun was low on the western horizon with light wisps of clouds in the western sky. The sunset consisted of the most magnificent array of colors I have ever seen in the world. There was red, orange, violet, purple indigo, and other indescribable shades of colors. I was spellbound and couldn't take my eyes off the spectacle until the sun finally sank beneath the horizon and darkness set in. I remember thinking, what a contrast between this gorgeous peaceful scene and this war-torn dangerous area.

The rehearsal took place on an island (which I can't remember) and was realistically done with live ammunition fire support from the destroyers and rocket ships. During a lull in the exercises we were anchored off shore with nothing to do, and I was standing a 1200-1600 watch on the bridge when a DUKW showed up with several marines in it. As at Rabaul they signaled me concerning their approval of an experienced warship supporting them, as indicated by our tally of Jap flags painted on the wing of the bridge. I think that someone remembered the *Sterett* rendering fire support to this embattled division during the battle of Guadalcanal.

Following completion of the invasion rehearsal the division boarded their transport vessels for transport to Okinawa for the big show. We, in company of two other destroyers headed to Ulithi in search of Jap subs. We arrived at Ulithi to find a British carrier attack force together with attached units refueling in preparation for joining with U.S. Navy Fifth Fleet. The British were assigned to Task Force 57, a part of Admiral Spruance's Fifth Fleet, but independent of Task Force 58. To communicate with the United States Navy some terms had to be added to the British general signal book. British signalmen easily adapted to terms such as CAP, Dumbo, Buzz-saw, etc.

The British Pacific Force (TF 113) under the command of Vice Admiral Rawlings RN, consisted of their newest and best equipped ships:

1st Battleship Squadron, HMS *King George V* and HMS *Howe*

1st Carrier Squadron, HMS *Indomitable, Victorious, Illustrious* and *Indefatigable*

4th Cruiser Squadron, HMS *Swiftsure, Black Prince, Argonaut, Euryalus*, HMNZS *Gambia*

Fifteen destroyers

The 1st Carrier Squadron carried over 200 airplanes consisting of U.S. Navy Corsairs, Hellcats, and Avengers; also, British Seafires (the Navy version of the excellent Royal Air Force Spitfire fighter), and the Firefly, a heavy fighter. TF 112, The Royal Navy service squadron consisted of ten oil tankers, five escort carriers for airplane replenishment, and a large number of repair and salvage ships.

TF 57 took up a position about 100 miles south of Miyako Retto, a location east of the Sakishima Gunto, about midway between Formosa (now called Taiwan) and Okinawa, but to the southwest of Naha, Okinawa. Miyako Retto was heavily fortified with many operational airfields, and this position was carefully chosen for the British so that TF 57 could keep the Jap kamikazes off our backs during the first two important days of the Okinawa invasion. The British were in position the evening of 26 March and launched fighter sweeps and bomber attacks the following day on the airfields of Miyako rendering many of them inoperative. The next day the British returned to work over airfields not previously covered the first day—they also went to work attacking Jap coastal shipping. Admiral Rawlings adopted a trick from the U.S. Navy fast carrier procedure book. He positioned cruiser HMS *Argonaut*, which had the latest radar, and destroyer HMS *Wager* thirty miles forward of his task force to function as pickets so that the main task force could prepare a suitable welcome for the impending air attack. Admiral Rawlings had to call off his air strikes for 29-30 March because of a typhoon southward of his area of operation, and his need to refuel—two days later he resumed operations.

Starting in March task forces, task groups, and individual ships were arriving daily at Ulithi from all parts of the South Pacific and departing daily for Okinawa and Kerama Retto in preparation for the pre-bombardment of Operation Iceberg (code name for the Invasion of Okinawa). We were assigned to the Seventh Fleet which included Task Force 54. TF 54 was composed of the older battleship, *Tennessee* (14-inch main battery) as flagship, three *Maryland* class battleships with 15-inch main batteries, two *New Mexico* class battleships with 14-inch main batteries, the *New York* and *Texas* battleships with 14-inch guns, and the oldest battle wagon in the fleet, the *Arkansas* with 12-inch guns. TF 54 had seven heavy cruisers, three light cruisers, twenty-four destroyers and eight destroyer escorts. There was also a group of fifty-three LCIs and LSMs, fire support rocket and mortar ships. These ships along with the destroyers would also participate in the pre-landing bombardment.

During the pre-invasion bombardments and aerial bombings minesweepers were busy sweeping and destroying mines. These ships were always the first ones in and the last ones out. They were pretty much the unsung heroes of every invasion, and the invasion fleet could not afford to attempt a landing in unswept waters. While they were sweeping at five knots they had to defend themselves from attack by air, shore guns, submarines and suicide boats. The destroyers and CAP gave them as much cover as possible, but it wasn't always enough; nevertheless, we did a pretty good job of protecting them to the extent of our limitations.

Prior to the arrival of TF 54, our minesweepers had cleared a channel near Kerama Retto and the nearest island to the east. The cleared channel was marked with radar-reflecting buoys and TF 54 slowly moved northward through the cleared channel on 26-27 March to take up assigned positions for beach bombardment on the west side of Okinawa. Air photographs of Okinawa indicated few defenses of the beaches, yet there were targets to be knocked out with the help of air spot for naval gunfire. At this point in the campaign the Japs controlled all airfields on Okinawa, and we had no army air to fly air cover for us, so we had to depend entirely on our own CAP.

As early as mid March, Vice Admiral Mark Mitscher's fast carrier Task Force 58 was operating about 100 miles east of Okinawa, flying recognizance flights over Okinawa and the Nansei Shoto as far north as Osumi Gunto, just south of Kyushu. Mitscher's Task Force 58 was composed of four Task Groups designated TG 58.1, TG 58.2, TG 58.3, and TG 58.4. While one TG was rearming, the others were operational, striking land targets, Jap Navy surface targets, or covering our surface ships as CAP. TF 58 began launching pre-invasion strikes on Okinawa and other islands of the Nansei Shoto towards the end of March to 1 April. The first Jap blood seems to have been drawn when the destroyer *Haggard* from TG 58.4 sank a Jap submarine on 23 March. On 24 March 112 planes from TG 58.1 sank an entire eight-ship Jap convoy about 150 miles northwest of Okinawa. Also on 24 March in a pre-invasion bombardment battleships *New Jersey, Wisconsin, Missouri* and five destroyers shelled the southeast coast of Okinawa, while *Massachusetts, Indiana* and six destroyers shelled another section of the east side of Okinawa. On 29 March three task groups made bomber strikes on airfields on Kyushu. It was task groups from TF 58 that provided CAP for the invasion ships of the invasion screen.

By 1 April (L-Day for the landings on Okinawa) the Kerama roadstead just west of Okinawa in the Kerama Retto was crowded with service and repair ships, warships of all classifications and sizes, plus a few crippled ships—survivors of kamikaze attack. It was a place where ships could go to refuel and obtain minor repairs, and seaplanes could operate from. The kamikazes didn't bother the roadstead very much; however, there were suicide swimmers and boats that did cause some alarm. One night two Jap suicide swimmers swam out to an LST which was anchored close to the little island of Zamami, climbed aboard her cargo net which had been left trailing, shot and killed the deck sentry, and escaped. I believe it was the same night when another Jap suicide swimmer gained entrance to a destroyer through the hole in her bow and caused some commotion. I don't remember if any sailors were shot in that incident.

The invasion landing procedures had been well honed since the first landings on Guadalcanal back in 1942. Mistakes of each island amphibious landing had been corrected on the way to Okinawa and it was now a really smooth operation. With hundreds of ships carrying troops, supplies, and armor approaching the landing beaches, there had to be a system for keeping ships from colliding while reaching their assigned areas. This was accomplished with the use of color codes for each section of beach.

The northernmost invasion beach on the west side of the island was designated Green 1. The next sections Green 2, Red 1, Red 2, and Red 3, were assigned to the 6th Marine division. The 1st Marine division was on the right flank (south) of the 6th and went in on Blue 1, Blue 2, Yellow 1, Yellow 2, and Yellow 3. The next set of beaches were designated Purple 1, Purple 2, Orange 1, Orange 2, and were assigned to the Army 7th Infantry Division. The southernmost set of beaches, White 1, White 2, White 3, Brown 1, Brown 2, Brown 3, and Brown 4, were assigned to the Army 96th Infantry Division.

Several hundred landing craft of all sizes and types moving in to shore from the transports required a large control group of officers to direct traffic. This was accomplished with five transports (control vessels) anchored about 4,000 yards from shore (line of departure) controlling specific areas of the beach. The transports flew flags that corresponded to the color of the beach they controlled. Guide boats went in with the first waves and set up large colored markers, that could be seen at a great distance, for each landing area. Each guide boat and every landing craft of the first wave had a colored marker painted on them corresponding to the color of the beach where they were supposed to land. Each landing craft could immediately recognize the area where she should be heading. UDTs (Underwater Demolition Teams) had gone in three days previously to blow underwater obstacles. They charted reefs, tides, and water depth for each hour of the day. This provided the information needed to land each type of landing craft as determined by draft of the vessel and known water depth at a given time of day. Therefore, landing craft did not hang up on uncharted reefs as happened at Iwo Jima. Troops, armor, equipment, and all of the supplies necessary for maintaining an army in the field were unloaded systematically without the confusion and mistakes of early amphibious operations. Radar picket destroyers and picket submarines were stationed around the defense perimeter to protect the invasion fleet from submarine and surface vessel torpedo attack.

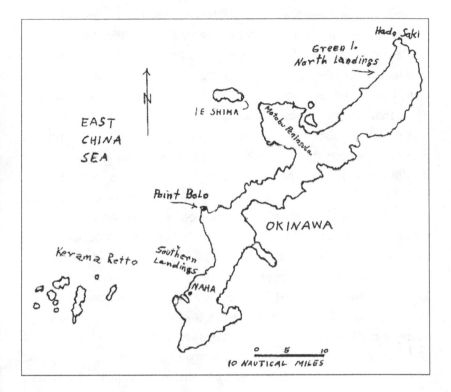

Plate 29: Okinawa Gunto, Kerama Retto, and Ie Shima.
(Drawing by Jerome S. Welna.)

During the night and early dawn the invasion force of 1,213 ships carrying 182,000 assault troops took up positions off the Okinawa coast. The 318 combat ships began their bombardment on 1 April at dawn and fired until 0830 when the troops began to land on the beach. This was the largest combatant fleet ever assembled in the history of naval warfare—it included over forty carriers, eighteen battleships, many cruisers, submarines minesweepers, patrol craft, salvage vessels, and auxiliaries. The armada included more than 148 destroyers and destroyer escorts. We were in position about 3,000 yards off Yellow 1; 1,000 yards inside the line of departure where the 1st Marine division was embarking to their landing area. It was a beautiful Easter Sunday with a clear blue sky and smooth water for the landing craft. The crisp cool air was welcome to me in comparison to the tropics where we had spent so much time. Except for a Jap mortar battery that dropped a few rounds on the beach here and there, our troops were mostly unopposed—the two major airfields (Yontan and Kadena) being captured within the first forty-eight hours of the initial landing. Kamikaze attacks were minimal the first day with only four ships being hit. An LST was severely damaged enough to put her out of the war for good while suffering twenty-four killed and twenty-one wounded. Three other transport ships were hit and suffered a total of thirty-two killed and sixty-six wounded.

Even though there was no significant defense of the beaches, we knew that when the troops moved in far enough to be out of support range of navy guns, there would be stiff resistance from the Jap defenders. What no one knew was the true nature of the Jap fortifications in the hills of southern Okinawa that stretched from a position in the hills east of the Hagushi beaches to Naha. With ancient Shuri Castle as its anchor, these fortifications consisted of deep tunnels and limestone caves with steel reinforced concrete—a fortress almost invulnerable to air bombardment and naval barrage. Nevertheless, our admirals and generals knew that the island was a

Japanese Gibraltar, and that resistance would continue to the last Jap soldier. Intelligence had advised us that the Japs had moved 2,000 kamikazes into the area prior to 1 April. This meant that the navy would catch hell in about three or four days.

To prepare for the onslaught of the kamikazes, Admiral Turner established sixteen R.P. stations (radar picket stations) encircling Okinawa. They were numbered 1 to 16 clockwise from bearing 007T north of Point "BOLO" which was the station center. The pickets of the outer screen were stationed from forty to seventy miles from the transport area and were in the direct approach of Jap aircraft from Japan, China, and Formosa. Close radar pickets were stationed twenty to twenty-five miles from the transport area in the inner screen and were engaged in detecting, tracking, and reporting on aircraft in the vicinity of the transport area.

The purpose of the outer radar pickets was to provide early warning of enemy aircraft, surface and undersea craft, and to function in fighter direction. Certain destroyers were designated as FD (fighter director) destroyers and had special equipment and teams for communicating with the CAP. These FD destroyers controlled the units of the CAP that were assigned to them by the central fighter director unit located in the *Yosemite* (the headquarters command ship). FD destroyers could then vector CAP on to the tails of oncoming aircraft.

I remember one case where the FD put a CAP behind an incoming kamikaze and the fighter pilot said, "I don't see him." Several seconds later FD gave him a slight correction in elevation, and then received a confirmation from the pilot of "splash one."

Each FD destroyer was assigned two LCS ships (landing craft support). The LCS ships were stationed in close proximity to the FD destroyers to enhance the detection of low-flying aircraft or surface units. We called the LCS ships the Pallbearers because one of their major functions was to pick up survivors from destroyers that had been hit.

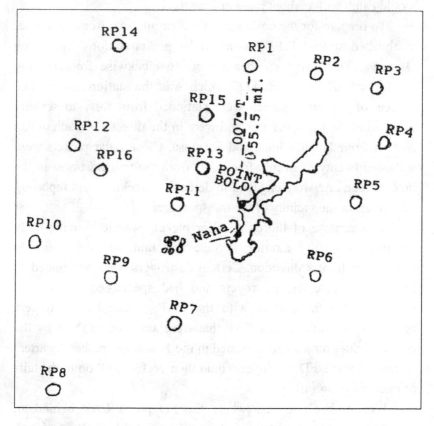

Plate 30: The approximate locations of radar picket destroyers at Okinawa, April 1945. (Drawing by Jerome S. Welna.)

The second day (L plus one), kamikazes hit four ships within the inner invasion screen and sank one of them—the *Dickerson*. No destroyers or destroyer escorts were hit this day. The kamikazes were involved in attacking ships that were unloading cargo. This day kamikazes killed 132 sailors and wounded another 398 for a total of 440 casualties. The following day April 3 (L plus 2) kamikaze attacks picked up a little by hitting five ships, the carrier *Wake Island*, destroyers *Prichett* and *Foreman*, and two landing craft. *Wake Island* and *Prichett* were lucky in that they had no killed and no wounded. *Foreman* had no killed and three wounded. LST *599* had twenty-one wounded and LCT *876* had two wounded.

By this time we were on radar picket duty off the island of Ie Shima guarding the narrow passage between the island and the Motobu Peninsula of Okinawa. The Japs had an airfield on Ie Shima which had not yet been secured. Our job was to prevent Jap reinforcements from entering the landing area by sea or air. The next two days were quiet without many kamikazes able to penetrate the CAP protective screen; however, on 4 April an LCI(G) (gunboat) operating in the landing area was attacked by a suicide boat and suffered eight men killed and eleven wounded. The following day, 5 April, the *Nevada* took five hits from a Jap six- or 8-inch coastal battery near Naha that killed two men while wounding sixteen. Nevertheless, this tough old survivor of the attack on Pearl Harbor never stopped firing in the duel until the offending Jap battery was silenced.

The Japanese high command was predictable. Once they devised a strategy they never seemed to vary from it and Okinawa was typical. The rule of thumb for expecting a Jap counterattack was L-Day plus four, but because of bad flying weather that grounded the kamikazes, it developed that it was L-Day plus five. Therefore, on 6 April the awaited counterattack took place when several hundred kamikazes descended on the navy. This was the beginning of the sea-air naval battle that was fought mostly by destroyers and destroyer escorts, and quickly earned the title of the most ferocious air-sea battle in the history of naval warfare.

I was standing a watch on the bridge when it all started early in the morning of 6 April 1945. The destroyer *Bush* at RP #1 about fifty-two miles north of Okinawa was attacked by four kamikazes. The *Bush* shot one down and the CAP probably got the other three. The *Bush* was fighting for her life and repulsing one raid after another. Meanwhile reports were coming in over the MAN radio of simultaneous attacks on other destroyers. There were so many attacks being reported that we started keeping a tally of ships under attack, and it didn't take long to realize that we had a huge problem to deal with. We were soon ordered to relieve a destroyer that was hit, only to be ordered to move to another picket station to relieve another damaged destroyer. The destroyer that relieved us was then hit—this game of musical chairs went on all day with us escaping harm until dark when the attacks finally ceased. My guardian angel and lady luck were protecting our ship.

All day the sky was alive with burning kamikazes. They would gang up on a destroyer and even if the ship would shoot pieces off their airplanes, kill the pilot, and set their airplane on fire, the sheer numbers of kamikazes would almost guarantee a hit because the gunners could only fire on one target at a time. When they hit one airplane they would have to shift fire to the second one, than the third, and so on until the last one was on them. The speed of the airplane, and the trajectory, would act as a missile and carry him into the target vessel. The explosion of his fuel and bomb on impact would do tremendous damage to the ship, and would almost always cause mortality and serious wounds among the surviving crew. The CAP pilots were wonderful. They would dive through our flack to kill a kamikaze while completely disregarding their own safety. They killed more kamikazes than the destroyers, but considering the numbers we were dealing with, hits on the destroyers were inevitable.

The *Bush*, which had been repulsing attacks and knocking kamikazes down all day long, was hit by a lone suicider late in the afternoon. The Jap lost pieces of his airplane as he ran into a wall of 5-inch fire, but he nevertheless slammed into the *Bush* at the water line of the starboard engine room. The explosion of his bomb and fuel blew a two-ton engine room blower almost seventy feet in the air with such force that it knocked the SG radar antenna off the mainmast—the blower then landed on the port wing of the bridge. The *Bush* was on fire from the flaming gasoline and the destroyer *Colhoun* came in from a nearby picket station to offer assistance.

While the *Colhoun* was aiding the *Bush*, all fires were extinguished and watertight integrity was maintained so that the *Bush* could be saved; however, a flight of fifteen bogies suddenly came in and started piling into both ships. By about 1830 both vessels broke up and sank. There were suicide planes coming at the destroyers from all directions. There was fire everywhere—on shore, air, and on the sea. The onslaught was so sudden and heavy that radiomen on the ships couldn't keep up with all of the communications from ships and our CAP. To expedite vectoring the CAP to a kamikaze, the destroyers would fire one round at the Jap to draw the attention of the Hellcats and Corsairs of the CAP. One of the CAP lurking at higher altitude would then pounce on the Jap and shoot him down. There were so many targets in the air, so many Japs on fire, and so many ships pouring 5-inch, 40-, and 20mm ammunition into the air against Jap aircraft that the sky was dark with smoke from exploding AA ammunition and Jap planes burning. And still they kept coming! These were Japs eager to give their lives to kill Americans, and we were all fighting to save our lives and our ships. Japanese records released after the war stated that over 700 kamikazes were deployed on 6 April in an attempt to destroy the American fleet. U.S. Navy records indicate seventeen ships were crashed by kamikazes this day—fourteen were destroyers, destroyer minesweepers, destroyer escorts, and three were ammunition supply ships, one of which was an LST. By day's end 367 sailors had lost their lives, and 490 were wounded, some of them mortally, for a total of 857 casualties.

At dusk our CAP retired to their carriers so that they could land before dark, refuel, re-arm, and get prepared for the next day. We remained at our battle stations well after dark because there were still a few kamikazes roaming around, and they only had enough fuel for a one-way trip. We weren't bothered but some of the other destroyers were and had to shoot them down. Land-based army air was still unavailable because captured airfields were still not operational. We were waiting impatiently for the appearance of the specially equipped army night fighter aircraft; however, it would be several days before we could enjoy the pleasure of their company.

The following day, 7 April we were notified of a new Jap secret suicide weapon called Oka (a Japanese word for cherry blossom). The Oka was a rocket propelled human bomb consisting of a torpedo-like warhead containing 1,135 pounds of high explosive. (That was almost twice the amount of explosive in our torpedoes). The Oka (or Baka as we called it—Japanese word for idiot) was piloted by one man bent on a suicide mission. The Baka weighed in at 4,700 pounds and had a top speed of about 600 m.p.h. It was small and so fast that it was almost impossible to shoot down; however, it had to be transported under the belly of a Betty because it had a very short range and little flight time in the air. It was therefore vulnerable because the Betty and its fighter escort were slow and not very maneuverable due to the weight. This made it easy for our Hellcats to shoot down the escorts and Bettys carrying their Bakas. It was also easy for our destroyers with 5-inch guns to blow them up in the air before the Baka had a chance to disengage from the Betty. If, however, the Baka detached from the Betty and headed for a ship it was almost impossible to shoot it down. If the Baka hit a destroyer it would cut it in two and the ship would be gone in just minutes.

We were on picket duty in the outer screen west of the transport area where ships were still coming and going unloading supplies when twenty planes attacked the area—twelve were shot down by ships and the CAP. A kamikaze hit the battleship *Maryland* killing sixteen men and wounding thirty-seven. The destroyer escort *Wesson* was at a screening station between RP #1 and Ie Shima when one of the attacking planes peeled off and hit her while she was firing on three others. Her engineering spaces were badly damaged but she still managed to reach Kerama Retto on one shaft. She suffered eight killed and twenty-three wounded.

It was nearly dusk when we finally came under direct attack by two kamikazes. They suddenly dropped out of the clouds, and they appeared to be heading across our bow when they suddenly made a quick left turn and approached at a target angle of thirty degrees, elevation forty degrees, and were headed directly for our bridge. Our director must have had them on radar because our main battery immediately opened fire on them. The first plane was hit in the nose by one of our 5-inch shells and exploded into a million pieces and a huge ball of fire as he fell into the ocean. Our director then shifted fire to the remaining plane that was getting very close and strafing as he came in. Our 40's and 20's had opened fire indicating that he was getting very close. Our forward starboard 20mm gunner (my close buddy Bob Burns) shot the left wing off the airplane but he still kept coming in on a crash course. When I thought he was about to hit us, one of our 5-inch shells hit him in the nose and he blew up as did the first one. The explosion occurred almost over the ship and pieces of the airplane and pilot rained down around the ship and on us. When it was all over and we secured from general quarters, the seamen had to break out their brooms and sweep all of this stuff over the side.

While we were fighting off our two Jap attackers, the destroyer *Bennett* was hit in her engineering spaces by one kamikaze that caused severe damage including three dead and eighteen wounded.

We escorted her to Kerama Retto. She was able to go under her own power in spite of her extensive damage. Kerama Retto had fast become a graveyard for damaged ships—mostly destroyers.

We didn't know it at the time, but while we were fighting for our lives in repelling kamikaze attacks 6 April, the Japanese were executing a plan to wipe out our transport invasion fleet on the west shore of Okinawa. Their remaining super Battleship *Yamato* had left Tokuyama at 1520 6 April and sortied from the Inland Sea by Bungo Suido. At 1745, 6 April the submarine USS *Thredfin* patrolling off of Bungo Suido sighted and reported a large battleship and six smaller vessels traveling at twenty-five knots on a southwesterly course. At about 2000 the submarine USS *Hackleback* reported a battleship, a smaller ship, and eight destroyers still pursuing a southwestern course. These reports were immediately received by Vice Admiral Mark Mitscher of Task Force 58 who realized that this had to be the *Yamato*. Vice Admiral Mitscher dispatched patrol planes to locate the exact position of *Yamato* and keep her in sight until bombers and torpedo planes could be vectored to her for attack.

While Task Force patrol planes were looking for *Yamato*, she had turned west passing through Van Diemen Strait, cleared Sata Misaki, the southernmost point of Kyushu, changed course to about WNW, and sailed north of the lighthouse on Kusakaki Shima. The battle plan was to circle around as far from TF 58 as possible, by turning southwest into the East China Sea, and then southeast to a position about eighteen miles from where the transports could be attacked the evening of 7 April.

Admiral Mitscher had anticipated this and was determined that *Yamato* would not get very far. He prepared for a blocking action by ordering all four of his task groups to launching positions northeast of Okinawa. TG 58.1, 58.3, and 58.4, all were able to join TF 58 for the attack. Much to their chagrin, TG 58.2 was unable to participate because fueling was not completed. Searches were flown by TG

58.1, and 58.3 at daybreak of 7 April, but strike planes did not lift off the decks of the carriers until the exact position of the *Yamato* was verified.

The keel for *Yamato* was laid down in 1937 and she was completed in December of 1941. She was the largest, most powerful battleship in existence. She displaced 72,809 tons fully loaded and her main battery consisted of nine 460mm (18.1-inch) guns. These guns shot a projectile weighing 3,200 pounds 22.5 miles. By comparison, our new fast battleships carried nine 16-inch guns that fired a projectile about twenty-one miles weighing 2,700 pounds. *Yamato* had a cruising speed of twenty-five knots, but she could attain a maximum speed of 27.5 knots. Our new fast battleships were faster—they could attain a maximum speed in excess of thirty knots. On paper the *Yamato* was superior to anything we had in our navy. This may have been a false illusion to the Japanese because, as demonstrated in previous battles, our ships were faster and more maneuverable, and our crews were much better trained.

At 0823 a search plane from the USS *Esssex* located *Yamato* and her task group southwest of Koshiki Retto. The pilot reported her on a course of 300 degrees, speed twelve knots—she was undoubtedly traveling faster than that. Admiral Deyo was advised of this information so that he could prepare an intercepting plan of action. Admiral Deyo and his staff immediately drew up a battle plan labeled TF 54 consisting of six battleships, seven cruisers, and twenty-two destroyers. The object of the plan was to keep the Japanese away from the transports by keeping his ships between Okinawa and the *Yamato* task force.

Two navy PBY flying boats operating out of Kerama Retto located *Yamato*, light cruiser *Yahagi*, and eight destroyers about 1015 in the morning. The *Yamato* task force was just starting to turn south and began firing on the two patrol planes, but never came close to hitting them. The two patrol aircraft stalked *Yamato* for five hours, much to the chagrin of Japanese Admiral Ito. His gunners were not well trained and couldn't shoot them down and he couldn't evade them. He had to realize that devastating air strikes were about to begin.

When the *Yamato* task group turned south and set a course for Okinawa we were alerted because this force was headed for us on the outer picket line. We all knew that there was one hell of a battle shaping up if air strikes from Task Force 58 couldn't stop *Yamato*. At exactly 1241 the first two air strikes from the carrier USS *Bennington* hit the task force with bombers, and torpedo planes— *Yamato* received several bomb hits and a torpedo hit. At the same time torpedoes from Avengers of the carrier USS *San Jacinto* sank the destroyer *Hamakaze* with a bomb and torpedo hit. The cruiser *Yahagi* was hit in the forward engine room with a bomb and torpedo that wiped out the engineering crew and caused her to go dead in the water. For two hours and fifty-four minutes *Yahagi* was punished with twelve bomb and seven torpedo hits before she sank at 1406. *Yamato* lasted a little longer, she absorbed many bombs and at least 10 torpedo hits for three hours and two minutes before she finally sank at 1423.

When the battle was finally over, twenty-three officers and 246 men survived from *Yamato's* crew of 2,767 officers and men. Light cruiser *Yahagi* lost 446 men and officers, and destroyer *Asashimo* lost 330. Three of five destroyers were sunk and lost 330 killed and 209 wounded. Four additional destroyers were badly damaged and managed to slip away to Sasebo with heavy loss of their crews. Our losses were ten airplanes and twelve men. Naval historians to this day have never understood why Admiral Ozawa sent the *Yamato* task force out with no air cover. Once again this battle proved the battleship to be outmoded by air power.

Later in the afternoon we picked up a downed Hellcat pilot who had taken part in the battle to sink the *Yamato*. He was a young flight officer who had been shot down twice before. The third time he went down his airplane had been damaged by antiaircraft fire from the *Yamato* and he was forced to ditch. We also sent our whaleboat out to frisk a dead kamikaze pilot. Naval intelligence always wanted whatever information we might retrieve from dead Jap pilots. This pilot was carrying a scroll of cream colored silk that had Japanese writing on it. We had no idea what it meant—it was up to intelligence to figure it out.

During the height of the action a daring rescue was made to recover a downed pilot from carrier *Belleau Wood.* His Avenger had made bomb hits on *Yamato* from so low an altitude that the explosion set him afire and all three had to bail out. The two crewmen had parachute trouble and drowned, but the pilot managed to get into his rubber raft, from which he witnessed the death throes of *Yamato.* There he was spotted by two PBM pilots who had been following the battle in their PBMs. While one PBM pilot acted as decoy to attract enemy gunfire, the second one made a neat water landing, taxied toward the pilot, whose raft was in the midst of floating Japanese survivors, took him on board, made a jet-assisted takeoff, and subsequently landed him safe and sound at Yontan airfield.

About two hours later another PBM located Japanese survivors, made a water landing and took some prisoners. There were other prisoners taken that day and a few of them yielded some profitable information. In one case the prisoner confirmed the mass kamikaze attack on TF 58 that was planned for 11 April, which had already been mentioned by a prisoner taken 6 April. Admiral Mitscher took this boasting seriously and took proper action to thwart the attack— the boasting turned out to be correct.

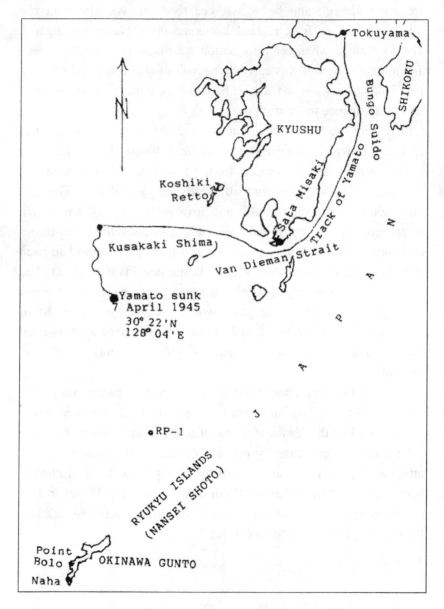

Plate 31: Sinking of *Yamato*, April 1945.
Map shows the course of *Yamato* after embarking from Tokuyama on
6 April 1945. (Drawing by Jerome S. Welna. Not to scale.)

While the battle to sink the *Yamato* task force was raging, the kamikaze raids continued and we were not wanting for targets to fire on. April 8 was an interesting day when a suicider came in on us in the late afternoon. He approached on our starboard side for his suicide dive. A Hellcat was on his tail pumping 55mm slugs into him. The air was heavy with a low cloud cover that made it easy for us to see the Hellcat's tracers going into him. He was on a collision course with us and even though we were making twenty-five knots we couldn't evade him. We requested permission to fire at him but the Hellcat pilot wouldn't give it. Just when he seemed certain to hit us the Hellcat pilot made a desperate, dangerous move. Apparently he had determined that the Jap was dead at the controls, so he pulled up on the port side of the Jap so that his starboard wing was under the port wing of the Jap, banked his airplane to port and flipped the Jap over. The Jap made a harmless nose-dive into the water and blew up not far from the ship. That was a real close call and we all breathed easier after that one! This was just one reason why all navy personnel loved our CAP pilots.

The day wasn't over. After our CAP retired just before dusk a lone kamikaze dropped out of the clouds and headed for our starboard quarter. We were at GQ and I was assigned to the after battle damage control party. Our ship was making a hard right turn at twenty-five knots or better in an effort to evade this Jap. I was kneeling down near the torpedo shack watching this guy and trying to figure out where he might hit so that I could get out of there. I finally decided that he would hit right where I was—I could see our 40s and 20s tearing into him, and he was on fire, but he just kept coming. I had just about decided to run forward to escape his possible point of impact when I saw Shorty Lynn crouched down by the door to the machine shop at the quarterdeck on the port side. He was frantically waving at me to make a run for it and join him. He figured he was in a safer place than I was. Shorty was also part of the after damage control party, and like me, he had nothing to do but stay safe until we got hit. In a split second the kamikaze was almost on us and I began running to join Shorty. I had only run a few feet when the Jap hit the water just a few feet from the ship and exploded with a big bang. The force of the explosion blew me thirty-five feet across the quarterdeck, between the torpedo mounts, in a wall of flame to Shorty's location where I crashed into the port rail. I picked myself up and discovered that I wasn't hurt as I said something stupid to the effect that that was a hell of a ride. I guess that my guardian angel was once again looking out for me; however, I was properly dressed for the occasion. In addition to my tin hat I was wearing my kapok life jacket, a long sleeve shirt, earplugs, and protective sunglasses. I was untouched by the fiery blast that blew me through the air and burned all of the paint off the side of the ship from the quarterdeck aft to the stern.

That was the last aerial action of the day. It must have been an hour or so later that I was walking forward when I met the chief corpsman walking towards me. He looked at me for a second, his mouth dropped in astonishment, and his eyes got big. He said "Jerry, I heard that you were blown overboard in the explosion and I have you on the MIA list." I said something to the effect that rumors of my demise were somewhat exaggerated.

That evening we were ordered to RP-1. There were two new seamen in my sleeping compartment from Colorado. These men were inductees and older than the usual new crop of seamen replacements. They were not happy about being in the navy, or assigned to destroyer duty, but they did their jobs as ammunition handlers. When I entered the compartment they met me with a pessimistic comment; one of them said, "by this time tomorrow evening we'll all be dead." Their attitude was backed by the fact that no destroyer had ever lasted more than two days at RP-1 without being sunk or severely damaged. I don't remember how I answered him, but I do know it was cheerful and optimistic.

The morning of 9 April was routine as usual with a call to general quarters and gun drills a half-hour before dawn. The CAP arrived on time after daylight and the routine condition watch was set. In the afternoon emergency drills were conducted and closely observed by the captain to satisfy himself that general procedures were done efficiently including speed, thoroughness, and every detail including battle dress. I can state unequivocally that constant drilling was one of the great secrets to our navy's success—it carried me through many close calls.

In the late afternoon the CAP had to leave and return to their carriers before dark. As usual we went to general quarters about thirty to forty minutes before sunset—this day the time was 1850 and sunset occurred at 1930. About five minutes following the departure of the CAP our CIC reported a large formation of bogies about forty miles distant coming in from the northwest. The captain immediately ordered flank speed—twenty-five knots, and then announced the following over the ship's loudspeaker system:

> *Attention—this is the captain speaking—we have Jap planes en route heading directly for us—if you characters ever want to sleep with a blond again, you had better shoot down these bastards as soon as they come up.*

Our guys in the engine room got our speed up real fast and the captain maneuvered the ship to bring all guns to bear on the incoming targets. The gun boss (gunnery officer) received orders to open fire as soon as the targets were within range.

The weather was clear with good visibility. Our gun director locked on to the formation of twenty-five Jap Vals. As they approached closer five of the Vals peeled off and started straight towards us. Before closing within gun range the first Val (of the five) peeled off and circled around several miles behind us. Lieutenant J. G. Roy Cowdrey was a superb gunnery officer in the main battery gun director. Roy blew the second Val out of the sky with 5-inch fire when it was still four miles away. Roy then shifted fire to the third Val and also blew it away with 5-inch fire. When it hit the water the odds were now cut in half. The two remaining Vals were heading directly for the bridge and they were strafing the 40- and 20mm gun crews and other exposed personnel as they approached. By now the fourth and fifth Vals were close in and were receiving fire from our 40s and 20s. Below the starboard wing of the bridge on the 01 level Steward's Mate James Bailey and his gun crew ignored machine gun bullets hitting all around them, to shoot a wing off of the third Val. It exploded in the water less than fifty yards off the starboard beam. One wheel of the Val hit the forecastle and wedged under the starboard anchor chain. I watched as the force of the explosion catapulted the dead pilot over our stack, still strapped in his chair, turning end over end. He hit the water no more than five yards from the port beam, broke from his chair, and his parachute (which was still strapped to him) opened up and blossomed out. What was a suicide pilot doing with a parachute?

The fourth Val was now close in and headed for the bridge. They liked to crash the bridge if possible because it was the most likely place to score critical hits that would paralyze ship handling. If the attacking plane lost altitude from a hit it could still do a lot of damage by hitting vital engineering spaces at the water line. This Val, (the fourth) was hit and on fire from our gun fire, yet its speed carried it to the water line where it exploded into the starboard wing of the mess hall below the bridge. It blew a ten foot wide hole in the hull at the water line, tore up the deck plates exposing the fuel bunkers below, and wrecked the diesel generator which was located in a compartment within the "U" of the mess hall, thus putting it out of commission. It also blew out part of the cofferdam (bulkhead) between the forward fire room and the starboard wing of the mess hall. For a brief time the exposed fuel tanks were on fire, but the rush of seawater into the ship quickly helped the forward damage control party extinguished it.

The hit severed all electrical cables on the starboard side of the ship and also cut off all power on the port side of the ship. With all of the circuits out it was impossible to reset the breakers. The Chief Engineer Leonard Woods finally restored power with the emergency jump system. He and the guys in engineering were also able to trim the ship with ballast.

As I remember it we were dead in the water for over one hour without power for our guns, radar, and other vital needs. During this time we were a sitting duck for any Jap kamikaze that came along, and that is exactly what happened. The number one Val that had circled the ship to the rear of us at the start of the attack a few moments earlier showed up again. I had gone back to the number four 5-inch gun mount to see how the boys were getting along. The number three and four 5-inch gun mounts had no blast shields, and their gun crews were completely exposed. I looked up and sure enough, this Jap was back and setting up for another hit on us. The gun captain spotted him at the same time as I did, and quipped, *"here comes our mail boys."* He was referring to the fact that we hadn't received mail for over two weeks. The pointer and trainer already had a bead on the Jap which they had to do by hand since they had no power. They had one chance, and only one, to get a round off in time to get him before he got us. They fired one round and knocked him down; however, after he was hit his glide path took him down on the LCI that had caught up behind us. He clipped the mainmast of the LCI and fell on her bow where a 40mm gun was located, killing the entire gun crew. There are different accounts of what happened concerning this attack; however, this is what I saw.

Fortunately our communications were still intact and our captain was able to get action and damage reports off immediately. A relief destroyer was ordered out to assist us if necessary, and relieve us of our picket duties. We were ordered back to Kerama Retto for emergency repairs of battle damage. For a while it looked as if we would have to be towed back to Kerama Retto; however, we did manage to make it on our own power.

Dusk was rapidly changing to darkness and I went up to the quarterdeck where the 20mm gunners were sweeping up pieces of Jap aircraft. I picked up a piece that had Japanese printing on it— I've had it in my possession all these years. From there I went up to the starboard hatch of the mess hall to see if the guys on forward damage control needed any help. They were just bringing Bill Friest out of the mess hall in a stretcher. He was covered with oil and had a dazed look on his face. He was lucky to be alive—he had been sitting down behind the diesel engine when the Jap hit. He was sheltered by the diesel engine from the main thrust of the explosion, but was suffering from shock and concussion. The forward damage control party seemed to have everything under control so I continued on and the next guy I ran into was a buddy that I played chess with in off-hours. He was on forward damage control and checking watertight doors, one of which he was passing through from the mess hall to the forward seaman's compartment when the Jap hit. He was blown into the seaman's compartment from the explosion and was also lucky to be alive. He carried concussion lesions on his back for several weeks. He also carried two 25 caliber machine gun slugs in his kapok life jacket that saved his life during one of the Jap strafing attacks. As for me, I was also lucky. I acquired a bruise in my left leg that turned out to be an imbedded tiny piece of shrapnel that I carried for over twenty years before it worked its way to the surface. I also wound up with a sprained wrist. I have no idea of how either one of these minor injuries happened.

It was amazing that no one was killed, and only nine men had minor wounds. No Purple Hearts were awarded—I always thought that Friest should have received one, but even he was classified a minor wound.

Darkness finally set in and it was about that time when the electricians restored some of our power. We secured from general quarters and most of us in the torpedo gang gathered in the torpedo shack. I crawled up on the workbench and went to sleep. I guess I had the hell scared out of me and I was exhausted. I remember the special sea detail being set for a tow to Kerama Retto, but I don't remember anything else until morning when I discovered that we were in Kerama Retto, mooring to a repair ship, and had gotten there under our own power. That was no small accomplishment, considering the extent of our damages.

We received a warning from command that the Japs on the island were attempting to harass damaged ships by sending out swimming suicide bombers to create havoc among the crew by boarding ships and killing crew members. We therefore set sentries armed with Thompson submachine guns at strategic locations to sound the alarm and repulse them if necessary. We were lucky because no suicide swimmers appeared.

A few days after arriving in Kerama Retto it was Sunday and church services were held on the repair ship we were moored to. Even sailors who professed to be atheists attended. I don't remember being at the service more than fifteen or twenty minutes when the general alarm went off and everyone made a break for their battle stations. There was some firing at the south end of the roadstead, but no planes appeared where we were. That was the last action for us in the war.

There were destroyers with damages of every kind imaginable. There was one destroyer anchored about 800 yards from us. It was all by itself, not near a repair vessel, and for good reason. The ship had completely lost all topside structures from forecastle to stern. It appeared as if someone had knocked the entire superstructure off it and had then taken a giant can opener and opened up the main deck from forecastle to the stern. To put it another way, all that was left was a hull. It took several days for us to learn the identity of the ship, which turned out to be of the *Fletcher* class. I can't remember the name of it, and I presume that it wasn't worth repairing. We couldn't find out how many of the crew were killed and wounded. I don't remember any one of authority wanting to talk about it. In the days that we were at Kerama Retto I only saw one man on that ship and I couldn't tell if he was a crew member or from a repair ship.

One day a *Sumner* class destroyer moored to the other side of the repair ship we were moored to. I was known to have served on a *Sumner* class destroyer and our torpedo officer asked me if I would go aboard and offer assistance if needed. They were not in need of my services and were busy gathering up their dead for transfer to a burial party. Their CIC had been hit and it was a real mess. Since I was of no help to them I returned to the *Sterett* in a somber mood.

The first day of our arrival repairmen came aboard to remove the engine of the Jap airplane and the pilot's body from the mess hall. Engineers from one of the repair ships came aboard to assess the damage and decide just what to do with the ship. Depending on the amount and kind of damage, they had to determine whether we should be repaired at Kerama Retto, Pearl Harbor, or the states—we were all hoping for a yard in the states. An engineering officer appeared one day looking for our captain and chief engineer, and announced that they would be coming aboard with many tons of steel plate. Our engineers now had to shift ballast so that the ship would list to port far enough (several degrees) so that the steel plating could be attached below the water line. I forget how much the ship had to be rolled over to port, but it required quite a few degrees to roll it enough to expose the ten-foot hole beneath the water line. I had a bunk along the port hull, and while the ship had a port list I was sleeping partially against the hull.

Plate 32: USS *Sterett* DD 407 showing kamikaze damage to ship's starboard side received off Okinawa 9 April 1945. (Official Navy photograph taken at Kerama Rettc, Ryuku Islands, 11 April 1945.)

The port list also made eating in the mess hall interesting. If you could find a table that hadn't been damaged or destroyed, food and coffee wanted to slide off the table. I built a shim that I could put under my tray to even things up. The engineers and repairmen finally got the steel patch attached and then they finished shoring it up with lumber on the inside and righted the ship. We still had a slight inconvenience—we had to climb over two-by-four shoring to get to our tables to sit down. I don't believe anyone complained; after all, we were all still alive and in one piece with only nine men (including me) slightly wounded!

Friday 13 April was a dark day for the navy. At first light over Kerama Retto the loudspeakers of all ships blared that President Roosevelt was dead. This news hit the navy very hard because Roosevelt was considered the best friend the navy ever had—the news was truly demoralizing. The reaction to the news was apparent in all of our crew from officers to seamen—it just didn't seem the same now that he was gone. By order of the Secretary of the Navy every ship and duty station that had a chaplain held services for him on 15 April 1945. The form of the service was left to the chaplains and commanding officers of ships that had no chaplains.

For us the fight for Okinawa was over, but for the surviving battle groups of the navy the fight would continue for another eight weeks until 21 June. During that period they would continue fighting not only the kamikazes, but the strain of remaining at their battle stations for days and sometime nights to be ready to respond at a moment's notice to the sacrificial pilots bent on death. During the fight for Okinawa sleep became a luxury of the past—sailors went days and nights with very little rest. The battle of Okinawa would, in the end, be the most costly battle in the history of naval warfare. According to official navy records, the United States Navy lost thirty-four ships sunk, 386 ships damaged enough to be out of action for the remainder of the war, almost 5,000 sailors killed or missing in action, and almost 5,000 wounded. At the time it seemed to us that the battle for Okinawa would never end. The problem for the navy was that the Japs had plenty of airplanes, and even though they didn't have enough trained fighter pilots to fly against us, they did have plenty of young men willing to kill themselves by flying into our ships. And, if ten suiciders flew against a ship, and nine were shot down, the one that hit could usually kill several men, wound many others, do a lot of damage and possibly sink the ship.

The destroyers on the radar picket stations absorbed the brunt of the Jap attack.

Commodore Moosbrugger wrote:

> *The performance of the personnel of the screening and radar picket ships, both individually and collectively, was superb throughout the Okinawa campaign. Acts of heroism and unselfishness, fighting spirit, coolness under fire, unswerving determination, endurance, and qualities of leadership and loyalty exceeded all previous conceptions of standards set for the U.S. Navy. Never in the annals of our glorious naval history have naval forces done so much with so little against such odds for so long a period. Radar picket duty in this operation might well be a symbol of supreme achievement in our naval traditions. The radar picket station groups took every blow that the Japs could inflict and absorbed terrific punishment in personnel casualties and material damage, but the mission was successfully completed.[2]*

---

[2] CTG 51.5, Action Report, 20 July 1945, Captain Frederick Moosbrugger, Commander, Radar Picket Destroyers. An abstract of his Action Report was sent to all destroyers, posted on our quarterdeck, and quoted in the ship's newspaper.

Chapter 14

UNCONDITIONAL SURRENDER

Japan Surrenders, 2 September 1945

A few days later we received orders to proceed to Pearl Harbor for further assessment of our needed repairs. Our course took us to Guam—on the way we rendezvoused at sea with another destroyer operating at a radar picket station on the southeast side of Okinawa and transferred all but one firing run of our 5-inch ammunition—they would need it! I'm not certain of the name of the ship, but I do remember that it was a *Benson* class destroyer. I also remember their young officer who supervised their competent crew in the handling of the ammunition. I think we accomplished the transfer in less than two hours.

We were midway between Okinawa and Guam and I was on watch on the bridge. The time was about 1400 when I heard a dim roar that became louder and louder as the seconds passed. Since our hit at Okinawa, the "JU" telephone circuit that I manned was also tied in with the fire rooms and engineering spaces. Someone from the forward fire room called me for information concerning the droning noise that could be clearly heard in all of the fire rooms and engineering spaces. Our crew was understandably on edge following our experiences at Okinawa. Someone in CIC cut in on the conversation and identified the noise as coming from a flight of B-29 bombers on their way to bomb Japan. We were having some further conversation concerning the situation when the officer in charge of CIC cut in and laced me up one side and down the other for engaging in conversation. He was incorrect because protocol had long since been abandoned—he treated me as if I was an apprentice seaman who had just come aboard ship. He told me that I was to speak only when addressed by an officer, that I was to make no comments about anything whatsoever, that I was not to contact CIC on my own—if CIC wanted to talk to me they would contact me. His arrogant attitude really ruffled my feathers because during our days of combat at Okinawa, the captain had issued orders that members of the deck crew were to disregard protocol and report any visual sea or aerial contacts immediately to CIC and the bridge—we were still in a condition red zone (war zone) and the order was still in force.

A couple of days later I was standing my usual 1200 to 1600 watch on the bridge and the same officer was in CIC. We were approaching Guam and the captain was on the bridge sitting in his chair on the starboard side. There were several friendly aircraft in the air. Normally it was unwritten protocol that I notify CIC that the captain was on the bridge—this day I didn't because of that smart S.O.B. in CIC. I was standing at the captain's side as he watched all of the aircraft in the sky while intermittently glancing at me. I knew exactly what he was thinking, but said nothing. Finally, he could restrain himself no longer and he asked, "Mr. Welna, is CIC reporting those aircraft?" I answered, "No sir." He then said "Ask CIC why they aren't reporting those aircraft." Instead of prefacing my question with "The captain wishes to know," I asked CIC, "Why aren't you reporting those aircraft?" The ensign replied in a nasty tone of voice, "Because there are too many." When I repeated the answer to the captain he then said, "Ask CIC who is in charge." I of course knew, but I followed protocol and asked CIC, "Who is the officer in charge?" (I normally would have said, "The captain wishes to know who is in charge of CIC.") The ensign answered with his name and a set of expletives about how dumb I was because I didn't know that he was in charge of CIC. When I repeated the officer's name to the captain he immediately said, "Tell the ensign to report to the bridge on the double." In a very authoritative voice I told the officer, "Report to the bridge on the double!"

The captain ripped him up one side and down the other. He informed him in no uncertain terms that he was derelict in his duty, and that his lackadaisical attitude would not be tolerated. The captain lectured him for ten minutes in front of me and several other enlisted men on the importance of reporting all aircraft before sending him back to CIC. I maintained a poker face during the episode. Reports of all aircraft within range of our radar began coming in immediately when he returned to CIC. When I got off watch I went back to the torpedo shack to expect a visit from the ensign. I was sitting on the workbench and sure enough, he showed up. He was angry, and when he was through talking I smiled and informed him that I had followed his orders of the previous day explicitly. He was angry because he had been exposed as the dope that he was and there was nothing he could do to me.

From Guam we proceeded east to Hawaii and Pearl Harbor. Our radiomen were piping radio programs through the ship's speaker system while underway, and we had the privilege of listening to the almost continuous news reports of the advancement of our troops in Germany. On 29 April 1945 German commanders in Italy signed surrender terms—this was the beginning of the collapse of the German government. On 30 April 1945 Hitler committed suicide and Admiral Doenitz took over what was left of the German government. It was quite obvious that it was just a matter of days before the government of Germany would collapse and the war there would be over. General Jodl signed the unconditional surrender of Germany on May 7, 1945.

It was a relief to feel and enjoy the safety of Pearl Harbor after many months in the war zone. We no longer had to sleep with our clothes on in anticipation of air or submarine attack. While in Pearl Harbor four of my buddies and I went on liberty in Honolulu to visit the Royal Hawaiian Hotel and Waikiki Beach. We rented a box camera and took a bunch of pictures of all five of us enjoying ourselves on our first liberty in several months.

We were only in Pearl Harbor a couple of days before we left for Bremerton, Washington, and the Puget Sound Naval Shipyard where we were to receive permanent repairs. I remember coming on deck at about 0630 in the morning as we were passing through the Strait of Juan De Fuca. Vancouver Island was clearly visible to the north and I got my first glimpse of pine trees in almost four years—what a pleasure to see something besides palm trees. The air was brisk and invigorating with a high cloud cover and no indication of rain. I took several deep breaths and reveled in how wonderful it was to be back in the great northwest of the United States. I went down to the mess hall for a leisurely breakfast where the conversation among the guys was all about how happy they were to be back in a mainland port, and how the war in Europe was obviously coming to an end.

We tied up in Bremerton early in the afternoon and liberty was declared immediately. I went ashore in the evening and took the ferry to Seattle. The first bar I entered had their juke box playing "Don't Fence Me In" by Bing Crosby. I will never forget how wonderful it was to be back in civilization—especially when I heard his recording. The next day the ship was put in drydock and repairs began in earnest with the temporary steel scab and shoring being removed. From that time on until the completion of repairs we had to eat in a mess hall on the dock—the food was very good. After the stuff we had to eat in the tropics we thought we had died and gone to destroyer heaven. Our captain declared a thirty-day survivor leave for the entire crew. The crew was divided into two segments with half going on leave first, and the second going on leave when the first group returned—I chose the second group.

I sent a telegram to my fiancee, Lorayne, in Chicago instructing her to come to Seattle prepared to get married. At that time we had been engaged to be married for about two years. The navy had arrangements with the old Fry Hotel in Seattle for sailors and their families to live there at a very nominal rate. I put her up there and a navy chaplain married us the next day. We had a great time in Seattle with some of my shipmates and their wives. When the first group came back I took my leave and we went down to San Diego to spend some time with my family. Dad gave us some gas coupons and loaned us his car so that my bride and I could visit many of the historical sites in southern California. It was a very enjoyable honeymoon.

When we returned from San Diego, the ship was still not completely repaired, and we still had about six weeks to be together before I had to return to sea. While we were gone the *Laffey* DD 724 had arrived from Okinawa, under her own power, and was in the drydock next to us. She had come under attack 16 April at RP1 by at least fifty kamikazes closing in on her from every direction. The CAP destroyed many planes before they came into range of *Laffey's* guns; however, during the battle that lasted eighty minutes, *Laffey* was attacked by twenty-two kamikazes and hit by six. She also suffered four bomb hits and much strafing. In spite of tremendous damage to the ship, her gunners were still able to shoot down nine enemy planes. At the end of this action only two 20mm guns were still able to fire. This was probably the most vicious attack that any destroyer ever suffered during the battle for Okinawa. *Laffey* had thirty-one killed and seventy-two wounded. All of the crew from captain to seamen were commended for their outstanding performance and heroism in this action. As Rear Admiral Joy remarked, *"Laffey's performance stands out above the outstanding."*

I took Lorayne aboard the *Laffey* (which was a sister ship to the *Barton,* and which I had served aboard earlier in the war) to show her what damage occurs during a battle. I also took her aboard the *Sterett* to show her the hole that the kamikaze made in her side, but I don't think she ever grasped the full impact of what she had seen aboard either ship. Even experienced sailors don't fully appreciate what it's really like until they experience a real battle.

I sent Lorayne back to Chicago in early July because we were due to leave port the next day. We steamed down the coast to San Diego for refresher training. We had a large turnover in personnel of both officers and enlisted men, and we had to go through a refresher-training period and be accredited by a naval inspection party to determine our readiness for battle. Remember Baby Blue Eyes? He was a member of the inspection party that came aboard to inspect us and release us for battle duty. He was also the warrant officer that had been duly initiated into the "Ancient Order of the Deep" when we crossed the equator back in 1944. When he climbed up the ladder onto the quarterdeck I was the first one that he saw. He looked at me and said "remember me from the polliwog initiation? There better not be one cotter pin anywhere that isn't properly set." The twinkle in his eye told me that he was kidding.

After completing our inspection, we were ordered to Pearl Harbor for more gunnery practice which included four parts: shore bombardment, target sled towed by a target tow vessel, target sleeve towed by an airplane, and a radio controlled unmanned drone airplane. These drone target planes were difficult to hit because the controller could quickly maneuver them out of the way if you were getting too close. We had been going through intense gunnery exercises for about two weeks when we were assigned to screen the battleship *Wisconsin* while they went through their gunnery exercises. They had a green crew of officers and men in their secondary antiaircraft batteries, and they were requiring a great deal of practice to perfect their gunnery. One day we were screening her, starboard side to, while she was firing her 20mm guns on an aircraft towed sleeve. I saw her tracers going over our ship, and one of our new boots (seaman) was standing on our quarterdeck watching the firing. I called to him to get out of there but I wasn't fast enough. A stray 20mm shell hit him in the chest and dropped him. He wasn't dead when we transferred him in a stretcher to a hospital ship by breeches buoy[1] while under way, but I doubt that he survived that kind of injury. I felt sorry for the kid because he hadn't been around long enough to know what the navy was all about—I often wonder what finally happened to him.

The *Wisconsin's* gunners hadn't done very well and the orders came down for us to do some firing runs on the sleeve and drone. On the first pass of the sleeve our gunners not only hit it, but also shot it off the towline. The drone then came over and our guys shot it down. The sleeve returned and our guys hit it on the first pass—it returned and our guys shot it off the towline again. The captain of the *Wisconsin* evidently had had enough of the antics of our little destroyer, and he called the target practice off. We all wondered what he had to say to his gun crews that evening.

It was evident that with the intense gunnery training we were going through, we were headed for the invasion of Japan. After what we had been through at Okinawa we weren't very happy at the thought of what lay ahead of us. Because of certain changes in our antiaircraft armament, and the increases in intensity of the battles that had taken place while we were in Seattle, we knew that we would be in the thick of the fight—we were sick of the war and wanted it to be over.

In early August, while still training at Pearl Harbor, we were getting reports that the Japanese were ready to surrender, and on 6 August the first atomic bomb was dropped on Hiroshima. Two days later the Soviet Union declared war on Japan. We were all angry as hell and ready to take on the Soviets. We had done all of the hard

---

[1] The breeches buoy is composed of lines strung from one ship to another while both are under-way so that personnel, mail, ammunition, etc. can be transferred from one ship to the other.

work and now they wanted to walk in and take over the situation and dictate the surrender and peacetime occupation of Japan. On 9 August another atomic bomb was dropped, this time on Nagasaki. On 14 August Emperor Hirohito announced the unconditional surrender of all Japanese forces. The next day the U.S. Navy was ordered to cease fire on Japanese forces. We immediately went on peacetime watches. We were only on peacetime watches for a day or two when several incidents occurred that caused Admiral Nimitz to rescind his cease fire order.

We received word that a cruiser had been torpedoed. Since the command had not released any details as to location, date, or time, we assumed that it happened 15 August. We were also informed that all Japanese forces were not surrendering, and were therefore directed to proceed as usual with wartime routine, which meant that Jap ships and aircraft were to be attacked and destroyed until further notice.

It was years later that I finally learned the story behind the sinking of the cruiser that was reported lost 15 August 1945. The ship was the heavy cruiser *Indianapolis* en route from Guam to Leyte Gulf with no destroyer escort. (This was the same ship that had just delivered parts of the atomic bomb to Tinian in the Northern Marianas for assembly at Guam.) She left Guam 28 July with an ETA (estimated time of arrival) at Leyte Gulf of 1100 31 July. This ETA was sent in a message to Rear Admiral McCormick aboard the battleship *Idaho* to whom *Indianapolis* was to report upon arrival at Leyte. The message arrived so garbled that it could not be deciphered, and her communications officer never asked for a repeat, thus Admiral McCormick never received it.

By about 2300, 29 July the unescorted *Indianapolis* (having no antisubmarine sonar gear) had reached a point where the direct course from Guam to Leyte, and from Peleliu to Okinawa, intersect. These were well known heavily traveled shipping lanes, and a Jap submarine lurking there had a good chance of sighting a target.

When the unescorted *Indianapolis* appeared on the scene, the Jap sub commander fired a spread of six torpedoes at the short distance of 1,500 meters (just short of one mile), two of which made direct hits on the *Indianapolis*—at that short range he couldn't miss. The two violent explosions made short work of the ship and she sank in less than fifteen minutes. A surviving chief radioman said that he had sent several SOS messages, but no one was sure if they were actually transmitted because of the immediate loss of electric power when the torpedoes hit.

No definite statistics are available, but best estimates indicate that about four hundred men were killed out of a crew of 1,199 in the two explosions. Approximately eight hundred men abandoned ship, but only 316 survived eighty-four hours in the water; over 450 men must have died in the water due to drowning, wounds, exposure, and sharks. Early in the morning of 31 July an army C-54 land based plane flew over the area on its way to Leyte. The crew of the airplane saw flares and tracers fired by the survivors and thought it was a naval battle of some sort. When they reported it to naval command at Leyte they were informed that the navy knew all about it and not to be concerned. It was 2 August before the hapless survivors were spotted by a land based navy patrol plane on a routine flight out of Peleliu. Once the alert was sounded, five DEs (destroyer escorts) were ordered to the scene; still, no one ashore had figured out what ship they belonged to. It took the DEs from the night of 2-3 August until 8 August to round up all of the survivors that by this time had spread out over the ocean. It wasn't until a message from DE, *Cecil J. Doyle*, on 3 August informed shore command that the *Indianapolis* had gone down, and that the survivors they were picking up were from that ship.

These nagging questions still persist today: Why was the *Indianapolis* ordered to proceed unescorted through a known area of Jap submarine activity? Why didn't the first report of flares and firing to the navy shore command at Leyte, by an army plane on 31

July, alert anyone that a ship was missing, or possibly sunk? How could a heavy cruiser disappear from a navy command without creating questions when it failed to report to Leyte for assignment to Admiral McCormick?

Admiral Nimitz ordered a court of inquiry, which was held at Guam from 13 August to the twentieth. The results of the inquiry were not made public. The first notice of the sinking was announced on 15 August, the day after the Japanese agreed to unconditional surrender. The press criticized the navy for the delay in reporting the sinking, and their news stories fired up the public. Then Secretary of the United States Navy, James Forrestal, felt the pressure of the press, and against the advice of his admirals ordered Captain Charles Butler McVay III, Commanding Officer of the *Indianapolis*, to be brought to trial by general court-martial. I can find no record of an officer of the United States Navy ever being court-martialed for losing his ship in battle. The charges were (1) culpable inefficiency in the performance of his duty, and (2) negligently endangering the lives of others.

In December of 1945 court-martial proceedings were held in Washington D.C. Commander Hashimoto, captain of the Japanese sub that torpedoed the *Indianapolis*, was flown to Washington to testify. This resulted in more angry editorials in the press followed by a critical resolution of Congress; however, Commander Hashimoto's testimony vindicated Captain McVay of the charge that he was guilty of hazarding his ship by not zigzagging. Commander Hashimoto testified that "had the *Indianapolis* been zigzagging it would have made no difference to him." I don't remember what Captain McVay was found guilty of, but the court later recommended that his sentence be remitted and he was restored to duty; however, I don't believe he ever commanded another ship.

When one considers the magnitude of the Naval Pacific War, it becomes obvious that honest mistakes can and did occur. In the case of the *Indianapolis* some unforeseen errors in procedures and communications occurred that resulted in a horrible tragedy. These errors were manifested by the chance position of an enemy submarine, and the converging course of the *Indianapolis* that happened to be in the wrong place at the wrong time. Procedures for keeping track of ships, and changes in communication procedures, were quickly initiated to prevent a reoccurrence of the *Indianapolis* disaster.

The formal unconditional surrender by the Japanese was officially signed on board the battleship *Missouri* 2 September 1945. Events had happened so suddenly that we had trouble adjusting to the cease-fire. When Emperor Hirohito of Japan announced his willingness to agree to an unconditional surrender on 14 August, many Japanese units didn't receive the order to cease fire, or refused to believe it, which resulted in many engagements occurring between that date and 2 September. In addition, many battles occurred for many months following the official surrender with many Japanese personnel being unnecessarily killed because of their refusal to surrender. It wasn't until the early 1970's that the last Japanese soldier finally gave up.

We set sail from Hawaii on 25 September with task force 57.5, which consisted of the battleship *Mississippi, North Carolina,* carrier *Enterprise*, and some other destroyers. We were on our way to New York by way of the Panama Canal. I found the peacetime navy difficult to adjust to. Instead of four hours on watch and eight hours off, and battle stations morning and evening, I drew one watch about every 24 hours—the rest of the time was boring. Since we no longer had our torpedo mounts (they had been removed at Bremerton and replaced with 40mm antiaircraft mounts), I had no torpedo mounts to service, and had been transferred to the gunners mate division. I spent my free time reading, playing chess, and trying to figure out if I should reenlist in the navy or return to civilian life?

We had been at sea for several days when we ran into the periphery of a typhoon. Worse yet, it became necessary to refuel at sea from the *Mississippi* in heavy weather because the task force commander had delayed our refueling, and we were already pumping ballast to maintain stability (pumping sea water into fuel bunkers to replace used oil). My watch station had been changed to helmsman and I had the watch when it was time to refuel. Being a helmsman was not one of my better attributes. Even in calm weather I could never steer the ship to my satisfaction—even a snake couldn't follow my wake. Now that we were sailing parallel to the *Mississippi*, and almost close enough to start firing lines so that fuel hoses could be hauled over,[2] the OOD wisely sent for one of the quartermasters who was gifted at steering a straight course in such an operation. I was happy to have him relieve me of the responsibility. With the two ships sailing that close, the huge waves were alternately pushing the ships apart and then together. We were on a mountain of water one minute and down in a trough the next; and, with our decks awash and the ship pitching and rolling thirty degrees, it took a lot of skill to steer the ship and avoid a collision in that situation. It was a very dangerous operation and we broke five fuel hoses in the process. Each time a hose broke it sprayed oil all over our ship and the side of the *Mississippi*. A breaking line would whip and if it happened to hit a man it could kill him, injure him severely, jerk him overboard, or even cut him in two. It was very fortunate that we had no injuries among the deck force in this most difficult operation.

---

[2] Lines are fired by a line-throwing gun from the refueling ship to the fueling vessel. That line is then secured to a larger line that is hauled over to the refueling ship. The fueling ship has the larger line secured to the fueling hose that is then hauled over to the refueling ship, and the hose end is then placed in the fuel bunker receptacle so that pumping oil can commence.

I had gone down to help in the fueling of the after bunkers. When the operation was finished and we had broken away from the *Mississippi*, the medical officer announced that each crewmember would receive a shot of brandy at the clap shack (sick bay). We had gotten soaking wet refueling as we frequently did, and I thanked the chief corpsman for the libation and then asked, "Why now, when the war is over? We never got a shot of brandy for getting drenched during the war." I never got a satisfactory answer—translation, drink your brandy and shut up.

A couple of nights later we were engulfed by the typhoon with over 100-mile an hour winds, a black night, wild seas, and I had the mid-watch on the helm, (0000 to 0400). The ship was taking better than forty-five-degree rolls while plunging into mountainous waves, and bouncing around which made it difficult to keep her on course. When we would climb atop a mountainous wave the ship would hang there for a second before plunging down with the stern out of the water. At that moment the screws were exposed and racing to the point where they vibrated the whole ship. The rudder was also out of the water and steerage was impossible at that point. As she settled into the downhill travel of the wave, the stern, rudder, and screws would settle in the water and I could regain control of the ship. As we plunged into the base of another wave the green water would engulf the bow, bridge, and superstructure. At that instant it seemed like we were headed for the bottom of the ocean, then the water would spill off the bow and superstructure as we climbed the wave towards its apex. Once on top the bow would come out of the water back to the sound stack on the keel, hang there for a moment, and then come crashing down to repeat the process all over again. I had one eye on the compass and the other on the PPI scope so that I could see where we were in relation to the other ships in the task force. I was doing just fine and we had just hit the top of a wave with the screws and rudder out of the water. As the stern settled into the water I attempted to correct the yawl of the ship and discovered

I had no rudder—the steering gear had failed! I immediately hit the alarm button and yelled out that I had no rudder. At this instant we were approaching the top of the wave and I looked dead ahead to see the big black hull of the "Big E" (carrier *Enterprise*), and we were headed straight for her amidships section. The OOD came racing over and grabbed the wheel, and the captain tore out of his emergency cabin on the bridge and raced into the pilothouse. The OOD confirmed that we had indeed lost our steering gear. The JOD was sent back to the secondary con to see if he could gain steerage from there. He had no more luck than I had had, and so the bridge was a beehive of activity with the captain shouting orders to gain control of the ship by alternating power from one shaft to the other. This was accomplished by increasing the turns on the starboard shaft while slowing down the port shaft. This transfer of power to the screws caused the ship to turn away from its collision course with the "Big E." The ship was then steered by alternating power from one shaft to the other until a better emergency plan was developed. I do not remember the "Big E" or other ships in the task force altering course. It was expected that we would solve our own problem.

The engineers down below couldn't locate the reason for the power failure on the steering gear, and the only thing everyone knew was that we were in big trouble. Finally, someone got the idea to pull the deck plates up from the aft steering room in the after crews compartment to gain access to the rudder assembly. A block and tackle was rigged to the rudder assembly and men from the compartment provided the muscle required for steering the ship. From that moment until many hours later, when steerage was finally restored, the ship was steered by that method with orders for corrections coming from the bridge. The OOD complimented me on my astuteness and quick reaction to the emergency—I was never able to learn the cause of the mechanical failure.

We finally sailed out of the typhoon and into smooth seas once again. I was looking for something to do when I discovered that the boatswain was looking for someone with nerve enough to paint our war record on both wings of the bridge—we didn't have room enough on the main battery director which was the usual place for the record of kills. The boatswain created some rigging that made it possible for me to suspend myself over the side of the bridge to do my work. I was working about thirty feet above the rushing sea below, but that didn't bother me because the sea was calm and the weather was so beautiful. The yeoman produced stencils of a battleship, cruiser, destroyer, and airplane, all of which I painted black. I also had stencils for the Jap flag to represent specific enemy units destroyed—one for the battleship, one for the cruiser, three for the destroyers, thirteen for aircraft destroyed, and nine half flags for assists in destroying enemy aircraft. There was also one German flag signifying one German aircraft destroyed. I also painted an island with a palm tree and six Jap flags signifying six invasion bombardments. By the time I finished with my handiwork I had taken up most of the available space on the bridge wings. I was proud of my work, and everyone seemed happy with it.

We arrived at Panama City the afternoon of 8 October and on 8-9 October we passed through the Panama Canal and moored at the Coco Solo Naval base at Colon where we spent three days of liberty. The task group was written up in the local paper; however, most of the article talked about one destroyer (the *Sterett*) and its battle record. I laughed to think that my artwork drew that much attention. I can't verify the story but we were told that one of the senior admirals contacted the Pentagon in Washington to verify our battle record.

Liberty in Colon was an experience. Like all good sailors, the first thing that two of my torpedo buddies and I did was to head for the most popular bar. After "splicing the main brace" we ventured out into the town to view the local sites. Some of the fellows hired a horse-drawn carriage and driver to squire them around town to see the sights, but we preferred to visit local shops and just wander around on foot. In our exploring we came to a place called Cash Street, a wide street about one block long with a parkway running the middle length of the street. On the opposite side of the street were small rooms, (cribs) each with a door opening to the sidewalk of the street—each crib was occupied by a prostitute. There were at least a couple of hundred sailors milling around on the sidewalk with SP's trying to disperse the crowd while the women were all trying to get the sailors into their rooms. Most of the prostitutes were black except for one woman who sat in a beach chair at one end of the cribs nearest the downtown center of Colon. She appeared to be part black and part Caucasian. She was barefoot, wore a blue low cut evening dress, had red hair, and was smoking a long black cigar. She was talking to a black woman sitting in a chair next to her and seemed to be oblivious to all of the activity going on around her. I took her to be the madam of the operation.

We were watching the show in amazement from the opposite side of the street when a chief petty officer came walking down the street in front of the cribs. A door suddenly opened and one of the women grabbed him, hauled him into her room, and slammed the door. In no more than five seconds the door opened and the chief came rushing out of the room hat in hand as if he had been hit in the butt with a cattle probe. We nearly died laughing at the spectacle. By this time we had seen enough of Colon and went back to the ship. Two days later we cast off our moorings and left for New York. As we were passing Cape Hatteras we hit a little rough water, but nothing like the conditions that have given Hatteras its reputation. For Hatteras the water was about as smooth as it ever gets. One of the seamen came to me while I was sitting on a stowage box on the fantail enjoying the weather. Being a Pacific sailor who had no experience with really rough weather, except for the typhoon we had recently come through east of Hawaii, he asked if this was as rough as the Atlantic gets. I laughed—he was a young seaman who came aboard just before we left Hawaii, and other than the typhoon, he hadn't experienced rough water. He was eager to learn about seamanship and had a million good questions. I gave him a little indoctrination concerning knowledge he didn't get in boot camp or would ever get out of books.

We entered New York Harbor on 17 October 1945. We were part of several task groups of Task Force 57 that were assembling for the celebration of the return of the fleet for Navy Day. The battleship *Missouri* leading the various task groups had already preceded our task group (57.5) into the harbor and up the Hudson River. The capital ships (battleships, cruisers, and carriers) were flying their admiral flags for the first time since the start of the war. All of the ships were flying signal flags describing their score of enemy ships sunk and aircraft destroyed. This was the first time since the start of World War II that the public was allowed to visit aboard U.S. Navy warships, and people had come to New York from many parts of the country to witness the event. They were amassed in huge numbers along the shore to witness this most impressive armada the world had ever seen, pass before them. To the crowd of spectators this must have been a thrilling sight.

Since our ship was scheduled for decommissioning we broke from the caravan of ships as we rounded south Brooklyn. As we came closer to the shore we saw a huge crowd of people on land off our starboard quarter—there must have been several thousand of them that had gathered at what I believe was then known as Battery Point to watch the fleet enter the harbor. Apparently they could see our battle score painted on our bridge because we heard a tremendously loud cheer from the crowd (more like a roar) that lasted for as long as we were in view. We entered the Brooklyn Navy Yard and tied up port side to. Liberty was immediately declared and I went ashore with Dave Vestal, and one of the engineers, (whose name I can't remember). A street photographer took our picture on the street. I cherished that picture and had it for years; however, with all of the moving around it somehow disappeared.

Because our ship was to be decommissioned we had all of the free time we had money for. While many of the sailors had to remain aboard their ships to entertain the public, we relaxed and toasted them from our favorite bar. I had some relatives in New York and they invited me to have dinner with them one evening. The next evening I went ashore with Dave and Bob Burns to visit all of the cabarets we could find. The New Yorkers were wonderful to us and treated us like heroes. We didn't have to buy many drinks and the girls were attracted to us like flies to Scotch tape. It turned out that the people had been exposed to many land-based navy men, but never to so many seagoing sailors sporting numerous campaign ribbons and battle stars. We walked into one place where a floor show was starting. The MC was at the microphone and when he spotted us he stopped the show to announce to the crowd that some combat fleet sailors had just entered, and he asked the crowd to give us a big welcome. There was much applause and when we sat down I felt like royalty—the first round of drinks was on the house. We had similar welcomes everywhere we went, and the New Yorkers were really celebrating Navy Day.

A couple of days later both officers and men started to disappear from the ship. They were being detached in preparation for decommissioning. All my buddies were being transferred and it wasn't long before I was the only torpedoman left on the ship. I phoned my high school buddy Bob Benson (who had tried to enlist in the navy with me) who was in New York working with the U.S.O. as an entertainer. We got together and he took me backstage to many of the New York stage plays and introduced me to the performers. He also took me to cocktail parties that were frequented by entertainers, and even to a Halloween costume party that included several army officers and their wives and a dry land sailor.

They were service personnel that had something to do with the U.S.O. I also met an air force officer from the 8th Air Force—and that is one party I'll never forget. I had a great time in New York.

We soon learned that our ship was being stripped prior to being sold for scrap. It gave us all a melancholy feeling to lose our ship that had been home to us for so long, and had served us so well in some of the greatest sea battles ever fought in the history of naval warfare. Guns, communication gear, radar, other equipment and tools that we had used and cared for over the years were being removed—even our personalized foul-weather jackets had to be turned in. I really hated to part with my jacket—I have never been able to replace it with one of similar quality.

I was standing a gangway watch one evening when the executive officer summoned me to his makeshift office on the bridge which had already been stripped of everything except the wheel. He informed me that on 31 October 1945 I was to be transferred to Pier 92 in New York City for one night, and then on to Great Lakes Naval Training Station at Great Lakes, Illinois, for separation from the service. He then made a sales pitch for me to reenlist in the navy. He made an issue of how much the navy would continue to need men of my experience and record; however, I had already decided that I would try civilian life, continue my college education, and should I decide to continue a naval career it would be as a commissioned officer. The next evening I reported to Pier 92, spent the night there, picked up my first class train ticket to Great Lakes in the morning and was on my way to end my naval career.

At Great Lakes I found myself in the same barracks, same floor, where I had begun my enlistment as a boot almost three years before—I wonder what the odds were against that happening? The old barracks was immaculately clean and hadn't changed one bit. The navy was exceptionally well organized and processed us rapidly. A couple of days later on 7 November I received my final pay, honorable discharge, and I was once again a civilian. That evening I was back in Chicago with my wife at the home of my in-laws.

My naval career had ended with feelings of melancholy. While I was happy to be back with my wife, I was missing my buddies that I had grown so close to, and had shared so many experiences with. I was also saddened about the decommissioning of the *Sterett*, the ship that had served us so well in so many engagements. As Secretary of the Navy James Forrestal said, "the *Sterett* was a gallant fighting ship superbly handled by her officers and men." And now she was headed for the scrap heap. At least she didn't suffer the indignity of being sold into some third rate navy where she would deteriorate from neglect. I am proud to have been a destroyer sailor and to have shared with her superb crew the reputation of such a splendid little destroyer.

Plate 33: The author, Petty Officer Jerome S. Welna,
November 1945 at discharge from service.

Plate 34: Author Jerome S. Welna.

EPILOGUE

My immediate concern now that I had become a civilian was to find a job. What I soon learned was that following the German surrender back in May, the army began discharging men by the hundreds of thousands. By the time I was separated from service, these fellows had taken up most of the available jobs, and had also filled up the available space in the colleges and universities. To add to the problem, industries were rapidly changing from war production to peacetime goods. These factors made jobs scarce when I attempted to enter the job market with no formal training that prepared me for employment—of what use was a torpedoman to a prospective employer? I had the option of returning to naval service, but there were problems with that also. I knew from contacts with my former shipmates who were still on active duty that most torpedomen were now stationed on carriers or on island bases. Neither prospect appealed to me; in addition, our first child was due in February or March and I didn't want to be gone for that occasion.

Contrary to the stories I have heard concerning the problems some veterans had in adjusting to civilian life, I had none. I stored all of my combat experiences somewhere in the back of my mind and never spoke of them for over fifty years. When on occasion I finally started speaking, I always tended to mention the pleasant things, not the unpleasant ones. It so happened that my new father-in-law was a regional manager for the Fuller Brush Company. He offered to train me to sell Fuller Brushes, and the idea appealed to me. After two weeks of training I was ready to venture out on my own as a salesman. I had to go door to door to sell my brushes to housewives. My new career immediately became profitable enough so that I could buy a second hand car (a junk heap) for more flexibility in making my calls, and I was soon making twice more money than the guys working in the grocery stores.

Six months later I moved my wife and daughter to San Diego, California, where I continued selling brushes. Even though I was doing well income-wise, my objective was a college degree in logging engineering. The desired school for that major was the University of Oregon; however, since I wasn't a resident of the state, they wouldn't talk to me. I finally contacted the California State Polytechnic College at San Luis Obispo, California, and was accepted in the school of agriculture, which was my second choice, but turned out to be my best choice. I soon discovered that I had an affinity for science and agriculture. I was entering my senior year when recruiters from all the military services appeared on the campus and the navy offered me a commission in the Naval Reserve—it was very tempting, but I declined. Two weeks later the Korean War broke out, and had I accepted the commission I would have been on active duty twenty-four hours later and my education would have been once again interrupted. In January of 1951 I accepted a research position with Salsbury Laboratories of Charles City, Iowa, even though I would not formally join the company until the end of March when I would receive my degree.

Upon graduation I immediately entered their graduate work program in diagnostics, and later established their dealer education department. With the cooperation of the research division I developed the most comprehensive school of poultry diseases in the world. Our students came from all parts of the industry in the United States and the world including university departments and the veterinary profession.

During this period I worked and studied with Dr. Kathel Kerr, one of the nation's leading specialists of internal parasites of food producing animals and public health, and Dr. Neal Morehouse, the nation's leading specialist of protozoan diseases of farm animals. I also authored several poultry disease manuals, other scientific papers, and edited company product manuals and publications. By this time in 1955 I was classified as an associate scientist and was enjoying national recognition throughout the animal health industry. Our family had now grown to three girls and one boy.

After completing my advanced education I accepted a position with the Animal Feed Division of Doughboy Industries in 1958 where I headed up their poultry production unit. After almost four years with Doughboy I formed my own consulting company which I managed until 1971 when I joined the Animal Health Division of Schering-Plough Corporation, one of the premier pharmaceutical companies of the world, where I held several management positions in the company until I retired in 1994. At that time Schering-Plough retained me as a consultant for an additional three years.

I now spend my time doing limited consulting work, writing, caring for my invalid wife, and managing the family finances.

Appendix 1

AGP5   June 22, 1982

Mr. Jerome S. Welna
3332 Dove Court
San Diego, California 92103
U. S. A.

Dear Mr. Welna:

We are pleased to send you the enclosed set of
Philippine Liberation Medal and Philippine Republic
Presidential Unit Citation Badge in connection with
your request for decoration(s) for your service(s) in
the battles/campaigns for the defense/liberation of
the Philippines during World War II.

Please acknowledge receipt of same.

Sincerely yours,

FOR THE CHIEF OF STAFF:

Incl:
  as stated

ELADIO D. TILOS
Major, PA (GHQ)
Asst Adjutant General

370

Appendix 2, dated April 8, 1976, explains why it took twenty years for me to receive these decorations.

REPUBLIC OF THE PHILIPPINES
DEPARTMENT OF NATIONAL DEFENSE
GENERAL HEADQUARTERS, ARMED FORCES OF THE PHILIPPINES
Camp General Emilio Aguinaldo, Quezon City

AGW3   April 8, 1976

Mr. Jerome S. Welna
3532 Dove Court
San Diego, California   92103
U. S. A.

Dear Mr. Welna:

This is to acknowledge receipt of the letter dated
June 26, 1972, from the General Services Administration
of the United States of America.

Limited funds and the enormous requests coming from
your country, as well as from ours, have made it difficult
for us to meet promptly the increasing demand for the Philippine Liberation Medal. Hence, we have resorted to the
policy of issuing the decoration on a first come first
served basis. It is out of stock at present.

We shall accommodate your request when the decoration
is again available.

Sincerely yours,

FOR THE CHIEF OF STAFF:

JUAN D. VALLEJOS
Major,   PA (GHQ)
Asst Adjutant General

371

Appendix 3

Presidential Unit Citation for the *Sterett*

THE SECRETARY OF THE NAVY
WASHINGTON

The President of the United States takes pleasure in presenting the
PRESIDENTIAL UNIT CITATION
to the
UNITED STATES SHIP STERETT
for service as set forth in the following
CITATION:

"For extraordinary heroism in action against an enemy Japanese Task Force during the Battle of Guadalcanal on the night of November 12–13, 1942. Fighting boldly and with determination against units of the powerful enemy Fleet intent on bombarding our airfield at Guadalcanal, the U.S.S. STERETT successfully engaged three Japanese vessels at close range during the thirty-four minutes of furious action. Scoring numerous hits on an enemy light cruiser, she then closed range to 3000 yards and fired a full salvo of torpedoes to cause two large explosions and assist in sinking a battleship. When an enemy destroyer was sighted at 1000 yards from her starboard bow, she immediately took it under fire and, with two torpedoes and two five-inch salvos, exploded and sank the vessel before it could open fire. With her after section severely damaged and burning and with both after guns disabled as the remaining enemy ships concentrated their gunfire on her, she fought desperately to control the damage and succeeded in retiring from the battle area under her own power. A gallant fighting ship, superbly handled by her officers and men, the STERETT rendered invaluable service in defeating a major enemy attack at this crucial point in the Solomon Islands Campaign."

For the President,

James Forrestal

Secretary of the Navy

Appendix 4

Battle History of the USS *Sterett* DD 407
7 December 1941 to 2 November 1945

USS Wasp operation in reinforcement of MALTA, 14–20 April and
3–17 May 1942

Guadalcanal Tulogi Landings, 7–9 August 1942

Capture and Defense of Guadalcanal, 10 August–13 November
19942

Battle of Guadalcanal (Third Savo), 12–15 November 1942

Consolidation of Southern Solomons, 8 February–20 June 1943

New Georgia Group Operations

New Georgia-Rendova-Vangunu occupation, 20 June–31 August
1943

Vella Gulf Action, 6–7 August 1943

Treasury-Bougainville Operation, 27 October–15 December 1943

Rabaul Strike, 5 November 1943

Rabaul Strike, 11 November 1943

Marshall Islands Operation, 26 November 1943–2 March 1944

Gilbert Islands Operation, 13 November1943–8 December 1944

Air attacks designated by CinCPac on Defended Marshall Islands
Targets

Asiatic-Pacific Raids, 1944

Truk Attack, 16–17 February 1944

Marianas Attack, 21–22 February 1944

Marianas Operation, 10 June–27 August 1944

Neutralization of Japanese bases in Bonis, Marianas, and Western
Pacific, 10 June–27 August 1944

Capture and Occupation of Saipan, 11 June–10 August 1944

First Bonins Raid, 15–16 June 1944

Battle of Philippine Sea, 19–20 June 1944

Capture and Occupation of Guam, 12 July–15 August 1944

Capture and Occupation of Tinian, 20 July–10 August 1944

Palau Yap, Ulithi Raid, 25–27 July 1944

Liberation of Philippines, 7 December 1944–1 February 1945

Supply and Protection of Leyte

Resupply of Mindoro

Luzon Operation, 12 December 1944

Lingayen Gulf Landing 4–18 January 1945

Okinawa Gunte, Nansei Shoto Operation, 17 March–11June 1945

Accredited Enemy Units destroyed:

> One BB, 13 November, 1942 (assist)—Battle of Guadalcanal (Third Savo)
>
> One CL, 13 November 1942 (assist)—Battle of Guadalcanal (Third Savo)
>
> One DD, 13 November 1942 (sunk)—Battle of Guadalcanal (Third Savo)
>
> One DD, 6-7 August 1943 (sunk)—Battle of Vella Gulf
>
> One DD, 6-7 August 1943 (assist)—Battle of Vela Gulf
>
> One enemy submarine, August 1944 (unconfirmed)
>
> 13 enemy aircraft confirmed (destroyed)
>
> 9 enemy aircraft confirmed (assist)
>
> Many enemy aircraft (unconfirmed)
>
> Numerous barges destroyed
>
> Six invasion bombardments—many shore batteries destroyed

Appendix 5

Battle History of USS *Barton* DD 722,
30 December 1943 to 29 October 1944
—the period of time I served aboard as a member of the ship's company.

Operation Neptune—Invasion of Normandy—6 June 1944 to 25 June 1944

Accredited German units destroyed, 6 June to 24 June (night and day) 1944
> One enemy aircraft (Ju-88 bomber)
> Additional unconfirmed German aircraft
> Unconfirmed German E-boats
> Numerous German gun emplacements, tanks, and infantry units

Bombardment of Cherbourg—25 June 1944:
> Numerous German gun emplacements and infantry units destroyed

Appendix 6

Acknowledgements from the nation's
highest ranking naval officers

Fleet Admiral Ernest J. King, Commander-in-Chief of the U.S. Fleet: *Fought boldly and with distinction.*

Fleet Admiral C. W. Nimitz, Commander-in-Chief of the U.S. Pacific Fleet: *Well done--Your great work is an inspiration to us all.*

Admiral William F. Halsey, Commander of the South Pacific Forces: *An example of the fighting spirit in our destroyer force.*

Bibliography

Ambrose, Stephen E. *D-Day*. New York: Simon and Schuster, 1994.

Budiansky, Stephen. *Battle of Wits*. New York: Simon and Schuster, 2002.

Calhoun, Raymond, C. *Tin Can Sailor*. Annapolis, Maryland: Naval Institute Press, 1993.

Costello, John. *The Pacific War*. New York: Rawson, Wade, 1981.

Eisenhower, Dwight, D. *Crusade in Europe*, New York: Random House, 1997.

Hara, Tameichi, Captain, the Imperial Japanese Navy. *Japanese Destroyer Captain*. New York: Ballantine Books, Inc.: 1961.

Liddell-Hart, B.H. ed. *The Rommel Papers*. New York: daCapo Press, 1953.

Hughes, Terry and James Wade Costello. *The Battle of the Atlantic*. New York: The Dial Press, 1977.

Kilvert-Jones, Tim. *Omaha Beach*. South Yorkshire, Great Britain: Pen & Sword Books Limited, 1999.

Miller, Russell. *Nothing Less Than Victory*. New York: William Morrow and Company, Inc., 1993.

Morison, Samuel, Eliot, *The Two-Ocean War; History of United States Naval Operations in World War II*, Fourteen volumes. New York: BBS Publishing Corp with arrangement of Little, Brown and Co., 1997.

Roscoe, Theodore. *United States Destroyer Operations in World War II*. Annapolis, Maryland: United States Naval Institute Press, 1953.

Smith, S. E. *The United States Navy in World War II*. New York: William Morrow and Company, Inc., 1966.

Von Luck, Hans. *Panzer Commander*. New York: Dell Publishing, 1991.

Index

CPSIA information can be obtained
at www.ICGtesting.com
Printed in the USA
FSHW021309030719
59639FS